FAITHBUILDERS

Pastor Rory Wineka

PREFACE
"O ye of little faith"... (Mt. 8:26)

When was the last time God did something in answer to prayer that you absolutely cannot explain? God challenged His beloved people to call upon Him prayerfully by faith, promising He would answer by showing them great things which they would not be able to figure out. (Jer.33:3) God has an eternal plan of love to bless us exceedingly abundantly above and beyond our prayer requests if we would pray fervently and righteously by faith in His infallible Word. (Eph. 3:20)

God has declared plainly in His Word that He has an eternal salvation plan to conform His saints into the image of His dearly beloved Son. This salvation plan has a simple Biblical pattern to it:

1. Without faith it is impossible to please God. (Heb. 11:6)
2. Faith comes by hearing the Word of God. (Ro. 10:17)
3. Faith must grow from faith to faith in maturity. (Ro. 1:17)
4. Faith must grow into habitual obedience by "the faith" of Jesus. (Ro. 1:5; 1 Jn. 3:7)
   a. "The faith" that enables saints to walk as Christ walked, rooted in Him. (Col. 2:6-7)
   b. "The faith" that enables saints to live a crucified selfless life of service. (Gal. 2:20)
   c. "The faith" that enables saints to examine themselves honestly for fruit. (2 Cor. 13:5)

i

    d. "The faith" that enables saints to finish their race fighting the good fight. (2 Tim. 4:7)

This indescribable gift of "the faith" flows out of God's gift of **eternal life**. Neither of these phrases, "the faith" or "eternal life", are found anywhere in the Old Testament because only Jesus could provide these New Testament gifts to us as needy sinners. (Ro. 3:23; 6:23) Jesus Christ had to come by faith to the earth as God's dearly beloved Son to defeat sin, Satan, and death that we might be saved by grace through faith in God's precious promises. (Jn. 3:16; Eph. 2:8-9) God lays out this pattern of truth this way:

    1. God's Word is **precious seed**. (Ps. 126:6)
    2. God's **precious seed** teaches us only Jesus' **precious blood** saves a sinful soul. (1 Pet.1:19)
    3. **Precious seed** also creates **precious promises** to be believed by faith. (Jn. 1:12; 2 Pet .1:4)
    4. **Precious promises** create **precious faith**. (2 Pet. 1:1)
    5. **Precious faith** assures saints that Jesus is our **precious cornerstone** of faith. (1 Pet.2:6)

Jesus also revealed this growth process of "faith to faith" in the three different titles He used to address His disciples as He trained them into deeper levels of maturity: **servants, friends, brethren**. As He taught them the key principles of abiding in His love, Jesus told them He no longer saw them as **servants** but as **friends** who now know "all things" He had heard from His Father. This new level of intimacy reminded them that the same love God had for Jesus, He had for Jesus' disciples. (Jn. 15:9, 15) Then, after His resurrection, Jesus called His beloved disciples **"brethren"**, as they had finally grown after three years of training into "the faith" of Jesus Himself. (Jn.20:17; Acts 3:16) The first time Paul used this phrase "the faith" came in Acts 3:16 when he deliberately used the emphatic article "the" to teach the new Jewish Christians the power of true faith. Jesus taught that the same Spirit that moved Him to fulfill His mission would move them to fulfill their mission with His authority. (Mt. 28:18-20; Jn. 16:13-15) Sometimes, we as Christians forget that Jesus gave us His Spirit to do greater works than He did, as Peter's first sermon in one day saved far more souls than Jesus' three years of sermons did! (Jn. 14:12)

As demonstrated often in Scripture, God blessed many who sought Him by faith, sometimes granting them miracles to grow them from faith to faith. (Mt. 9:29) These **faithbuilders** were only given to people who already acted by faith in trusting God by taking Him at His Word.

However, God's miracles do NOT produce Biblical faith in people who do not know Him. For example, God did ten astounding miracles to prove His authority over Egypt's false gods to Pharoah, but those miracles did not change Pharoah's life or attitude. Jesus also performed many Messianic miracles that gave infallible proof of His deity, as Isaiah 35 predicted 700 years earlier. But the religious Jews refused all God's evidence and crucified Jesus. (Jn. 9) Hard-hearted sinners will always refuse God's most persuasive miraculous evidences. (John 9; Rom. 4:21; 8:38; 2 Tim. 1:12; Heb. 6:9; 11:13)

In conclusion, as we start this journey of growing from faith to faith, into "the faith" of Christ, we will examine God's Biblical examples of how He grows His vineyard to bear fruits of faith. (Jn. 15) Jude called upon saints to contend for "the faith" as we strive to keep ourselves in the love of God daily. (Jude 3, 21) In the following chapters, as I share many personal and Biblical **faithbuilders,** may God graciously grow us into a more intimate relationship with Jesus as God answers Jesus' effectual fervent prayers. (Jn. 17; Jas. 5:16) God desires that we, as saints, be far more in love with Jesus than we were the day before as He graciously grants us **faithbuilders** to grow us from faith to faith, and as we use, "above all", the shield of faith to quench all the fire-filled darts of Satan. (Eph. 3:20; 6:16)

Each chapter closes with practical questions of application. God wants us to grow in convictions that shape character and conduct so that we will one day be "Jesus with skin on" as He perfects us in His eternal and internal love. (Luke 12:48; 1 Jn. 4:12, 17) These questions should help to remind us daily that God loves us just as much as He loves Jesus, His dearly beloved Son. (Jn. 17:26)

DEDICATION

I dedicate this book to my precious wife and helpmate, Pat, who has been my best friend and encourager as we have served God together during our forty-one years of marriage and ministry empowered by God's abundant answers to prayer. I praise God for His indescribable gift of a prudent woman who possesses a "PhD in common sense" as her enlightened eyes of understanding aided me greatly in discernment and decision making. Her influence as the godly mother and discipler of our beloved three children has been priceless as our children have grown up to serve our Lord too. Solomon described my loving wife best when he wrote, "Her children arise up, and call her blessed; her husband also, and he praiseth her. Give her of the fruit of her hands; and let her own works praise her in the gates." (Prov. 31:29, 31)

I thank God from the depth of my heart for my mentor, Pastor Noel Irwin, who fully convinced me I was called to preach as a young pastor. His impact on my life as his "young Timothy" was priceless as he engrafted the durable riches of hope within me that shaped and confirmed my calling as a preacher of the powerful riches of God's grace. Noel is now in glory with Jesus after he fulfilled his mission on earth and heard from his Lord: "Well done thou good and faithful servant."

I also want to thank my daughter Christine for all her labor in love as she helped me with editing and creativity of thoughts for this book. Thanks also to my secretary Chris Segers for all her valuable help in editing and brainstorming of ideas. Thanks also to Matthew Code who provided the artwork in the train illustrations used in the book.

Finally and most importantly, all the glory goes to God for the lavish unsearchable riches of His love that saved my soul forty-three years ago and changed my life through many **faithbuilders** in answer to prayer that shaped the heart of this book. (I Cor. 10:31; Eph. 3:20)

CONTENTS

MY DAMASCUS ROAD FAITHBUILDER
"For God so loved the world"... Jn. 3:16
CHAPTER ONE

One day as Saul of Tarsus was journeying down the Damascus Road, God's glorious and gracious light from heaven pierced Saul's heart with deep conviction that changed his life forever. Trembling and astonished by Jesus' presence as the Lord of life, Saul asked, "Lord what wilt thou have me to do?" Jesus then instructed Ananias to care for Saul as a "chosen vessel" to bear God's name to all mankind. (Acts 9)

My "Damascus Road" took place in July of 1971 when four of my roommates, whom I had known from kindergarten through college, and I journeyed to Rehoboth Beach Delaware as five heathens who were chasing all that the world had to offer that summer. However, God had His agenda for that trip that far outweighed ours.

After we arrived late on a Friday night, I went to bed exhausted from having no sleep for two days. My friends went to the local bars on the boardwalk until closing time. When they got back to our cabin, they noticed a coffee house next door that was still open. To their disappointment, there was no booze, but they had met four very friendly Southern Baptist Christians from Louisiana, who invited them to breakfast the next Saturday morning.

When they informed me of the invitation the next morning, I

had no interest at all in being around "religious kooks" while on my much needed vacation, but they persuaded me to enjoy a "free meal" and then we could leave immediately for the beach. So, I joined them half-heartedly at best!

Much to my surprise, our neighbors made no effort to push their God on us, outside of praying before we ate. Our "new friends" were quite personable and very funny. After about two hours, which flew by quickly, we departed. As we left, they asked us to come to dinner that night and continued the invitations the next several days.

When Wednesday evening's dinner was done, they asked us to stay for "devotions", and we felt we owed them that, even though none of us knew what "devotions" meant. The man read John 3 and shared how Jesus died for sinners out of His great love for all mankind. All of that meant absolutely nothing to me personally, having grown up in a home with no Bible or any church attendance that I recall. I simply tolerated the religious "nonsense" as mythical. However, they then said we were going to voluntarily pray in a circle by holding hands around the table. If someone didn't want to pray, they simply squeezed the person's hand next to you.

I was not expecting what happened next! Two of the young ladies began crying as they prayed for our eyes to be enlightened by God's love and that we would sense His Presence in the room as He spoke to us of our need for a Savior. All of my friends and I passed on praying, and the session

2

ended. Much to my surprise, I was not offended at all, but was instead pierced by their genuine love for us.

After devotions, they asked us to stay for popcorn and a skit they had planned. We spent the next three hours laughing and talking about all kinds of things, as they simply tried to be "Jesus with skin on" to us. This was my first experience with genuine Christ-loving saints, and I was drawn in powerfully by God's radiant light shining through their unconditional love. (2 Cor. 3:18; I Jn. 4:17)

As we were about to leave, I walked out onto the porch to catch some ocean breeze as the temperature was still around eighty degrees at 10:30 p.m. One of the young ladies followed me out and sought permission to ask me a personal question. I said "sure" as my mind was very open to her sincerity and friendship. She asked me if I was truly happy, and I informed her that I couldn't possibly be happier as a single school teacher with great friends and a special girlfriend back home. She then asked me if I found out the next week that I had terminal cancer, how that would affect my joy. I was stunned by the piercing question and was somewhat speechless. Before I could answer, she responded that such news would rattle her, but would have no effect on her joy at all as a Christian whose eternal hope was anchored to Jesus Christ her Lord. Then she smiled and walked away saying, "Think about it".

The next day our new friends asked us to spend the day with them at the beach. At first I thought "how boring," but I really wanted to get to know them much better. After playing cards for a while, one of the young ladies asked me if I wanted to go for a walk. I agreed, and we headed down the beach to a quieter place where we could hear better and have more privacy for her loving agenda.

She then proceeded to ask me if she could ask me a personal question, and I thought "Oh-oh", but her smile and compassionate kindness softened my heart. She asked if I had thought about the question asked me the night before, and asked me my thoughts on life and death. She proceeded to ask me if I was a "sinner." Although I wasn't real sure of the meaning of the term, I told her "most likely" because I stated I knew nothing about Jesus or the Bible, but was pretty sure my life didn't line up with its standards. She smiled and proceeded to share the gospel of God's love for me as a sinner who needed a Savior. Her persuasive love touched me deeply as she wasn't "preachy" but sincerely loved me and spoke to me in a very embracing and enlightening way. Her love grabbed my heart because I grew up in a home where I never once recalled either of my parents stating their love for me.

I then shared with her my appreciation for her caring enough to lovingly tell me the truth, but that I was a perfectionist who didn't want to give up my lifestyle. I believed it was impossible for me to change my ways. She then responded that if I believed by faith that what she told me was true, that Jesus would move inside of me and change me from the inside out. Then she said, "What do you have to lose? If I'm lying to you, or Jesus is just a myth, there will be no change and you will go on living as you are now. However, if I'm telling you the truth, and you prayerfully admit your need of Jesus, by faith, and ask Him to save your soul with all your heart, He will change you from the inside out. Think about it. That's all I ask; for your eternity and soul are at stake".

That night I began thinking about their tears of love shed on Wednesday night that melted my iceberg heart. The next morning I surrendered, having no idea how all this "salvation stuff" would work out. I prayed a simple prayer by faith asking God to save me as a sinner who needed help from heaven. As God saved my soul, He paved the gracious loving path for many **faithbuilders** to come.

After that morning, I headed home to go on a two-week fishing trip in Canada, even though my new found Christian friends begged me to stay one more week with them, as they were leaving in seven days for Louisiana. So as I got into the car, they handed me a New Testament as God started a miraculous journey of faith.

Many years after my conversion experience, I began to think of the first time I remembered ever thinking about God. As an eight-year-old boy, my father took me on my first Canadian fishing trip down the Pickerel River in Ontario. As we headed downriver to our lodge, I remember the sheer cliff granite walls that stood one-hundred feet coming up from the river's water straight up into the air. I thought within my mind that there had to be a God that made such an awesome wonder, although my father had never taught me that God existed. We, as a family, never went to church or had any spiritual discussions. There existed no Bible in our home. This event on the Pickerel River reminded me of Jesus' statement that even if the people would not declare Him as King and Lord that "the stones would immediately cry out". I am eternally grateful to my gracious God that although my father on earth told me nothing about Jesus that my Father in heaven spoke to me through creation that day as indeed "the rocks cried out", and the ears of my soul heard His still small voice. (I Kings 19:12; Ps.19:1-3; Luke 19:40)

FOOD FOR THOUGHT (Phil. 4:8): "Examine yourselves whether ye be in the faith." (2 Cor. 13:5)

1. Have you had a life changing "Damascus Road" encounter with the living Christ, and if so, when specifically? (2 Cor. 5:17)

2. How does God's Spirit bear witness with your spirit that you are God's child? (Rom. 8:16)

3. When was the last time you loved someone enough to tell them the truth in spite of your fears? How did that turn out? (Jn. 3:16)

4. How do you daily remind yourself you are dead to sin and alive unto God? (Rom. 6:11)

5. How important is Biblical repentance to true salvation decisions? (2 Cor. 7:10-11)

FAITHBUILDERS OF ANSWERED PRAYER
"Pray without ceasing"... I Thess. 5:17
CHAPTER TWO

After I got back home from the beach, I packed my fishing gear and my New Testament and headed to Canada with my friend who had been with me in Delaware. The travel time was twenty hours, so I opened the Bible in Matthew and began to read. Immediately God's Spirit began to speak to me in a still small voice as His words were engrafted into my heart and life. The eyes of my soul were enlightened by a holy book that wrapped its arms around my conscience and began to shape my concept of God as a loving Savior who sent His Son into an evil world that would reject His love gift. (Jas. 1:21-22; Eph. 1:18)

At this time, I was a college prep English teacher who had to read a book every three days to develop a new reading program in the inner city school in which I taught. What amazed me the most about reading the Bible is that I had always been a very avid reader, but I had never read any book that pierced my heart with such life-changing convictions that reshaped my values so radically and so quickly. In twelve hours of reading, I began to hate what I used to love, and began to love what I used to hate, "Christians". (Rom. 5:5; 2 Cor. 5:14)

When we finally arrived at our fish camp, I had read half the New Testament, and couldn't wait to finish it. In the process of reading, I began to underline the things I didn't understand, which was quite a bit. I just kept reading, knowing that my appetite needed to be fed, as I had for the first time in my life truly tasted of God and knew deep within my soul that He was a good, gracious, loving God. (I Pet. 2:2)

We unloaded our gear and immediately went fishing. We were out on the lake about an hour when it began to rain. We caught our limit of twenty walleyes and headed in for dinner. The next two days it rained nonstop, yet we continued to catch our twenty fish limit daily. We had eaten fish every meal for two days and still had our limit to bring home to the USA. So that night I recommended to my friend that we return to Delaware if it was raining the next morning as we awakened.

The next day it rained, so I went to the owner of the lodge and told her we wanted to leave and would pay for the two weeks of our reservation. She graciously told us we only had to pay for one week knowing I would return as I had been there often in the past; she also knew I was fanatical about fishing, and saw me as "good advertising" for her camp as I had always caught my limit of fish!

So we packed up and headed home. After being on the road for one hour, the sun came out and all clouds disappeared, but I looked at my friend and said "keep driving" as my nose was once again embedded in my Bible. By the time we reached Ohio, I had finished the entire New Testament, and my mind was spinning with thoughts about how my character and conduct needed to change, as I counted the cost also of those decisions. (2 Cor. 5:17)

When we got home, we hung up our wet clothes and fishing gear in our rooms and grabbed our beach stuff and headed to Delaware, about another eight-hour drive. As we were pulling out of the drive I yelled for my friend to stop so I could get the mail as our roommates were all working. I grabbed the mail and threw it on the counter in the kitchen. As I did that, one envelope addressed to me slipped out from the rest. It was from the young lady who walked with me on the beach. The first sentence stated, "Rory I must immediately apologize for my selfishness as I have been praying that the weather would be so bad in Canada that God would bring you back to us before we leave Saturday for home in Louisiana."

I remember that sentence today word for word even though that letter was written forty years ago. That letter became my first personal **faithbuilder** and answer to prayer. My heart leaped with joyful anticipation about how big my God really was to move His creation that always obeys His voice. She went on to say that part of her reason was that a marine captain named Doug was going to visit them soon and that she wanted me to meet him. Because of my athleticism and him being an All-American college football player, she felt he would identify with me, and I with him.

We finally arrived in Rehoboth Beach, which I found out years later was the name of one of the wells dug by Isaac in Genesis 26 as a picture of God's sustaining His people's needs in the deserts of life; this well also foreshadowed Jesus' bringing God's people living water in John 7. When we arrived at the coffee house, two of our friends were gone to the airport to get the Captain who would only be there that night. When he arrived, it was like meeting the brother I never had as he spent five hours walking me through the whole New Testament; he answered all my questions that arose from my underlinings of Scriptures I didn't understand as a new Christian. My new journey of faith increased its pace that night as I learned that the Bible contained all the answers and precious promises I needed for life and godliness. Now I would need to learn how to diligently add virtue to my faith, which Jesus Himself would give me as He touched me from on high with His virtue. (Luke 6:19; 2 Pet. 1:1-5)

Many years later as a pastor, I was putting together the prayer sheet for our church's Wednesday evening prayer meeting that weekly preceded our evening Bible study. Our study that night examined the faithful widow's persistent prayer in Luke 18, teaching how God hears and answers persistent effectual prayers. The passage closes with "when the Son of man cometh, shall he find faith on earth?" (Luke 18:8) The context of this passage asks when Jesus returns, will any Christians and churches still be taking prayer seriously and persistently? So after thinking about the seriousness of Jesus' question, I asked my secretary the next day to randomly choose and call twenty churches to find out what time their Wednesday evening prayer meeting started. To my surprise, nineteen of twenty churches did not even have a prayer meeting at all! When churches no longer understand that God's house is first "the house of prayer", they frequently become entertainment centers to gain money as "a den of thieves", robbing God of His glory as Jesus taught in Matthew 21: 13. Oh, how the righteous have fallen!

Rory Wineka

FOOD FOR THOUGHT (Phil. 4:8): "Lord I believe, help thou mine unbelief" (Mark 9:24)

1. **Did God ever do something supernatural in your life? If so, what was it? (Eph. 3:20)**

   Now unto him that is able to do exceeding abundantly above all that we ask or think, according to the power that worketh in us,

2. **How big is your God and why? How is that reflected by your prayer life? (Ps. 139; Isa. 56:6-7)**

3. **Do you believe that in the Christian's life there are no coincidences? (Acts 17:28)**

   for in him we live, and move, and have our being, as certain also of your own poets have said, for we are also his offspring.

4. **How have you been God's balm of Gilead in healing others spiritually? (Jer. 7:14; 8:22)**

   Is there no balm in Gilead; is there no physician there? why then is not the health of the daughter of my people recovered?

5. **How have you possessed your possessions through effectual fervent prayer? (Jas. 5:16)**

   Confess your faults to one another, and pray one for another, that ye may be healed. The effectual fervent prayer of a righteous man availeth much.

6. **Do you believe with childlike faith Jesus' promises regarding prayer? (Jn. 14:13-14)**

   13: And whatsoever ye shall ask in my name, that will I do, that the Father may be glorified in the Son.

   14. If ye shall ask anything in my name, I will do it.

Faithbuilders

I Thes 5:17 - Pray without ceasing

7. Do you have a God-conscious prayer life that seeks God throughout the day? If so, how does that help with peace and joy in your life? (I Thess. 5:17; Phil. 4:6-7)

⑥ Be carefull for nothing; but in everything by Prayer and supplication with thanksgiving let your requests be made known unto God. ⑦ And the peace of God, which passeth all understanding, shall keep your ♡s and minds through Christ Jesus.

8. Do you keep a prayer journal to help you bless God with a grateful heart? (Ps. 103:1-2)

① Bless the LORD, o my soul! and all that is within me, bless his holy name

② Bless the LORD, o my soul, and forget not all his benefits:

9. Do you keep a praise journal to record your personal **faithbuilders**? (Rom. 1:17; Eph. 3:20)

Now unto him that is able to do exceeding abundantly above all that we ask or think, according to the power that worketh in us.

10. Do you memorize Scriptures to enlarge your heart for powerful, Biblical prayer? (Heb. 4:12, 16)

⑫ For the word of God is quick, and powerful, and sharper than any twoedged sword, piercing even to the dividing asunder of soul and spirit, and of the joints and marrow, and is a discerner of the thoughts and intents of the heart.

⑯ Let us therefore come boldly unto the throne of grace, that we may obtain mercy, and find grace to help in time of need.

FAITHBUILDERS OF HOLY CHOICES
"Choose you this day whom ye will serve"... (Josh. 24:14)
CHAPTER THREE

After prayerfully growing in grace for two months, God began convicting me daily about moving back home with my parents to free myself of the many temptations hammering my saved soul as I continued to live with my roommates. The greatest temptation was the monthly parties filled with alcohol and the great potential for immorality. Two divorced female neighbors held a party bi-monthly, and our house held one the alternate months. These parties, as the word got out, were powerful magnets for nurses and secretarial pools from local corporations, partly because one of my roommates was "Mr. Ohio" in division I football.

The secondary temptation developed as one roommate began using and selling drugs, mainly marijuana. One night he offered me a little pill to get "somewhat high" because he knew I didn't like to drink and refused to smoke either cigarettes or his marijuana due to my athleticism. I accepted his pill and went to my girlfriend's house. When she, being a nurse, saw what I had, she refused to let me take it alone, but insisted on splitting it because she had never seen anything like it. The next day I found out that the pill was a horse tranquilizer which put a friend of mine in the hospital the night before due to his reaction to its potency. That scared me to the depth of my soul and finalized my decision to move out from my "friends" who would do such a thing to their good friend.

After living at home for three days, my only sister, Lynn approached me boldly and asked, "What has happened to you?"

I was totally surprised as she began to share that a "new brother" had moved in who for the first time in his life treated her respectfully, and we no longer had the animosity that had caused us to fight like "cats and dogs". She also noticed a very radical change in the way I treated my mother, who I never got along with either.

I then shared with her what had happened to me that summer in Delaware and that I had become a born again Christian. To the best of my ability I described to her some of the changes in my lifestyle and decision making; however, I could not necessarily explain them all, seeing I really had little to do with the life change which only God could explain and empower. (Mt. 11:28-30; 2 Cor. 5:17)

After her numerous questions, caused by the fact that we were a Biblically ignorant family that never went to church or owned a Bible, I simply opened my Bible and walked her through the clear passages in Romans 3:23, 6:23, and 10:13. I then explained the sinner's need of a Savior, and that I knew for sure that the power of the gospel actually worked miraculous changes in a person's life, mine!

Lynn then asked me how to pray to become a Christian. I simply told her to do what I was instructed to do in Delaware; just be

16

honest with God in telling Him that you realize that you are a sinner who cannot save her own soul; ask Jesus to forgive you, save you from yourself, and change you into all he wants you to be for His glory. I told her just to speak to Him as a friend, like she had been talking to me, because Jesus just wants to hear an honest confession of need. There are no "magic" words; simply humble yourself at His feet. (Heb. 4:16) My precious sister became a Christian that day granting me a great **faithbuilder**.

About a week later my father, Paul, approached me for the exact same conversation. I had always feared my dad but never had much of a relationship with him as he was far too busy building a new business from the ground up after he had gotten out of the Navy having served in the Pacific during World War II. He was also a very quiet man who was an only child and one of the rare victims of a divorce in the late 1920s, which caused him to be quite introverted.

After our one hour discussion, he went away thinking about his Christian relatives in Pennsylvania who took him in for a time after his mother's divorce. They were very loving, Christian people who sat around a piano as a family on Saturday night singing hymns to prepare their simple hearts for church the next day. These recollections moved him to come to the church I attended at the time, and on the first morning he came forward at the "altar call" to give his life to Jesus.

Years later my dad became a fine Christian man who was a

hungry Bible student and a very bold witness for Jesus. We had breakfast one day as he turned ninety, and he shared with me that his prayer was that God would take him quickly "when his day came" because my mom suffered much with memory loss from strokes before she died. The following week he had his annual physical and his doctor proclaimed him very healthy, being only on medicine for acid reflux. Two days later he fell backwards at home and hit his head on the cement driveway and died soon thereafter. God gave me yet another **faithbuilder** for my journal, that He takes care of His own to the very end, as God faithfully answered my Dad's prayer (Ps. 37:25). *PS 86:11 Teach me thy way, O Lord, I will walk in thy truth: unite my heart to fear thy name.*

One of the most powerful truths that God has engrafted into my life as an anchor to my soul is that godly people make God-honoring choices as a way of life. Our teachability and humility allow God as the Holy Potter to shape our hearts daily to make right choices. Teachable saints walk in God's truths and consequently have a healthy submissive fear of God. (Ps. 86:11) Then, as a result, God grants saints the power, based on that Biblical fear, to make the right choices daily, guarding the holy integrity of our values and our lives. (Ps. 25:21, 12, 14) May we all learn to "wait" on Him in daily prayers of utter dependency knowing that without Jesus we are nothing and can do nothing. (Jn. 15:5) *21: let integrity and uprightness preserve me; for I will wait on thee.*
12: what man is he that feareth the LORD? Him shall he teach in the way that he shall choose

One of Israel's greatest sins came from habitually choosing to ignore God's voice because they did not fear Him. Consequently the Jews listened to their own carnal voice of selfishness and

I am the vine, ye are the **18** *branches: He that abideth in me, and I in him, the same bringeth forth much fruit: for without me ye can do nothing.*

then started murmuring against their Lord even after He fed them manna from heaven. (Num. 21: 5-9) Therefore, God sent fiery servants among them and many people died from the snake bites. Then the people came crying to Moses to pray for them and their sins. God immediately told Moses to make a brass serpent and put it on a pole for all the people who had been bitten to "look and live" if they would believe by faith that God would forgive them and heal them. (v8)

The same problem exists today in our culture that has no fear of God. Many people are still being "snake bitten" by their carnal sins: adultery, alcoholism, divorce, drinking, drugs, lying, stealing, hatred, bitterness, murder, idolatry, and unbelief. Solomon nailed it when he said "there's nothing new under the sun". (Eccles. 1:9)

I find it most interesting that the medical symbol today is the snake on a pole, reminding all mankind that Jesus is the Great Physician who heals all afflictions. As Isaiah wrote, "In all their affliction he was afflicted, and the angel of his presence saved them: in his love and in his pity he redeemed them; and he bare them, and carried them all the days of old." (Isa. 63:9) I have two very good friends who are doctors and both of them say boldly that all doctors should be Christians because no one can explain healing and the supernatural workings of our bodies. The same God who healed the sinners in Moses' day, still heals all sinners who will "look and live" at Jesus Christ the Lord. (Jn. 3:16; 2Pet. 3:9)

The Lord is not slack concerning his promise, as some men cant slackness; but is 19 longsuffering to us-ward, not willing that any should perish, but that all should come to repentance.

But without faith it is impossible to please him; for he that cometh to God must believe that he is, and that he is a rewarder of them that dilligently seek him.

FOOD FOR THOUGHT (Phil. 4:8): "The secret of the Lord is with them that fear Him." (Ps. 25:14)

1. **Do I possess a healthy fear of the Lord that makes me wise to make daily choices? (Prov. 9:10)**

The fear of the Lord is the beginning of wisdom: and the knowledge of the holy is understanding.

2. **How can I improve my patiently waiting on God in decision making? (Isa. 40:31; Heb. 11:6)**

Isa 40:31 But they that wait upon the Lord shall renew their strength; they shall mount up with wings as eagles; they shall run, and not be weary, and they shall walk, and not faint.

3. **How do your choices affect your daily experience of joy in life? (Isa. 65:12-14)** ①

4. **How do I bear the burdens of other saints in effectual praying, as Jesus does for me? (Gal. 6:1-2)**

① Brethren, if a man be overtaken in a fault, ye which are spiritual, restore such an one in the spirit of meekness; considering thyself, lest thou also be tempted. ② Bear ye one anothers burdens, and so fufil the law of Christ.

5. **Do I pray Biblically enough for Jesus to answer all my prayers for His glory? (Jn. 14:13-14)**

13. And whatsoever ye shall ask in my name, that will I do, that the Father may be glorified in the Son.

14. If ye shall ask anything in my name, I will do it.

6. How do others see that I possess **"the faith"** of Jesus as I reflect His light and life? (Ro. 1:5)

By whom we have recieved grace and apostleship, for obedience to the faith among all nations, for his name.

7. How do I enjoy **"the faith"** of Jesus as His love enables me in my walk of sacrificial service to enjoy His **faithbuilders?** (Gal. 2:20) I am crusified with Christ: neverless I live; yet not I, but Christ liveth in me: and the life which I now live in the flesh I live by the Faith of the Son of God, who loved me, and gave himself for me.

8. How do you allow God to unite your heart to His daily to make good choices? (Ps. 86:11)

Teach me thy way, O Lord, I will walk in thy truth: unite my heart to fear thy name

9. Do you **"consider your ways"** before you enter God's presence in prayer? (Hag. 1:5, 7)

5: Now therefore thus saith the Lord of hosts; Consider your ways.

7: Thus saith the Lord of hosts; Consider your ways.

10. How effective is the leadership in your home in training your children to make godly choices on a consistent basis, no matter what the world thinks? (Josh. 24:13-15; Ps. 25:12) (14) Now therefore fear the Lord, and serve him in sincerity and in truth: put away the gods which your fathers served on the other side of the flood, and in Egypt, and serve ye the Lord. (15) And if it seem evil unto you to serve the Lord, choose you this day whom ye will serve: whether the gods which your fathers served that were on the other side of the flood, or the gods of the Amorites, in whos land ye dwell: But as for me and my house, we will serve the Lord.

21

ps 25:12 what man is he that feareth the lord? him shall he teach in the way that he shall choose

FAITHBUILDERS OF GRACE
"For by grace are ye saved through faith"... (Eph. 2:8)
CHAPTER FOUR

Before we could graduate from high school as seniors in 1966, we were required to attend baccalaureate a week previous. I could not understand why we had to sit through a "religious speech" in order to get our diplomas. So I hated the thought of wasting a whole evening with such nonsense.

As I sat in the auditorium, boredom filled my mind with thoughts of, "How soon can we get out of this place? We are seniors who did all you asked us to do. Let us go, please, to have some fun for a change!"

Just then the ceremony began and a tall, husky, good looking man walked out, who was later introduced as "Pastor David Burnham," and I thought, "Oh here we go...I've gotta spend the night listening to a boring pastor!"

But then he got up and began to speak, and the more he spoke, the more I was drawn in to hear "his story". He had played football in high school and was quite a star, later being an All-American football player in college. He was later offered a professional football contract which he refused.

He explained that his father Carl died of a heart attack as he pastored a church called The Chapel on Fir Hill. The church's leaders asked Dave to assume his father's role as pastor. After much prayer, Dave accepted the calling to pastor his father's church.

My heart was stunned in disbelief as I was a fanatical pro football fan who worshipped the Cleveland Browns. My Dad owned season tickets on the forty yard line when Jim Brown played for Cleveland. I thought, "What kind of nut would make such a foolish choice!?"

As Dave continued speaking, he had my full attention. When he was done, I remembered nothing but his decision to pastor and to not play pro football. Overall, I really enjoyed the dynamic way in which he stated things, and I thought, "If I ever have an interest in hearing about God, I would like to hear it from this man!"

Now let's flash forward five years to the fall of 1971. My salvation was almost sixty days old as I returned to teach college prep English and Latin and assist the varsity basketball coach in an inner city school. A most dramatic change of attitude dominated my heart the first day of classes, as I found a newly planted love in my heart for these teenagers, forty percent of whom were from broken homes. When I finished my last day of school the previous year, I couldn't wait to leave the stress and chaos of a school that was run by the kids due to a very weak principal. Teachers should have gotten combat pay for trying to teach in this "zoo". Students were daily robbed and assaulted by teenage "thugs," most of which had already failed twice by the seventh grade. Hallway walls were covered in graffiti. Seventy percent of the teachers requested transfers to other schools annually. The incorrigible students from other junior highs were transferred here as the "last stop" before being removed to juvenile hall or kicked out for the rest of the year. Seven of my former students are now in prison for murder! I really didn't want to come back at all, but now I saw these teens through Jesus' eyes. (Eph. 1:18) *The eyes of your under-standing being enlightened; that ye may know what is the hope of his calling, and what the riches of the glory of his inheritance in the saints,*

Shortly after returning to school, the shop teacher approached me once again, as he had the previous year, and invited me to his church for Sunday services. He said "I heard you had a religious experience this past summer."

I responded, "No. I became a Christian. I am not religious at all, as Jesus hated religion and spoke boldly against it for three years. Jesus is into personal relationships, not religion."

He smiled as he too was a very faithful Christian who fully understood the difference between religion and personal relationships with Jesus. Then I asked him for directions to his church, and he responded, "Didn't you go to Akron University? The church is one block away. You have to know where it is!"

To my surprise, I had parked next door to this church while in college, and walked past it for four years. That's how oblivious this heathen was until I came to know Jesus. I didn't have a religious circumspect bone in my body!

So I met my friend at the front door on the following Sunday evening. We sat towards the front enjoying the sweet music of the organ and piano. As I sat there, I thought about the other churches my neighbors took me to the past two months, but none of them had really "grabbed" my heart or attention, although all of them preached truth from the Bible. As I pondered these thoughts, the pastor walked out and I couldn't believe my eyes. It was Pastor David Burnham who spoke at my high school baccalaureate! I remembered saying to myself that night five years earlier that if I EVER had an interest in hearing about God, this is the man I think could get my attention!

As he began to preach, he had my heart's absolute full attention for the next forty-five minutes. I took so many notes on their little bulletin that there was no room left to write more! His message powerfully penetrated my heart as I felt like a buck private sitting in front of a five-star General, taking marching orders for the daily battles of life, especially as an inner city teacher! All the people could have left the room as I felt his message was just for me. What a **faithbuilder**!

I attended his Christ-exalting Bible preaching church, The Chapel, for the next thirteen years and eventually served under his leadership as one of his pastors for six years. More about that later!

With God there are no coincidences as He divinely meets all our needs in Christ. (Phil. 4:19) All things work for His glory and my good, as He daily guides my steps and decisions, protecting me as I walk His paths of righteousness, and He "connects the dots of my life." (Acts 17:28) God's precious promises give me a daily faith that He always takes care of His own as He grows us from faith to faith, (Rom. 10:17) as He builds us into "the faith" of Jesus through a maturity that enables us to "fight the good fight of faith". (Rom. 1:5, 17; 10:17; Col. 2:6-7)

Many years ago we took our children to Disney World and their favorite ride was "It's a Small World". After riding that ride at least ten times, partly because the line was short and it got us out of the hot sun, we finally headed home. For the next five days that tune burned in my mind as I often began to hum it over and over, "It's a small world after all".

Then a few months later I began to think of the first time I met my wife's great uncle. Tom Ambrose. After sharing my testimony of how Pastor David Burnham had spoken at my high school graduation and how I ended up on his pastoral staff many years later, her uncle got up and walked out of the room. He came back smiling and showed my wife and me a picture of David Burnham's mother and father, Agnes and Carl Burnham. He then explained why he had that picture as he had introduced them to each other in their younger days. I was stunned on how God's grace "connects dots" in our lives. It is indeed "a small world after all!"

FOOD FOR THOUGHT: Your life may be the only "sermon" some people will ever hear! (Mt. 5:16) *let your life so shine before men, that they may see your good works, and glorify your father which is in heaven.*

1. **Do you believe that Jesus is all you need? How has God proven that to you? (Rom. 8:28-39)**
   situations in the world may try to seperate us from God - us from him (vs 35), But we can conquure through God all things (vs 37) However, Nothing can seperate Gods love tword us (vs 38-39). It is always us who moves away from him, Not vice versa!

2. **How has God amazed you, going before and behind you, protecting you? (Ps. 139:5-6)** *⑤ Thou hast beset me behind & before, and laid thine hand upon me. ⑥ Such knowledge is too wonderful for me; it is high, I cannot attain unto it.*

3. **Do you daily ask God to search your heart and mind as He leads you in love? (Ps. 139:23-24)** *㉓ Search me, O God, and know my heart: try me, and know my thoughts: ㉔ and see if there be any wicked way in me, and lead me in the way everlasting.*

4. **How had God protected you even in the days before He saved your soul, as His eternal eyes of love were on you and His heart guided yours? (Matt. 6:26-34; Acts 8:28-32; 17:27-28)** *㉗ That they should seek the Lord, if haply they might feel after him, and find him, though he be not far from every one of us: ㉘ for in him we live, and move, and have our being; as certain also of your poets have said, for we are also his offspring.*

5. **What was the last specific faithbuilder God gave you? (Mark 10:27; Eph. 3:20)** *㉗ And Jesus looking upon them saith, with men it is impossible, but not with God : for with God all things are possible.*
   ㉓ Now unto him that is able to do exceeding abundantly above all that we ask or think, according to the power that worketh in us. **27**

6. What do you need to trust God for today? (Prov. 3:5-6)

⑤ Trust in the LORD with all thine heart: and lean not unto thine own understanding ⑥ In all thy ways acknowledge him, and he shall direct ~~their~~ paths.
thy

7. How do you strengthen yourself in "the faith" so you may finish your race well? (2 Tim. 2:1; 4:7)

2:1 Thou therefore, my son, be strong in the grace that is in Christ Jesus.

4:7 I have fought a good fight, I have finished my course, I have kept the faith.

THE FAITHBUILDER OF A PRUDENT WIFE
"A prudent wife is from the LORD"... (Prov. 19:14)
CHAPTER FIVE

Shortly after I became a Christian I came under great conviction about how I spent my money on the things I treasured. As my values shifted, the first thing I decided to quit was drag racing my Dodge Dart each summer. So I went to my neighbor's house to ask him if he knew anyone who was selling a "beater," an older model car that I would only need to pay liability insurance on because my insurance rates were costly for a twenty- three-year-old.

He told me that his boss at work had an older car for sale. So I jumped into my Dodge and drove to his house. He came to the door and faintly remembered me and asked me what brought me there. I asked to see the older car he had for sale and he was surprised because he had no such vehicle. My neighbor must have heard him joking around, but he apologized for the confusion and invited me in knowing we both loved to hunt.

As we were sitting and talking about hunting and fishing, his four daughters came home from shopping. They were all very friendly, but one of them named Pat changed the whole atmosphere of the room when she entered. We will come back to that observation later!

I went home then and called the young lady Debbie from Louisiana, who had walked with me on the beach and challenged me to think about Jesus. We had started talking on the phone in August, and the calls were getting longer and longer, running up quite a phone bill, but it was all worth it as she encouraged me in my growth as a new Christian.

The more we talked, the more serious our relationship developed. I decided to fly to Louisiana over my Christmas teaching break to stay with the Pastor who was in Delaware at the coffee house and visit my friend Debbie who also lived nearby. My main goal was to meet Debbie's family and explore the possibility of asking her to marry me.

I thoroughly enjoyed my first Christmas at her home with her godly family and seeing my friends from the coffee house again, but it was soon obvious the engagement was not a good idea for a few prayerful reasons. So I flew back to Ohio thanking God for making it very clear that I needed to seek a good Christian woman nearer my home who I could go to church with and grow close to under the guidance of my new home church and pastors.

As soon as I arrived home, I immediately went to see my next door neighbors, who were my "second parents", a dear couple who cared much for me, and were excited to hear any news about my possible engagement. When I got to their home and told them it didn't work out, they immediately said that they knew someone who wanted to go out with me. They had never said such a thing before. I asked who they had in mind, and they said, "Our friends' daughter, Pat, who you met a few months ago". I hadn't even noticed the couple playing cards with their backs to me. Here it was the man and his wife from whom I tried to buy the car that wasn't even for sale.

So I got her phone number that night from her mother and called Pat the next day for a date, but she turned me down. I discovered that her mom was scheming to get Pat away from a young man her parents didn't like.

I was somewhat confused and a little upset, my ego being hurt, because I hadn't been turned down in many years regarding dating. So I swallowed my pride and called again and asked just to go out for pizza with no strings attached at all. Pat agreed, and the evening went well as we really connected and had great conversation and fun. So I asked her if she would go to church with me the next Sunday, and that's when God began to knit our hearts together in Christ. Pat had become a Christian at a young age, when her neighbors had taken her to church but they quit going and consequently so had she.

Over the next few months we went to church every time the doors opened and got into a good neighborhood Bible study with a couple that helped me get my first Bible. Both of us began to grow exponentially as we absorbed God's Word and grew together in the grace and knowledge of Jesus Christ our Lord. We got married in 1973 and had no idea what God's plans were for our future together serving Him at the Chapel where we attended church.

Seeing we both grew up in dysfunctional homes which provided no spiritual training, we struggled somewhat in building our marriage, partly because we received no premarital counseling. So we had to work things out daily as we developed good conflict resolution skills in order to love each other unconditionally. (Jn. 13:34-35; 15:12) *This is my commandment, That ye love one another, as I have loved you.*

God immediately began to enlighten me to the incredible gift that He had given me in Pat by providing a Proverbs 31 priceless, godly, loving helpmate and virtuous woman to be my wife. Pat's spirit of contagious, merciful servanthood changed my life dramatically because there was none of that in the home where I grew up. Every day she was ministering to someone: me, our children, neighbors, family, friends, and strangers. She loved everyone unconditionally as she served Jesus. (Jn. 13:1-17)

When God began convicting me about the possibility of ministry, Pat was quick to remind me that she married a school teacher- not a pastor! But she also declared that she was more than willing to trust God, as a picture of Ruth, as He led us together on this possible new path of life.

Over the forty-one years of our marriage now, we have had one argument, which lasted all of five minutes. We reconciled that night, and I apologized for my foolishness. Our home has been a sanctuary of peace and rest for our three precious children and still is today. She has served our family all the days of her life with her love, cards and notes, cooking, and baking as a

32

woman whose candle never goes out even at night. Her children still today call her "blessed" knowing they have a mother who fears and loves her Lord as "her own works praise her in the gates" of our home. (Prov. 31:31)

Through this great **faithbuilder,** God indeed gave me an indescribable gift in a helpmate, a Biblical combination of Sarah, Ruth, Mary, and the virtuous woman who has done me "good and not evil all the days of her life". Thank God for His unsearchable durable riches of a life partner whose "strength and honor are her clothing" as "she openeth her mouth with wisdom" to spur me on to love and good deeds to glorify God. (Prov. 8:17-21, 32-35; 31:12, 25-26)

God often reminded His beloved Israel that "the LORD is thy keeper: the LORD is thy shade upon thy right hand." (Ps. 121:5) David as God's "sweet psalmist" often reminded the Israelites that they were a divinely protected and "kept" people, and that "kept" saints keep God's Word. (Ps. 30:3; 119:167) Peter reminded his persecuted Jewish brethren that they were "kept by the power of God through faith unto salvation." (I Pet. 1:5) Historically the Jews knew well the special meaning of the word "kept" reminding them of God protecting them as the "apple of his eye." (Zech. 2:8)

In conclusion, after being married to my wife and best friend for forty-one years, I fully know that I am a "kept" man. I praise my great God of unsearchable riches for crowning me with a

virtuous woman who loves Jesus and me with all of her heart! (Rom. 11:33; Eph.3:8)

11:33   O the depth of the riches both of the wisdom and knowledge of God! how unsearchable are his judgements, and his ways past finding out.

3:8   Unto me, who am less than the least of all saints, is this grace given, that I should preach among the Gentiles the unsearchable riches of Christ.

FOOD FOR THOUGHT (Phil. 4:8): "A virtuous woman is a crown to her husband" (Prov. 12:5)

1. How do you as a husband appreciate God's gift of a "help meet" who builds her house into a home with the wisdom of the unconditional love of servant-hood? (Gen. 2:18; Prov. 14:1)

Pro 14:1 Every wise woman buildeth her house: but the foolish plucketh it down with her hands.

Gen 2:18 And the LORD God said, It is not good that man should be alone; I will make him an help meet for him.

2. How do you as a wife strive to fulfill your God ordained role as a "help meet"? (Prov. 19:14)

House and riches are the inheritance of fathers: and a prudent wife is from the LORD

3. How are you training your children what to look for in a godly spouse? (Prov. 22:6)

Train up a child in the way he should go: and when he is old, he will not depart from it.

4. How are you building a growing marriage full of God's grace and mercy? (2 Pet. 3:18)

But grow in grace, and in the knowledge of our LORD and Saviour Jesus Christ. To him be the glory both now and for ever. Amen.

5. Is your home merely "Christian" or is it clearly Christ-centered? (Luke 6:46)

And why call ye me, Lord, Lord, and do not the things which I say?

6. **How is your home an incubator, teaching children to fear God? (Ps. 86:11)**

Teach me thy way, O Lord: I will walk in thy truth: unite my heart to fear thy name.

7. **How is the Lord building your home for His glory as you are His "watchmen"? (Ps. 127:1)** Except the Lord build the house, they labour in vain that build it: Except the LORD keep the city, the watchmen waketh but in vain.

8. **How has God sealed your home in agape unconditional contagious love? (Song Sol. 8:6)** Set me as a seal upon thine heart, as a seal upon thine arm: for love is as strong as death; jealously is cruel as the grave: the coals thereof are coals of fire, which hath a most vehement flame.

9. **How does God's eternal love protect your marriage and home from life's floods? (Song Sol. 8:7)**

Many waters cannot quench love, neither can the floods drown it: if a man would give all the substance of his house for love, it would utterly be contemned.

FAITHBUILDERS FOR SEEKERS AFTER TRUTH
"Seek ye the LORD while he may be found"... (Isa. 55:6)
CHAPTER SIX

Not long after I began attending The Chapel, I got very involved in their training programs to become a better servant-soldier to know how to effectually use all the weapons of God's Word accurately to "fight the good fight" of faith. Many godly men came alongside of me to sharpen and encourage me in daily seeking God's will and wisdom through personally knowing God's Word. (Jn. 7:17; 1Tim. 6:12; 2 Tim. 2:2)

My learning curve was like climbing a ladder of many rungs, not knowing where the next one would lead in practical application; my soul simply trusted God who had burned into my heart many faithbuilders as precious memories that built a precious faith, as Jesus did for the disciples on the Emmaus Road in Luke 24.

First, I enrolled in teacher training and began to help teach fifth grade boys, assisting the teacher who had initially invited me to The Chapel. This experience stretched me to understand child-like faith and made me learn to put God's bread of life on the bottom shelf where all could reach it and be well fed. I gained a far greater understanding of Jesus' living love for children and newborn Christians, as He had to fill my cup so I could fill theirs. I had no anticipation of all Jesus would teach me as he grew me into a better teacher, so I could give transferrable concepts of God's love to their hungry hearts which thirsted for

When I see the the lost world I see the sin in people & the failures of humanity, I need to see how christ loves them to have a burden for the lost not just a disappointment of them.

Faithbuilders

righteousness, as many of these boys were from good Christian homes.

Secondly, a man asked me to join the church's evangelism training so I could go out with men on Thursday evenings to visit people who had filled in a visitor card, knowing we would be coming without notifying them first. Though the training was excellent, it did not remove my fears of talking to strangers about the Lord's love. But all that soon changed, as I found myself seeing lost souls through Jesus' eyes. I couldn't keep my mouth shut, just as the new evangelists in the book of Acts. (Acts 1:8) *But ye shall recieve power, after that the Holy Ghost is come upon you: and ye shall be a witness unto me both in Jerusalem, and in all Judea, and in Samira, and unto the uttermost part of the earth.*

Thirdly, a new Christian Education Pastor joined the staff and heard that I taught inner city junior high and was now the head basketball coach. He asked me to lead a Monday night high school Bible Study to reach teens from a number of schools. The study was held in the home of a young man whom I later discipled one on one and who today is a pastor. The teens were easy to motivate and were so hungry to grow in grace that they actually inspired me. That study lasted for two years in the home of hospitable gracious and godly people who loved the teenagers dearly.

Fourthly, that same new pastor invited me to go on two mission trips; one during Christmas break to Bluefield West Virginia to minister in a small church and the other during the summer to an Indian Reservation in Red Lake Minnesota. These trips really took me out of my comfort zone and stretched me into an utter

whats stretching me into utter dependency?!

dependency on God, knowing only His divine enablement would allow me to be effective in service. The Minnesota trip was very hard due to the alcoholism, violence, and divorce that were rampant among the Indians. The pastor we worked with only saw seven people in 15 years come to know Jesus, and most of them died or were killed before they were saved for two years.

While God stretched my faith through these numerous ministry experiences and **faithbuilders**, He also stretched me in my teaching in the inner city. The school finally got a new principal who ran a "tight ship" both academically and behaviorally. In six weeks she had removed ninety-five percent of the incorrigible teens who had made it nearly impossible to teach those who wanted to learn. A student asked me to do an after school Bible study which soon had thirty teens coming. This was a direct result of my sharing Jesus on a consistent basis in my classes. Part of the curriculum had me teaching mythology in my English and Latin classes, so I taught how Jesus lived at the same time, and the people of Rome had to choose: religion based on idolatry and myth or a relationship based on factual truths given by God in the flesh. Our discussions motivated me greatly as the teens asked great questions as seekers after truth. I told them they had to make up their own minds personally, because I refused to coerce them into having "my faith."

While all these doors were being opened by God alone, He was stretching my faithfulness and people were watching, much to my surprise. Two pastors at my church began asking me to pray about going into the ministry as the church teens were like "putty in my hands" for God's glory, according to their observations and the feedback from parents. But I told them that I had no interest at all in pastoral ministry but would pray because I respected their opinions and wisdom. Also my "mission field" was my inner city youth who had no one to help them figure out life's issues. God began convicting me though about trusting Him for the impossible, as I did when He saved my soul. After all, I never wanted to be a Christian. As a matter of fact, I certainly wasn't looking for God in Delaware, but He surely sought me out through His loving vessels of contagious truth and light. (Mt. 5:16)

So I began to pray fervently for another **faithbuilder** and for God to reveal His will for me in His Word. After much prayer, I applied to seminary to see if I would be accepted. Shortly thereafter, my principal whom I had a great relationship with asked me to see her after school. So that afternoon I walked into her office to be informed that I could no longer mention the name of Jesus in my classroom. She told me that she would miss me as she knew my prayers. She stated that two wealthy Jewish men who had close friends on the local board of education demanded that my sharing about Jesus cease. So God rather quickly gave me another **faithbuilder** in answer to prayer. A few weeks later I got accepted into seminary to start on a whole new path of my journey to be in the center of God's will, attempting to bear eternal fruit for God's glory. (Jn. 15:16)

While all this was transpiring, my mentor pastor asked me to do the training of sixty teens for a larger mission outreach for that summer in which we would be ministering to three churches, with me leading one of the teams. So God seemed to be confirming my calling. Then I informed my principal I was resigning to attend seminary in the fall. My principal later called me and asked me to take a one year leave of absence, and that she would hold my teaching position in case my calling to ministry didn't work out the way I had planned. She also informed me that she was sensitive to this process as her brother started to enter the priesthood, but it never worked out for him. I thanked her for caring, but told her this was a matter of faith, and that I totally trusted God by faith or I wouldn't have resigned.

So a few weeks later we got onto two buses for a twenty-four-hour bus ride to Waskish, Minnesota where I would experience another major **faithbuilder**, something only God could do that would radically change my life!

FOOD FOR THOUGHT (Phil. 4:8): "Seek ye first the kingdom of God and His righteousness" (Mt. 6:33)

1. **What is there that you really need to trust God alone for? (Prov. 3:5-6)** ⑤ Trust in the Lord with all thine heart; and lean not unto thine own understanding. ⑥ In all thy ways acknowledge him, and he shall direct thy paths.

2. **When was the last time God burned a "life lesson" into your heart and what was it? (Luke 24:32)** And they said one to another Did not our heart burn within us, while he talked with us by the way, and while he opened to us the scriptures?

3. **Do you have a godly friend who helps you weekly to grow in grace? (2 Tim. 2:2; Titus 2:3-5)** And the things that thou hast heard of me among many witnesses, the same commit thou to faithful men, who shall be able to teach others.

4. **How is God's Word the final authority for your life and decisions? (Isa. 43:13)** Yea, before the day was I am he; and there is none that can deliever out of my hand: I will work, and who shall let it?

5. **How do you daily feed your heart with God's "manna" from heaven? (Jer. 15:16)** Thy words were found, and I did eat them; and thy word was unto me the joy and rejoicing of mine heart: for I am called by thy name, O LORD God of hosts.

6. Are you a person who gathers much or little manna from God daily? How many times have you completely read through your Bible in one year? (Exod. 16:17)

And the children of Israel did so, and gathered, some more, some less.

7. Do you have a God-fearing mentor discipling you in your walk with God? If not, what mature godly saint could disciple you in "the faith"? (Prov. 13:20; 2 Cor. 13:5)

13:20   He that walketh with wise men shall be wise: but a companion of fools shall be destroyed.

2 Cor
13:5   Examine yourselves, wheather ye be in the faith; prove your own selves. Know ye not your own selves, how that Jesus Christ is in you, except ye be reprobates?

MIRACULOUS FAITHBUILDERS
"With God all things are possible"... (Mt.19:26)
CHAPTER SEVEN

One of the awesome privileges of serving God on short-term mission trips is experiencing the Biblical reality that our Lord always has agendas far beyond our plans and expectations if His servants have a teachable, humble heart. I have been privileged to plan, go on, and lead fifty mission trips in the last forty years, but one trip dramatically changed my life: the **faithbuilder** of Waskish, Minnesota, a fishing village, population 135, where I took a team of twelve to do vacation Bible school for one week.

To set the context, my pastor mentor asked me to design and do all the training for three months to prepare high school youth to minister to children before the summer of 1976. The first night of the training the teens began to moan and groan because of the syllabus which called for devotions through daily Bible reading, personal Scripture memorization writing their own lessons, teaching children how to memorize Scripture, and a book to read to help prepare their hearts for the mission at hand. They complained because previous mission trip training had consisted basically of showing up and staying awake, and you got to go! I told them that in order to glorify God as His servant-soldiers, they had to prepare their hearts and materials. Jesus spent much time training his disciples before He sent them out two by two, and I was simply following His pattern to maximize our effectiveness. (Mark 6:7)

When we arrived in Waskish after a two-day, twenty-four hour bus trip, the teens were tired but ready for the challenge ahead. When we settled in, the church's leader asked me to preach the Sunday message and promote the VBS to the church, although she had minimal expectations regarding the Sunday morning attendance and VBS success. When I told her that I was not a preacher and had never preached, the teens said, "You preach to us all the time, but you just don't give an altar call!"

So on Sunday, I preached reluctantly and our teens promoted VBS, sang songs to lead worship, and gave good personal testimonies of God saving their souls and preparing them for this outreach to the community's precious children. After I preached, a thirteen-year-old young lady approached and asked if there would be anything for teenagers during the five-day VBS. I told her "no," but if she could bring at least three friends we would put a class together for them all. She smiled and said she would do that.

The next day, fifteen teenage girls showed up and stayed afterwards to begin building some great friendships with our fifteen young people as hungry hearts contagiously influenced their peer group. When VBS ended each day, they brought their lunches and stayed all afternoon. By the end of the week, all fifteen teenage girls had accepted Jesus as their Savior, and had built strong relationships with my team of servants.

When we boarded our bus for the long journey home, the tears flowed as all the teens exchanged addresses with the promise of correspondence through the summer, which they did do. So as we headed out, I told our teens that we were going to maximize our time on the trip home by evaluating each other, thinking about the changes we saw God make in each life through the week, and the effectiveness we had individually as a team.

God blessed us exceedingly beyond our prayers and greatest imaginations, and the young people praised Him all the way home and encouraged each other. Even though sometimes the evaluations were very honest and a little "brutal," it was always done in love. Through this process our teens bonded in ways that only God could explain, as they sensed His Presence every day in the midst of sharing His precious Word to precious lost teens and children who needed unconditional love.

As we got about two hours from home, the teens finally finished their evaluations of each other so I told them to relax and just have fun the rest of the trip. Much to my surprise they said, "No. We are not done yet, as we are going to evaluate you!"

They began to share how they at first hated the way I set up the training, and how bad their attitudes were, and that some of them wept when they found out that they were going to actually be in my group, as our team split into three groups for three different locations in Minnesota. By the time the two hours were done, they had greatly encouraged me and urged me to pray about becoming their new youth pastor, as the current youth pastor had just announced his resignation to pursue further training in seminary. I told them that was the church's decision, not mine, and that I had two years of seminary in front of me yet. But what they didn't know was that their evaluation finally one-hundred percent confirmed God's answering my prayers about whether to leave teaching to enter the ministry, and not to take a leave of absence with full assurance God had called me to full-time ministry.

To help explain my prayer journey, I was somewhat confused about God's will when we left Akron on the bus for Minnesota because of three opportunities in front of me. After I told my principal about possibly resigning, she begged me to reconsider and offered me all college prep classes, and the school newspaper leadership to replace the 200-student difficult study hall I ran annually.

The second opportunity came through a highly respected Christian principal at a top quality non inner city school where no Jewish students attended who might be offended by my sharing Jesus in the classroom. He offered to hire me immediately for a position to teach college prep English, Latin, and offered me the head coaching basketball job too.

So confusion ran through my mind as I prayed asking God what I should do: go back to my current school and just love the teens to Jesus, but not share my faith in Jesus; go to the new school with the great offer from the Christian principal, or go to seminary.

As we arrived at our halfway point on the trip up to Minnesota, I roomed with one of the pastors who would lead another team in another location. My heart ached as I shared my confusion as I wanted to be in the center of God's will. I didn't want to make a good choice, but the best choice possible, as I thought all three choices could be from God.

He responded, "Rory, God is not the Author of confusion. Only one of these doors is from God, with the other two being from Satan's distracting and unholy voice. You most likely will have great clarity by the end of the week. Just keep seeking His face through His Word and prayer and He will clarify His will for you." (Acts 6:4; Mt. 7:7) *Ask and it shall be given you; seek, and ye shall find; knock, and it shall be opened unto you.*

That's exactly what God did when He showed up in Waskish, Minnesota that week as Jesus answered prayer exceeding abundantly above and beyond our requests as He fulfilled His agendas for those teenage girls. All the glory goes to Him alone for saving souls and changing lives as He granted a whole community and our team many **faithbuilders** (1Cor. 10:31). Many of our team from that trip faithfully serve Jesus as full-time pastors and pastors' wives today, but unfortunately, one of the young men is in prison serving a life term for multiple murders. *weather therefore ye eat, or drink, or whatsoever ye do, do all to the glory of God.*

A few years later, another **faithbuilder** occurred for my disciples as we went on a retreat where God showed up miraculously. After spending twelve months training six of my key disciples, I took them on a wilderness camping trip to the

Georgian Bay in Ontario, Canada. God blessed abundantly as we studied the life of Peter as a fisherman who had great potential but lacked maturity as he often displayed his "little faith". Peter had great moments of exalting Christ and also committed great sins by denying His Lord, as one day Jesus rebuked him, calling him "Satan." (Mt.16:23) The young men each worked on giving their testimonies and Biblical devotionals on what they learned from Peter's life, as each afternoon they had to lead a Bible study for the whole team. The weather and fishing were awesome as God's creation spoke to us daily. (Ps. 19) One night around midnight we were fishing as God lit up the sky with flashing lights of green, blue, white, and red as He displayed the Aurora Borealis in its full glory. Most of the men had never seen this before.

Towards the end of the week, a bear came into camp looking for food, but God protected us as he left without hurting anyone or damaging our food supply which was well-sealed in strong coolers. On the last day, we packed up all our gear and put it into two boats as we headed out of a little canal into the main bay area. As we turned the corner, the small waves soon grew to six-foot waves as the winds started to howl. The narrowness of the channel kept us from being able to turn back as many treacherous shoals lay on both sides. The smaller boat with two men in it had little weight from supplies, but it still began to take on water quickly, as one man began to bail water with his ball cap. Our larger boat with four men and all the heavy gear also began taking on water coming over the front windshield. As the boats continued filling with water, so did our hearts with fear as we silently called out to God for divine protection. A few minutes later, a huge rubber raft with two 175 horsepower motors shot over the top of a huge wave and came right to us. It was the Canadian Coast Guard who took four of our men into their raft plus all heavy gear like tents, camping gear, and ice chests. They went before us smashing down the waves as they escorted us several miles into safe harbor. We thanked them from the bottom of our grateful hearts as we stood soaking wet on the dock of the marina. After we had all changed into dry clothes, I went into the marina to see the owner who I knew because I had been going to this fishing area for twenty-five years. I asked the owner how often he had seen the Coast Guard in his forty-five years of owning the marina, and he responded "Never, not once in all my life going back sixty-five years of living here at the mouth of the bay"!

I returned to that area many times after that and still never saw the Coast Guard, and neither did the marina owner or his family to the best of my knowledge. I believe with all my heart that God sent those men to rescue us as his dearly beloved servants. Five of the six young men with me later became pastors, and the sixth man became a doctor who used his medical practice for glorifying Jesus Christ. This **faithbuilder** changed all our lives as our Redeemer burned into our souls scriptures we share as praises on the eight-hour trip back home. God reminded us well of the days Jesus rescued His beloved disciples from raging storms which had greatly frightened seasoned fisherman like Peter. This wasn't one of the lessons I had planned for my

50

disciples to learn about Peter's growing from faith to faith. (I Cor. 10:31; Luke 24:32)

In closing, God always goes before and behind His servants with divine protection for those saints trying to fulfill their mission in life to grow in "the faith" of Jesus. (Ps. 139:5-6; Jn. 17:4; 2 Tim. 4:7) **Faithbuilder** miracles grant servants precious memories that "stack stones" reminding us that in Him alone we live and move and have our being. (Josh. 4:6; Acts 17:28; I Jn. 4:9) For example, on two separate mission trips the brakes went out on our church bus loaded with teenagers as we went through red lights of major intersections, and both times no traffic came into us. I was driving on one of those trips, and I will never forget the fear in my heart as I hit that brake pedal that went all the way to the floor as I stared at the red light. Neither will I ever forget the relief in my soul as God shielded us as our perfect hiding place. (Ps. 119:114) *Thou art my hiding place and my shield: I hope in thy word.*

Another **faithbuilder** occurred when a pastor friend had lost his position for honoring God's Word at a church that was far more interested in entertaining people than in telling them the truth of Jesus. He soon incurred debt, having no income. After my wife and I prayerfully discussed his need, we decided to send him what we could, seeing our discretionary funds were limited. So we secretly mailed him a "love gift" of $50.00 trusting God to replenish our small savings account. Two days later we received an anonymous gift for $500.00 in the mail reminding us of God's precious promise to those who faithfully cast their bread upon the waters. (Eccles. 11:1) Then a few

Cast thy bread upon the 51 *waters: for thou shalt find it after many days.*

months later, people we barely knew from church sent us a "love gift" of $1500.00 just "to help us out". My wife and I have experienced these types of unexpected financial blessings many times over the last thirty-five years, with the most recent "love gift" coming just a few weeks ago as we got ready to go on vacation. God always takes care of His own children! (Ps. 37:25)

I have been young, and now am old; yet have I not seen the righteous forsaken, nor his seed begging bread.

FOOD FOR THOUGHT: "If God be for us, who can be against us?" (Ro. 8:31)

1. **How do you trust God with all your heart in your decision making? (Prov. 3:5-6)** (5) Trust in the LORD with all thine heart; and lean not unto thine own understanding. (6) In all thy ways acknowledge him, and he shall direct thy path.

2. **How do you seek Him with all your heart daily in making life's choices? (Mt. 6:33)** But seek ye first the kingdom of God, and his righteousness; and all these things shall be added unto you.

3. **Do you have a teachable seeking heart that is attentive to His still small voice? (I Sam. 3:9-10)** (9) Therefore Eli said unto Samuel, Go, lie down: and it shall be, if he call thee, that thou shalt say, Speak, LORD; for thy servant heareth. So Samuel went and lay down in his place. (10) And the LORD came, and stood, and called as at other times, Samuel, Samuel. Then Samuel answered, Speak: for thy servant heareth.

4. **Are you so in love with God that your prayers allow Him to do the impossible? (Luke 1:13,37)** (13) But the angel said unto him, Fear not, Zacharias: for thy prayer is heard: and thy wife Elisabeth shall bear thee a son, and thou shalt call his name John. (37) For with God nothing shall be impossible.

5. **When is the last time God miraculously answered prayer for you? (Jer. 33:3; Eph. 3:20)** 33:3, Call unto me, and I will answer thee, and shew thee great and mighty things, which thou knowest not. 3:20, Now unto him that is able to do exceeding abundantly above all that we ask or think, according to the power that worketh in us.

6. **How do you remember your faithbuilders to always foster gratitude and worship? (I Sam. 12:24)**

Only fear the LORD, and serve him in truth with all your heart: for consider how great things he has done for you.

7. How are you more in love with God than you were a year ago? (Ps. 119:159; Phil. 1:9-11) *(9) and this I pray, that your love may abound yet more & more in knowledge and in all judgement; (10) That ye may approve things that are excellent; that ye may be sincere and without offence till the day of Christ; (11) Being filled with the fruts of righteousness, which are by Jesus Christ, unto the glory and praise of God.*

8. How does God going before you and behind you daily shape your thinking? (Ps. 139:5-6) *Thou hast beset me behind and before, and laid thine hand upon me. Such knowledge is too wonderful for me; it is high, I can not attain unto it.*

9. How do you see God making you more than a conqueror through His love for you? (Rom. 8:37) *(36) As it is written, For thy sake we are killed all the day long; we are accounted as sheep for the slaughter (37) Nay, in all these things we are more than conquerors through him that loved us.*

10. How is your church training teenagers to serve God in missions and ministry, and how do you see them growing in wisdom and stature as Jesus did as a teenager? (Luke 2:52)

and Jesus increased in wisdom and stature, and in favour with God and man.

FAITHBUILDERS THAT SHAPE OUR TESTIMONY
"Let your light so shine before men"... (Mt.5:16)
CHAPTER EIGHT

One summer my son and I traveled to Golden Lake in Ontario, Canada on a fishing trip for a father-son bonding time around the joys of creation's loud voice and iron sharpening iron fellowship. One evening after cleaning our fish and having dinner, we sat on the porch staring at all the stars God had created and were amazed at how so many more were visible than at home.

As we were getting ready to go into our cabin for the night, my son spotted something far in the distance and asked, "Dad, what is that sparkling stuff over there? It looks like a million fireflies dancing around!" I told him I wasn't sure but would try to find out the next day.

So at lunch the following afternoon I asked the lodge owner what that could have been in the distance, and he responded, "Oh that's just a little city about thirty miles away set on the side of a hill."

As my son and I once again sat on the porch that night, I began to share with him Jesus' description of a true Christian as we turned to Matthew 5:14-16. Jesus taught that when God saves a soul and changes a life, life change is obvious to all that see God's grace engrafted into that person's character. When Jesus moves into the heart, His light literally dispels darkness as we

55 *what darkness is in me that prevents anyone to see my light!*

become the light of the world. Jesus told His disciples, "A city that is set on a hill cannot be hid." (Mt. 5:14; cf. Ps. 18:28)

In Acts 4:12-13 the Jewish people marveled easily seeing the boldness of Peter and John as they declared the need for people to turn to Jesus for salvation. These "unlearned and ignorant men" spoke so powerfully that the crowd recalled that they had been with Jesus, who had so changed their lives into lights of love shining forth for His glory. Recall that these same men ran from the cross and now risked their lives to tell the truths they had been taught. Peter had even denied knowing Christ as He was on trial. Changed lives are the most powerful tools of God in reaching people for His Kingdom. (Luke 17:21)

Neither shall they say, Lo here! Lo there! For, behold, the kingdom of God is within you.

My son Stephen and I later discussed how creation is God's voice to our world and how His daily creation makes all mankind without excuse to the reality that there is an all-powerful Creator who made the universe. (Ps. 19; Rom. 1:20) We then talked about the perfect order of God's creation demonstrated by how a weatherman can predict daily the exact time the sun will rise and set, because God faithfully orders His universe which always obeys Him.

To strengthen these word pictures of creation I then pulled a bare hook of my tackle box and asked him how many fish we would catch with just that hook. He laughed as he explained to me that fish weren't stupid! Then I covered the hook with a rubber worm and he immediately he said, "That will get them every time", as we had caught many bass that week with that set-up of hook and bait. Then I explained that the Greek word for temptation means a "baited hook", and that Satan knows exactly the bait he needs to catch us in sin so he can damage our testimony and put out our light so it cannot shine for Jesus. (Act 1:8; ICor.10:12-13) My son still uses these word pictures today as he trains teenagers as a youth pastor in our church.

Two months after God redeemed me from myself, He granted me a great **faithbuilder** of testimony. I was lying under my car changing the rear end gear in order to go racing at a local drag strip with two of my roommates that night. I heard a car pull into our driveway, and I crawled from under the car to see two very attractive young ladies who were seeking one of my roommates named Terry. I informed them that he was working late but would be home in about an hour. They proceeded to ask me my name and I told them "Rory." They said in harmony, "Oh, you're the preacher!"

I responded "What in the world do you mean by that?!"

One of them said, "Terry used to call you the teacher, but a few weeks ago he started calling you the preacher, as he told us how much your life had changed from a trip you took together."

When Terry arrived home, I immediately confronted him over my new "title" as preacher. He then explained to me that it was a title of respect because he loved to hear me answer his questions about Jesus, and how easy it was to believe what I said because he saw the changes in my life. Then he shared, with a big smile on his face, one specific example from a party we were at the previous weekend at our neighbors', when I left early alone, having had no alcohol whatsoever. When he came home I was sitting on the couch reading my Bible. Then Terry said quite emphatically, "Rory, that is just not the old you, the teacher; it's the new you, the preacher!"

I thanked Terry for the explanation but admonished him to never call me "the preacher" again, because it was embarrassing; more importantly, it was a title I certainly did not deserve or want!

A few weeks later God gave me another testimony **faithbuilder**. My roommates and I were water skiing one hot day on a local lake. One of my friends needed to leave for work in twenty minutes so we stopped the boat to bring in the current skier to allow my friend his last run before we had to take him back to the parking lot. I shut off the engine to get him setup in the water. When I tried to start the engine again the battery died so I had to remove the engine cap to try to start it by a rope around the flywheel. After many frustrating pulls on the rope, my anger began to burn as I grew up with a very "short fuse" when I got frustrated. So I tried one last hard pull and the rope flew back and snapped me hard in the corner of my eye. I used God's Name in vain! Immediately, the still small voice of God's Spirit spoke to my soul inaudibly, "NO! You do not curse your Savior". Soul stirring conviction sent chilling "goose bumps" running up my arms on a ninety-five-degree day!

Brokenness and sorrow filled my heart with grief for my sin committed against my most precious Savior, and in the presence of all my roommates. I then noticed one of my friends, Larry, smiling at me. He had been with me in Rehoboth Beach and on the Canada fishing trip where it rained for three days. I asked him what was so amusing! He responded, "I have been with you a lot since Jesus obviously saved your soul, and this is the first time I've heard you swear in thirty days and the 'old' you swore constantly!"

Then God's grace struck me with the evidence of my life change, which I hadn't noticed at all, as my friends beheld "the city on the hill" of my light shining! I grew up in a home where God's name was spoken only in vain as a curse word. I certainly didn't say to myself that my language had to change now that I was a Christian. The words spoken to me at the beach came roaring back, "If I'm telling you the truth about Jesus, He will change you from the inside out!" (2 Cor. 5:17) Also, many years later my friend Terry contacted me to tell me he finally became a born-again Christian whose life God had also changed into "a city on a hill" for all his family and friends to clearly see. (Acts 4:13) ~~Therefore~~ Therefore if any man be in Christ, he is a new creature: old things are passed away; behold, all things are become new.

Two women have impressed me over the years as prayer warriors who embodied the Biblical principle of testimony as living lights for God as "a city set on a hill." The first lady, Betty Ann Moore, prayed for me for three years as a teenager because of the bad influence I had at that time on her churchgoing son. I didn't know this until I became a Christian, and my neighbor lady who went to church with her told me of her intercessions for me. My wife and I just last week had lunch with her as we have stayed in touch with Betty Ann the last forty-three years. She still stands strong for God to this day. (Mt. 5:16)

The second woman, Annabelle, was known as the prayer warrior in her town, and if any serious prayers were needed, her neighbors and church friends called her. I got to know her very well by living in her home as I deer hunted many years with her son Dick. In her later years of life, Annabelle fell and broke both feet. As I walked by her bedroom one night I saw her sitting on her bed and we began to share about Jesus. I asked her how she was doing in the healing process and how she managed to get around, as her bedroom was at the stop of a long steep staircase. She smiled and said, "God allowed me to get these two broken feet so I would have more uninterrupted time for prayer. To Him be all the glory!" How many prayer warriors have you met in your life who approached God's throne effectually and fervently in prayers that availed much for Jesus? (Jas. 5:16) Confess your faults one to another, and pray one for another, that ye may be healed. The effectual fervent prayer of a righteous man availeth much. (Profit)

Recently I took several men from my church to my hunting camp to help with a work day. After laboring for many hours cutting and splitting wood we stopped for a lunch break. One of my hunting friends from our club said, "You know what I love about the men of your church? None of them have to tell me they are Christians. They don't have to advertise their faith. It's real! I have met so many 'so-called' Christians over the years which have to tell you they are God's children because you would have never guessed. And on top of that they work harder on work days than the men who are partners in this club. These guys are welcome here any time!" Praise God for **faithbuilders** from true saints who are "Jesus with skin on" as real people to a real world. (I Jn. 4:17)

Herein is our love made perfect, that we may have boldness in the day of judgement: because as he is, so are we in this world.

FOOD FOR THOUGHT (Phil. 4:8): "A city set on a hill cannot be hidden". (Mt. 5:14-16)

1.   How has Jesus truly changed your life as a Christian? (2 Cor. 5:14, 17) *(14) for the love of Christ con- straineth us; because we thus judge, That if one died for all, then were all dead. (17) Therefore if any man be in Christ, he is a new creature: old things are passed away; behold, all things are become new.*

2.   How does Jesus' love (constrain) you daily to not sin? (Ro. 6:4, 11; 2 Cor. 5:14) *(restrain) (4) Therefore we are buried with him by Baptism into death that like as Christ was raised up from the dead by the glory of the Father, even so we should also walk in newness of life. (11) Likewise reckon ye also yourselves to be dead indeed unto sin, but alive unto God through Jesus Christ our Lord.*

3.   Anyone seeing your light shining more brightly daily? (Prov. 4:18) *But the path of the just is as the shining light, that shineth more and more unto the perfect day.*

4.   Do you meditate on His Word daily to absorb His glorious light? (2 Cor. 3:18) *But we all, with open face beholding as in a glass the glory of the Lord, are changed into the same image from glory to glory, even as by the Spirit of the Lord.*

5.   Do you keep a **faithbuilder** journal to help you remember God's miracles? (Eph. 3:20) If not, when will you begin your "blessing book" to pass on to your family and friends? (Ps. 103:1-2) *(3:20) Now unto him that is able to do exceeding abundantly above all that we ask or think, according to the power that worketh in us, (103:1) Bless the Lord, O my soul: and all that is within me, bless his holy name (2) Bless the Lord, O my soul, and forget not all his benefits.*

6.   How persistently do you pray for God's will to be done? (Mt. 7:7; I Thess. 5:17) [7:7] Ask, and it shall be given you; seek, and ye shall find; knock, and it shall be opened unto you: [5:17] Pray without ceasing.

7.   Is your life so threatening to Satan that your name is on his lips? Why? (Acts 19:13-17)

8.   Do you know any people who live up to the testimony of Samuel and Moses as effectual prayer warriors for the kingdom of God's eternal glory? (Jer. 15:1) (13) Then certain of the vagabond Jews, exorcists, took upon them to call over them which had evil spirits the name of the Lord Jesus, saying, We adjure you by Jesus whom Paul preacheth. (14) And there were seven sons of one Sceva, a Jew, and chief of the priests, which did so. (15) And the evil spirit answered and said, Jesus I know, and Paul I know; but who are ye? (16) And the man in whom the evil spirit was leaped on them, and overcome them, and prevailed against them, so that they fled out of that house naked and wounded. (17) And this was known to all the Jews and Greeks also dwelling at Ephesus; and fear fell on them all, and the name of the Lord Jesus was magnified.

|Jer 15:1| Then said the LORD unto me, Though Moses and Samuel stood before me, yet my mind could not be toward this people: cast them out of my sight, and let them go forth.

63

FAITHBUILDERS: STACKING STONES
"Forget not all his benefits"... (Ps.103:2)
CHAPTER NINE

One of the most practical and powerful Biblical principles that I have learned in thirty-seven years of ministry is that wicked people have short memories. This ingratitude greatly limits their worship and limits God's **faithbuilder** blessings to them and their families. (Ps. 78:1-8, 41-42; Ps. 106:13) The Israelites habitually ignored God's prophets as their faithless familiarity bred contempt. (Jn. 4:44)

After the era of the murmuring multitude of Moses' day, whom God allowed to die in the wilderness after forty years of disobedience, God trained a new generation under Joshua, whose name means "Jesus". This generation foreshadowed Israel's godly remnant, who would receive and believe the truths that Jesus preached in the gospels. (Jn. 1:11-12)

One of God's first commands to Joshua, after they crossed the Jordan River in flood stage as a **faithbuilder**, was to stack twelve stones as a memorial to the next generation of children. (Josh. 4:1-7) These stones were to remind the Israelites of God's faithful provisions to them as the apple of His eye because of the eternal covenant God made with Abraham to build His nation Israel. (Isa. 49:16; Zech. 2:8)

Therefore, when I started seminary, my wife and I began to stack the stones of God's miraculous faith builders that deepened our faith into "the faith" of Jesus in one year as we saw God's hand upon us. (Gal. 2:20) We believed that He would never leave or forsake us and would meet our every need in the riches of Jesus Christ. (Phil. 4:19; Heb. 13:5, 8) But we weren't sure exactly how He would carry out His precious promises to build our precious faith, giving us all we needed for life and godliness on our journey of faith. (2 Pet. 1:1-4)

The first **faithbuilder** occurred when the transmission went out on our only car two months into seminary. I called a teacher friend of mine, who ran the joint vocational auto repair classes at his school, for advice. After talking about our limited finances and how this was my only transportation to commute to seminary, he made a few phone calls. He found a used transmission with very few miles on it and proceeded to negotiate a price with a friend of his who owned a junkyard. He called me two days later telling me my car would be ready in two days at absolutely no cost to me. This teacher and I stayed close for the next twenty years and he eventually became a Christian.

The second **faithbuilder** came as I led a Wednesday evening basketball outreach program for our young men at church. About five weeks into the program I separated my Achilles tendon and crawled off the floor in agony. As I lay there in the greatest pain I had ever been in, the thought ran through my mind, "God, do you have the right guy here? I have no money, only major medical insurance; what's going on here? I'm rather confused by all this!"

A friend drove me to a nearby emergency room where I was told that I would be on my feet soon as they sent me home without even a pair of crutches. Three months later I was still on crutches. But during those three months, God kept stacking stones of grace and mercy.

The third **faithbuilder** came as I had to figure out how to get to seminary because I couldn't drive. I called the school and asked if any other students lived near me. The secretary informed that a man named Rufus Hofelt lived about eight miles south of me and gave me his phone number. Rufus agreed to pick me up and get me home as long as I needed help, and he carried my books to classes for three months because my crutches occupied both hands. Today we are on the same church staff, together, after thirty-five years of being in separate ministries.

The fourth **faithbuilder** came as I was invited to our church's men's breakfast while I was still on crutches. A stranger approached and offered to get my food for me as we walked through the buffet line. He asked me my name and discovered that his niece was in the teen Bible study I led on Monday evenings. He shared how it had changed her life. He then asked me if I was the former teacher who taught college prep English and told me he was a college professor who had just finished a book to be used in his computer classes. After submitting the book to his publisher, the company told him it was way too wordy even for them to edit and told him to try to find someone else who could help. So, he asked me to edit two chapters to see if his publisher liked my work. A week later, I gave him his edited chapters with about twenty percent fewer pages. He mailed the edited chapters to the publisher who told him to hire me immediately. He gave me an advance of $1000.00 which just happened to cover our three house payments and three electric bills that we were in arrears, leaving us about $20.00 for much needed food supplies. I later received $1500.00 when I finished the whole book, which again paid "bills due" and left us around $35.00 for food. Being that I couldn't work on crutches, this was a God-ordained perfect job that paid our bills for a few months. Great is our Lord! (Ps. 145:3; Eph. 3:20)

The fifth **faithbuilder** surprised my wife as she went to pay her bill at our children's doctor's office. The nurse at the billing window asked, "Who are you?" My wife said she didn't understand the question because this lady had dealt with my wife many times before. The nurse then explained that our doctor gave us a fifty percent discount and that he had never done that before for anyone to the best of her knowledge. So the nurse asked what kind of relationship we had as a family with the doctor. My wife explained that I used to be his daughter's English teacher before I went to seminary. Then the nurse was more surprised because the doctor was an orthodox Jew giving help to a Christian. I thank our great God "we **know** that all things work together for good to them that love God" according to Romans 8:28. That verse doesn't say we **understand** how they work out, as I heard a pastor once say.

The sixth **faithbuilder** came when my wife approached me a week before Thanksgiving asking if we could afford to make a meal for our whole family. It was a very special time for her, as she was a great cook who laid out quite a spread for all to enjoy. However, we were already well behind in bills and had no money for discretionary spending. That day I left for seminary and she went to the local post office one mile from our house, leaving our doors unlocked because we lived in a safe neighborhood. When she came home and opened the back door, she was shocked to see several bags on our kitchen table. As she walked closer, she noticed "Happy Thanksgiving" written in crayon on one of the bags, all of which were filled with all the fixings, including a twenty-pound turkey for a great Thanksgiving dinner! We still have no idea who gave us this memorial stone as a **faithbuilder**.

The seventh **faithbuilder** came in December as my wife asked if we could afford to go out to cut a fresh Christmas tree. We still had minimal funds that were all needed for food and a few presents. Several days later, a friend rang our doorbell while he held in his hand a fresh-cut tree already decorated! He then handed me an envelope with $80.00 in it from the church softball team I played on for three years. Next, he took me to his trunk which was filled with beef and chicken that lasted us for the next five months. This act of incredible love brought new life to Psalm 37:25, "I have been young and now am old; yet have I not seen the righteous forsaken or his seed begging bread". I had memorized that verse in my mind, but God engraved it into my heart that day and unto this day.

When i have a need go to God - let him work out the details. I dont need to drop 68 subtil hints to anyone. or help someone in hopes of a return of "something". Love people like Christ and walk with God - Fulfill my reasonable service, Be faithful and dont manipulate - Gods got it!

The eighth **faithbuilder** came when one of the pastors at church saw me still on crutches after three months. He stopped me to ask what the doctor was saying about my condition and when was I going to be freed from the crutches. Unfortunately, I told him I hadn't seen a doctor, due to finances, since I was in the emergency room three months previous. He immediately called a well-known orthopedic surgeon in our church and got me an appointment the next day. After x-rays the doctor said, "All I can say is that your healing is almost complete, and that is a miracle. From what I can tell, you should have had surgery, but The Great Physician has perfectly put your tendon right where it should be. The downside is that without the surgery you will most likely never have full strength in your leg. The upside is get rid of the crutches in about a week".

The ninth **faithbuilder** came as my wife and I were invited a few days later to our youth group's annual "Prom Alternative" Luau at a local State Park. Our church provided a well-known Christian singing group and a five-star dinner, as our teens wore suits and prom dresses to enjoy prom without the pressures of alcohol, drugs, and sex that their peers pressed upon them. As all the teens were getting off the bus, my wife and I sat in the first seat with me on my crutches for one more day. The youth pastor asked me how our finances were doing, and I told him we were still behind on several major bills, but we had faith God would provide as He had the past nine months. He then asked if the church was giving me a monthly stipend to help with gas and books. I told him that the church was giving me $150.00 per month and that we were very grateful. He then said that they were not giving me enough, as we had a child born in October, and that the stipend should have been more. The following week he handed us a check for $1000.00. Our bills that we owed for house and electric bill payments totaled $990.00! We praised God's graciousness again for giving us ten extra dollars for food too. (Ps. 103:1-2)

As all these **faithbuilders** happened, other "little stones" were being stacked for our remembrance: an envelope with $200.00 in it under our windshield wiper after church; a stranger shaking my hand in the church hallway, leaving $150.00 in my hand as he walked away; anonymous cash gifts of $20.00 to $50.00 in the mail; people giving us vegetables and food supplies, and many other indescribable blessings of love for God's glory, as He reminded us that if He takes care of the sparrow of the field, how much more His dearly beloved servants! (Mt. 6:25-34)

God has blessed us, use that to bless others. Dont not give BC Im afraid we wont have anything left over - trust God that he will take care of us!

The tenth **faithbuilder** came as I finished my first year of seminary and received a call to interview at a local church for a full-time youth position. Being on crutches for three months enabled me to take many extra classes, so I only needed eighteen more hours to graduate rather than thirty-six hours. This put me in a position to enter ministry full-time and finish school part-time, possibly. I called my pastor and asked him to pray for wisdom for me for my interview. He immediately asked me not to make any commitments, as he had been trying to get me on his youth staff team. The interview went well, and I was offered a full-time position starting immediately, so I again called my pastor who went to see my senior pastor. I received a call one hour later asking me to start part-time, much to my delight, at my home church as a youth intern. God once again gave me the delights of my heart for trusting Him with all my heart. (Prov. 3:5-6; Ps. 37:4-5)

The eleventh **faithbuilder** came four months later as the Christian Education director at our church decided to pursue a doctorate and recommended that I take her full-time position. The senior pastor asked me if I could handle full-time with the eighteen-hour load I had to take to finish my seminary Master's Degree in Christian Education and Biblical Studies. I responded that I knew it could work, but I needed to sit down with the seminary president to discuss curriculum because all my core courses were finished with only four electives remaining. I left his office and headed to my car to tell my wife the potential of great news. As I walked out the office door, the seminary president was coming across the church parking lot. I excitedly shared with him the opportunity, and he assured me that he would arrange for me to do three independent studies from home, and I only had to take one course in which I would only have to come sixty miles to the seminary three times for small group discussions. Then he said, "This type of ministry offer from one of the finest churches in the country cannot be ignored or taken lightly. You are a perfect fit, and we will make this happen as I meet with your pastor for lunch." Praise God for another memorial stone to stack, reminding me that my all-knowing God opens His doors that no man can ever shut. (Rev. 3:7)

The twelfth **faithbuilder** actually ties two miraculous events together that occurred a few years apart. After my wife and I had been married one year, we sat at dinner at her parents' home after church one Sunday in the summer of 1974. My sister-in-law asked about a relative's house that was supposed to be for sale soon. After we discovered the house had indeed been put up for sale, my wife and her sister drove out to see it because I had no interest at all. Consequently, I went to church that evening.

When I got back to her parents' house after church, all my wife talked about that night and on our trip back to our apartment was this house her sister didn't want. Then, I found out her uncle had built the house, so I called him. He informed me that the price was very fair and that the house was well-built with upgraded materials. The next day, I called the real estate agent to make an offer. The agent informed me that she already had two offers, but both offers had contingencies to sell their houses first. I informed her that we rented and could buy now. After some negotiations, we agreed on the purchase price. As we sat down to sign papers, the agent asked me what sold me on the house, and I told her I hadn't seen it yet. She almost "fell off her chair" as she said that never ever happened to her before. Then she asked what bank we would approach for a loan, and I informed her that I would approach the local bank close to our apartment. Immediately, she challenged my choice by telling me that that bank was so conservative they would NEVER give me a loan because I historically paid cash for everything.

The next morning I went to that local bank, and a few weeks later they approved the loan, much to the surprise of my experienced real estate lady. Then, my wife and I finally drove out to see our new house. We kept driving for miles as I thought, "Where in the world is this place?" After driving past many cornfields into a beautiful rural setting, we came to the house that didn't even have a driveway in front of the garage! The elderly owner didn't even own a car, as her son lived next door. Therefore, a car had never been in the drive, so grass filled the supposed driveway area. When we walked into the house, it was so immaculate it looked like no one ever lived there. The precious owner cleaned three days a week, as she had nothing much else to do as a widow. She waxed the cupboards monthly. One bedroom had never been used. It had paper over the windows, because she didn't want to pound nails into the oak woodwork. She left us tools, a mower, a washing machine, and many other nice items because she was moving out of state. God gave us an indescribable gift of grace, as we still live in that house today, forty-one years later. Our three children have informed us we cannot ever sell this house because it is truly "home". That leads to the second part of the **faithbuilder** as God continued giving us stones of remembrance to stack to tell our children in the future. (Josh. 4:1-7)

Two years later as we were in seminary, we fell behind several times on house payments. Our little local conservative bank never charged us any extra fees for late payments. They worked with us, graciously, as long as our extra debt didn't last more than six months. Every time our debt approached that six month window, God provided the exact funds to pay our back payments without penalty. God granted us another **faithbuilder,** as we learned that God is never late in meeting our needs because everything is beautiful in His time. (Ps. 37:25; Eccles. 3:11)

The final **faithbuilder,** pertaining to our decision to go to seminary, came as I applied to get my retirement I had accumulated as a school teacher for six years. We had very little savings, so I decided to pull my money, even though I lost half of it because I wasn't vested yet. However, the retirement system informed me it would be a six-month wait, and that delay would really stretch our savings to the last penny at best! About four weeks later, I walked into the backyard where my wife was harvesting vegetables from our garden, and she asked me what I was smiling about. I handed her an envelope with a check in it for $4000.00. My retirement money came five months earlier than expected. This especially blessed my wife, who had some minor anxieties as to how we would pay our bills without me having a job. I had been praying fervently for God to somehow assure her that He would meet all our needs in His own way and time. That **faithbuilder** encouraged both of us that God's beloved children never beg bread or are ever forsaken! (Ps. 37:25)

FOOD FOR THOUGHT (Phil.4:8): "If God be for us who can be against us?" (Rom. 8:31)

1. What are some **faithbuilders** God can has used to deepen your faith? (Ps. 42:7; 1 Cor. 2:10)

But God hath revealed them unto us by his Spirit : for the Spirit searcheth all things, yea, the deep things of God.

2. When facing difficult decisions, do you know how to strengthen yourself in Christ? (I Sam. 30:6)

And David was greatly distressed; for the people spake of stoning him, bc the soul of all the people was grieved, every man for his sons and for his daughters : but David encouraged himself in the LORD his God.

3. How has God taught you that a faith that can't be tested can't be trusted? (1 Pet. 1:7-9) ⑥ wherein ye greatly rejoice, though now for a season, if need be, ye are in heaviness through manifold temptations: ⑦ That the trial of your faith, being much more precious than gold that perisheth, though it be tried with fire, might be found unto praise and honor and glory at the appearing of Jesus Christ.

4. How have you learned to wait on the Lord in effectual prayer for tough choices? (Ps. 27:14)

Wait on the LORD: be of good courage, and he shall strengethen thine heart : wait, I say, on the LORD.

5. What invaluable lessons of life are your children learning from your integrity? (Prov. 20:7)

The just man walketh in his integrity : his children are blessed after him.

6. What diligent disciplines enable you to receive God's engrafted Word? (Jas. 1:21-22) ㉑ wherefore lay apart all filthiness and superfluity of naughtiness, and recieve with meekness the engrafted word, which is able to save your souls. 75 ㉒ But be ye doers of the word, and not hearers only, decieving your own selves.

7. How does the peaceable wisdom from heaven guard your heart daily? (Prov. 4:23; Jas. 3:17) But the wisdom that Is from above is first pure, then peaceable, gentle, and easy to be intreated, Full of mercy and good fruits, without partiality and without hypocrisy. (23) Keep thy ♡ with all dilligence for out of it are the issues of life.

8. How do you see the beauty of God's holiness work in your life weekly? (Ps. 96:9)

O worship the LORD in the beauty of holiness: fear before him, all the earth.

9. How does God's wisdom guard your whole day as you walk with Jesus? (Prov. 6:22; I Cor. 1:30) when thou goest, it shall lead thee; when thou sleepest, it shall keep thee; and when thou awakest, it shall talk with thee.

10.   When is the last time God shined His candle onto your head as a faithbuilder? (Job 29:3) (2) oh, that I were as in month past, as in the days when God preserved me; (3) when his candle shined upon my head, and when by his light I walked through darkness.

11.   How does God renew your daily faith to fly like an eagle? (Ps. 103:5; Isa. 40:31) But they that wait upon the LORD shall renew their strength; they shall mount up with wings as eagles; they shall run, and not be weary; and they shall walk, and not faint.

12.   How does your life bless God in specific acts of sacrificial service? (Ps. 103:22) Bless the LORD, all his works in all places of his dominion; Bless the LORD, O my soul.

13. **What habits allow Christ's mind to guide you in your daily decision making? (I Cor. 2:16)**

[14] But the natural man recieveth not the things of the Spirit of God: for they are foolishness "to him: neither can he know them, because they are Spiritually discerned.

[15] But he that is spiritual judgeth all things, yet he himself is judged of no man.

[16] For who hath known the mind of the lord? that he may instruct ~~of the Lord~~ him? But we have the mind of Christ.

FAITHBUILDERS WHEN FAITH WAVERS
"Increase our faith"... (Lk.17:5)
CHAPTER TEN

Fatigue breeds distortion. There are days in the lives of Christians when God doesn't *seem* to make sense! The exhausted Christ, worn down by three years of spiritual warfare battling Satan and his religious rebels, the Pharisees and Sadducees, cried out in Gethsemane for God to remove the "cup" of the cross. Then on the cross, Jesus asked from the depth of His soul why God had forsaken Him. Our Savior knew the answers to these questions. Thank God that He allows us to ask real-life questions in days of real-life trials that test our faith. God knows that a faith that can't be tested can't be trusted. As God's growing us from faith to faith, "the faith" of Jesus grants **faithbuilders** that grow us in grace, as God richly rewards His beloved children for their perseverance. (Rom. 1:17; 1 Pet. 1:7; Heb. 11:6)

Matthew's gospel to the Jews, the apple of His holy eye, provided many infallible proofs of Jesus' deity in the first ten chapters: the virgin birth and Messianic miracles prophesied seven-hundred years earlier by Isaiah, Jesus' birth in the little town of Bethlehem prophesied six-hundred and fifty years earlier by Micah, and the forerunner John the Baptist prophesied four-hundred years earlier my Malachi.

Then chapter eleven opens with Jesus training his disciples how to follow Him so he could make them into faithful fishers of men. After Jesus' resurrection, they would be sent into the world to preach the gospel to reproduce reproducers to build His church that the gates of hell would not prevail against. (Mt. 4:19; 16:18; 28:19-20; 2 Tim. 2:2-3)

In this context, John the Baptist is awaiting beheading in a prison cell for doing God's will, rebuking Herod for his adulterous sexual sins. John had preached repentance and scathing prophetic rebuke to the Pharisees and Sadducees for training up a "generation of vipers", Satan's deadly snakes; Jesus' ax of judgment would soon fall onto Israel as He burned the chaff of religion out of the apostate nation and gathered the faithful remnant of wheat into his barn. (Mt. 3:2-12)

John, exhausted by spiritual warfare, allowed his fatigue to breed distortion, consequently sending two of his disciples to question Jesus as to whether he was really the Messiah. Why hadn't the ax fallen yet on the unrighteous roots of the religious leaders for their diabolical lies? Why hasn't Jesus yet purged His barn of the counterfeit religious God-defiling chaff? John didn't expect a gentle, meek, Healer-Servant! Sometimes our unbiblical expectations get us into deep self-inflicted trouble. All John had to remember was his own declaration to follow Jesus as the Lamb of God who takes away the sins of the world; remember the baptism of Jesus when John saw the heavens opened, and God said, "This is My beloved Son in whom I am well pleased." (Jn. 1:29, 36) In the end, I wonder if John is not really seeking information from Jesus but simply confirmation that Jesus is the Messiah. (Ps. 40:1-5)

All dearly-beloved saints of Jesus have walked in John's shoes of doubt when Satan's storms seduce our faith with questions that rock our Jesus-inhabited boat. John certainly understood his weaknesses when he declared that his greatest joy was hearing Jesus' voice as the Bridegroom, and thusly Jesus must increase and John must decrease. (Jn. 3:29-30) That's why God records the disciples, after three years of personal discipleship by Jesus, all running from the cross; God had prophesied that when the Shepherd is smitten, the sheep will scatter. All Christians must remember why God calls us sheep, because on our best day we are all dumb and dirty in our rebellious nature, prone to wandering into fields of self-destruction. (Rom. 3:23; 6:4, 11,23)

Jesus graciously answers John's disciples without rebuke to go and show John *again* all the things they have heard and seen; His Messianic **words** and miraculous **works** had never been done before in all Israel's well-recorded history: the blind see, the lepers are cleansed, the deaf hear, the dead are resurrected, and the poor people hear the gospel, as the common people always gladly listened to Jesus. (Luke 7: 4-6) Jesus later rebuked Philip for not paying closer attention to His words and works, as Jesus' miracles validated His words as God provided infallible proofs of His deity. (Mk. 12:37; Jn. 14:8-12)

Jesus then declares John's greatness, as being "more than a prophet", as the Forerunner prophesied throughout the Old Testament, who came in the Spirit of Elijah. Our Lord makes an interesting statement about the kingdom suffering violence, and the violent take it by force as they fight the war against sin, self and Satan. (Luke 7: 9-15) Jesus then stated that "wisdom is justified of her children", as good trees planted by God always bear good fruits. (Luke 7:19; cf. Mt. 7:16-20)

As God fearing saints, we must all seek a teachable spirit that fosters a listening ear to His still small voice so that we may walk by faith that unites our hearts to fear God submissively. (Ps. 86:11) As we engage in diligent disciplines, growing from faith to faith, God will reward us with the unsearchable riches of weapons of warfare to withstand satanic darts of doubt aimed at our hearts. (Heb. 11:6).

Three common causes of doubt appear throughout Scripture, reminding us of the power of Jesus' precious blood that cleanses saints from the fears and fatigue of warfare. The *first* and foremost cause of doubt results from our incomplete knowledge of how big our God really is in meeting our every need through Jesus our all-sufficient Savior. (Col. 2:6-10; Phil. 4:13, 19) The principle of God's protective peace is simple. When our concept of God is big, our problems will be small in comparison; but when our problems are allowed to be bigger than our God, doubt will definitely shrink the roots of our faith. (Isa. 26:3; Phil. 4:6-7; Col. 2:6-7; Heb. 12:1-2)

Today's saints have complete revelation from God, all we need for life and godliness, which John the Baptist and the Christians of Acts didn't have. (1 Pet. 1:10-11; 2 Pet. 1:1-4) We have a perfectly preserved Bible that is the final authority for all our decisions. (Jer. 26:2; Ps. 12:6-7; Prov. 30:5-6) When the frustrated disciples on the Emmaus road met Jesus, all He did was tell them all they should have known to destroy their discouraging doubts. (Luke 24:25, 27; 2 Tim. 4:2)

The *second* common cause is worldly thinking when doubts and discouragement arise. For example, what is the first thing you do when your feelings seduce your faith? Do you drop to your knees with an open Bible to approach the only two places you can receive grace: the Word of grace and the throne of grace? (Acts 20:32; Heb. 4:12, 16) Do you instead first run to people for your answers? What is your daily final authority that provides the absolute truths that foster common sense and rest in your soul? (Mt. 11:28-30) Struggling saints must seek God first, because His ways and thoughts are not our ways and thoughts. (Isa. 55:6-12) Praise God for His indescribable gift of His Word that is incorruptible seed that never returns void, but is engrafted into humble teachable hearts that seek his kingdom principles. (Mt. 6:33; Jas. 1:21-22; 1 Pet. 1:23)

The *third* common cause of doubt is the life-disturbing circumstances that assault saints as a result of living in Satan's wicked world where he is the god of this Laodicean church age (I Jn. 5:19). John the Baptist had doubts but at least he went to the Living Word, Jesus, for his answers. Surely Jesus' words pierced and blessed his heart as he heard, "And blessed is he whosoever shall not be offended in Me." (Luke 7:23) The psalmist cried out, "Great peace have they which love thy law: and nothing shall offend them." (Ps. 119:165) Whenever you see a colon in Scripture, the words that follow it are usually the "cause and effect" truth to be learned as saints possess a self-defining Bible. In other words, great peace is caused by the effectual truth in God's gracious words.

John the Baptist's circumstances didn't change as he was beheaded shortly thereafter, but I assure you Jesus' words comforted his soul, as his feelings no longer seduced his faith (Ps. 40:1, 5, 16). John certainly finished the work which God had given him to do, as he was welcomed home in heaven with "Well done" as a faithful soldier of Jesus His Lord. (Jn. 17:4; Mt. 25:21)

After being a youth pastor for one year, I was crushed by confusion as a tragic trial unfolded in which God "didn't make sense at all", as in the days of John the Baptist's imprisonment. A call came in early evening informing me that one of my key disciples, Doug, had been struck by a car as he rode his motorcycle home from school. He didn't even have time to hit his brakes, as a lady pulled into her driveway in front of him and the impact sent him face first into a big tree. He died shortly thereafter.

That evening I wrestled with my doubts as to what God was thinking, while my feelings seduced my faith as a new pastor who had much to learn about God's agendas in days of tragedy and trial. Doug had great potential to be my top disciple and disciple maker, as I had very little strong male leadership in the youth group, but he loved some vile music groups. He worked at our church camp with teens, so I challenged him to consider his influence upon them regarding "listening to the right voices". This was one of our themes in our youth ministry that I taught the teens about: the maturity factors of Biblical discernment and decision making. (Luke 8:8; Heb. 5:14) After a month of meetings, he burned his rock albums with no one asking him to do so. Doug's heart exploded with the joy of freedom as he looked forward to having junior high youth in his cabin the next week.

His death also meant my first funeral as a Pastor. My roller coaster emotions swirled the next few days as I wept walking down the church halls begging God to give me His words and wisdom to minister to our youth group and to Doug's family. (Jas. 1:2-8) God soon answered my prayers. (Jer. 33:3)

When I arrived at the calling hours early the night before the funeral, I couldn't believe the lineup several blocks down the street with hundreds of teenagers weeping and hugging. The calling hours lasted five hours as the Christian family stood at the head of the closed casket encouraging all the teenagers who came to pay their last respects, as Doug was dearly loved by his school peers and youth group. As the last visitor, the assistant superintendent of schools, came to me, she said, "I have never seen such love and faith in my life. I came to encourage this broken-hearted family, but they encouraged me. Whatever they have to sustain them in such a time as this, I need!"

The funeral went well as we praised God for the assurance that we knew Doug was in heaven with Jesus. After the graveside services, a young man approached me to tell me he needed Jesus "right now"! After we talked, he prayed right there in the cemetery to repent and to get right with God by confessing his sins and asking Jesus to save his soul. (2 Cor. 7:10-11)

As the week unfolded, I simply asked God to answer Jesus' own prayers for me and our youth group. (Jn. 17; Heb. 7:25) Almighty God immediately went to work in people's lives. First our teens began asking themselves if they were as ready to die as Doug was, knowing how much he loved His Lord and had been a light to his peers. (Mt. 5:16) The youth began to reach out to their peers at school, and we soon had eight home high school Bible studies meeting with over one-hundred and fifty teens attending weekly for two years. The youth began signing up for one-on-one discipleship as our youth group grew from one-hundred to one-hundred and eighty-five teenagers, many of whom were led to Christ by their peers. Our teens initiated ministries, all on their own, in backyard neighborhoods to reach children for Jesus and in local nursing homes as the "learners" became "doers." (Phil. 4:8-9; Jas.1:21-22) Almighty God inspired a revival, as He fanned the flames in teenage hearts of sacrificial service and personal growth and He granted many **faithbuilders** over the next few years. (Ps. 85:6; 138:7; Isa. 57:15)

The teenagers' ravenous appetite fostered a vision for service as we expanded our missions' ministry to four tiers to stretch their growing faith. Level one for sophomores involved doing

Vacation Bible School outreaches for children and teens in West Virginia and Virginia. Level two took our juniors to Indian reservations in Minnesota and North and South Dakota for cross-cultural exposure and insight. Level three took our seniors into the West Indies doing cross-cultural door-to-door "cold turkey" evangelism on eight different islands where we saw over 10,000 conversions with follow-up. The West Indies Voice of Victory (WIVV) ministry team put the outreach together as they trained our team in San Juan, Puerto Rico for two days before we departed by boat and plane to individual islands. The night before we departed each year, we shared testimonies over the radio announcing to which island we were coming. The nationals all had radios, and few had televisions. Every island welcomed us, to some degree, with loving open arms, thanking us for loving them enough to tell them about Jesus. Level four sent our college young people for the whole summer to places where our missionaries served as we worked closely with several major missions' boards in cooperation. God's revival fires in our youth group started with the sparks of Doug's death, as this ministry design eventually placed approximately fifty of our youth around the world as young adults serving as pastors, pastor's wives, and missionaries. We will examine the abounding fruits of this youth missions ministry design later, as it powerfully enflamed our mission of discipleship too.

Praise God that His ways are far above ours as we trust Him for **faithbuilders** "when God doesn't seem to make sense." (Isa. 55:6, 8-9) As in Joshua's days, many stones were stacked in remembrance of God's miracles that reverse circumstances for His glory. (Gen. 50:20; Ps. 115:1; I Cor. 10:31)

Sometimes in days of fatigue and distortion, saints forget that God answers our prayers three ways: yes, no, and wait. God's agendas are always fulfilled as we learn, in time, that often His ways are not our ways, and that in His time everything is beautiful. (Eccles. 3:11; Isa. 55:8-9)

For example, when I was a new Christian, my Sunday school class of one-hundred and fifty people prayed fervently for a little girl who had a brain tumor causing swelling and piercing pain in her head. Doctors installed a shunt to reduce fluids and pain. The day came for x-rays to see if the swelling had reduced enough so the doctors could remove the tumor. The report stunned us all, including the doctors that the tumor had disappeared! The medical team could not explain it all, but the prayer warriors could as God granted us all an Ephesians 3:20 **faithbuilder** for His glory alone!

A few years later, I had to make a pastoral call to a local children's hospital to visit a young mother with whom I attended high school. Her little girl had a brain tumor also, so I shared the story of the previous miracle and encouraged her to have faith that God, as the Great Physician, could heal her. Then, I cautioned her that God's will would perfectly happen in His time. Six months later the child died. I wrestled with God a little in my disappointment, as I had grown close to the precious little girl and her family. However, I soon remembered that the child was in heaven walking with Jesus and she was spared the further evil of growing up in this dark satanic world; God had attended to her needs in her last hours of life, granting her rest and peace as angels carried her into Jesus' arms. (Isa. 57:1-2; Luke 16:22) In days of fatigue we need to remember that we are winning when we think we are losing, as the disciples discovered when they saw the resurrected Christ, Who said, "Peace be unto you!" (Luke 24:36)

To make a closing application, God has two simple sources to train us to abide in His holy will as servants and soldiers: truth and trials. If we choose to ignore His truth, we then choose for Him to use trials to get our attention that He might eventually get us to listen to His truths. (Luke 8:8) Moses wrote, "Everything that may abide the fire, ye shall make it go through the fire, and it shall be clean: nevertheless it shall be purified with the water of separation: and all that abideth not the fire ye shall make go through the water." (Num. 31:23) In other words, God uses fire and water, or trials and truth, to purify our hearts to know Him better that we might know His will better.

Job learned this lesson clearly at the end of his life as he proclaimed that he had spoken rashly because of his limited "head knowledge" that needed to become "heart knowledge". God had opened his eyes with enlightenment "too wonderful" for him, which led Job to "abhor" himself as he repented in "dust and ashes." (Job 42:1-6) Now remember that God spoke to Satan about Job as an upright servant who feared God and hated evil to maintain his integrity. (Job 1:8; 2:3) This holy saint had to battle his wife, who belittled his integrity and told him to "curse God and die." (Job2:9) However, Job reminded his "foolish" wife that saints must accept "good and evil" from God, as Job committed no sins with his lips to challenge God in his initial trials. Although Job's faith wavered a little now and then in the midst of severe trials, he still faithfully proclaimed full trust in God. (Job 13:15) Job had full confidence that he would personally see his Redeemer due to his faith of "gold", purified by the trials God allowed Satan to bring upon him. (Job 19:25; 23:10)

Job's life reminds me of the word picture God uses in Deuteronomy 32:10-11, teaching us how an eagle trains her eaglets. The context of this passage shows us what happens to God's dearly beloved people who are the "apple of His eye" as He matures them for deeper levels of service. First, the eagle stirs up her nest to get her eaglets out of their "comfort zone" by knocking them one at a time out of the nest. Imagine the shock of the eaglet, who has been nurtured and fed from birth by "mama" eagle, who now thrusts it into a spiral towards the ground as wings flap in fear. Then "mama" swings under the falling eaglet spreading "abroad her wings" to bear them on her wings back to the nest. Then she knocks the same eaglet out again, repeatedly, until it learns to fly in order to survive. Then she deals with eaglet number two, continuing the "stretching experience" so they learn to use their wings, learning also "mama" will never leave or forsake them. I call this lesson the **"trembling precedes trusting"** principle as God reminds us that Godly fear produces Godly faith. (Ps.86:11) Then God uses our

Godly fear to teach us to make Godly choices. (Ps. 25:12) Job later proclaimed how His awesome God always did "great things past finding out; yea, and wonders without number!" (Job 9:10)

Jesus and Job had one great life lesson in common as they both learned obedience through their sufferings. (Heb. 5:7-9) May God as the Author and Finisher of our eternal salvation help us when our faith wavers as He grants us **faithbuilders** to perfect our choices to obey out of delight, not out of duty.

Rory Wineka

FOOD FOR THOUGHT (Phil. 4:8): "For I know that my redeemer liveth" (Job 19:25)

1. How do you rest in God's peace when you are confused? (Phil. 4:6-7) ⑥ Be careful for nothing; but in everything by prayer; supplication with thanksgiving let your request be made known unto God. ⑦ And the peace of God, which passeth all understanding, shall keep your hearts and minds through Christ Jesus.

2. How have you seen the light of Christ shine from a dying saint's life? (2 Cor. 4:11) For we which live are alway delivered unto death for Jesus' sake, that the life also of Jesus might be made minifest in our mortal flesh.

3. How has God softened your heart by life's heartbreaking troubles? (Job 23:16) For God maketh my heart soft, and the Almighty troubleth me:

4. Are you willing to go "outside the camp" of life to suffer for Jesus? (Heb. 13:13) let us go forth therefore unto him without the camp, bearing his reproach.

5. What has your faith cost you lately? (Col. 1:24) Who now rejoice in my sufferings for you, and fill up that which is behind of the afflictions of Christ in my flesh for his body's sake, which is the Church:

6. Do you possess joy that no circumstances can diminish? (Ps. 5:11) But let all those that put their trust in thee rejoice : let them ever shout for joy, because thou defendest them: let them also that love thy name be joyful in thee.

7. In tough days of life, has God's peace ever kissed you with His merciful truths? (Ps. 85:10)

Mercy and truth are met together; righteousness and peace have kissed each other.

8. How do you faithfully spread the peace of God as a beautiful vessel of His glory? (Isa. 52:7)

How beautiful upon the mountains are the
feet of him that bringeth good tidings,
that publisheth peace;
that bringeth good tidings of good,
that publisheth salvation;
that saith unto Zion,
Thy God reigneth!

FAITHBUILDERS OF JESUS' JOY

"That my joy might remain in you"... (Jn. 15:11)

CHAPTER ELEVEN

The most joyful people I have ever met were the radiant saints of the Virgin Islands. When we approached their little tin-roofed eight-foot square houses that had no windows or doors, they would come out smiling saying "Praise the Lord. Thank God He brought you to our island to help us reach our neighbors and families for Jesus!" These loving Christians knew we were coming as the news had been broadcast via radio from WIVV, West Indies Voice of Victory, in Puerto Rico. Even the non-Christians on the eight islands we worked on were amazingly friendly and open to discussions regarding Jesus Christ as Savior. These precious saints had Jesus' joy internally driving peace into their lives, though they possessed nothing: no televisions, no cars, and for most, no jobs as they lived off the land with fruits, coconuts, and vegetables, and off the sea with fish, conk, and crabmeat. Their freedom abounded as there was no need for even a police department because there was little crime on most of the islands, as people looked out for each other and there was nothing worth stealing. Being with these dear saints reminded me of Jesus' teaching that the poor in spirit are blessed bountifully as they lean on Him alone. (Mt. 5:3) *Blessed are the poor in spirit: for theirs is the Kingdom of heaven.*

Three life changing encounters on the island of Tortola touched me deeply regarding the internal and eternal joy no one could ever take from these beloved saints who lived with eternal perspective. The first **faithbuilder** occurred as we ventured down goat paths deep into remote areas where few people lived. One day, we came upon an older Christian lady who sat alone on her tiny porch eating her early lunch which consisted of a can of corn. She broke into an ear-to-ear grin revealing the few teeth she possessed and shouted, "Praise Jesus. Thank God you came all the way back here to see me as I have been praying for you and your team of high school people. Thank you for loving us enough to come to our tiny island to tell us the truth about Jesus." My heart broke as I looked at her modest "little shack" of a home. An old metal bucket functioned as her stove and an old car seat with a spring sticking out the side as her bed. She most likely had on the only dress she owned, as it was common for the "wealthier people" to have two sets of clothing: one just washed hanging on the line to dry and the one they wore that day. Our fellowship inspired us for the rest of the day as we spent six hours going from home to home giving out Bibles and lessons, and returning the next day, with their permission, to discuss personal faith in Jesus as Savior (Jn. 3:16). Not a single person on Tortola asked us not to return, as they welcomed our love and encouragement of fellowship!

The second **faithbuilder** came as a literal picture of the widow's mite in Luke 21. It's one thing to know a verse we have read, but God burned a word picture forever into my soul as I saw this passage lived out as a great blessing to our team. As we entered a widow's yard, five children ran around naked as they played while their clothes hung on a line. Their mother came out to greet us in Christian love and praise. Then she hurried into her tiny "shack" and brought out a glass jar with a few coins in it. She asked me to hold out my hand as she poured the "widow's mite" into my palm saying, "Please give this gift to WIVV as I fell in love with Jesus many years ago through their radio broadcast ministry. Thanks for coming to our island!" The two teenagers with me looked at me with tears in their eyes as I fought off crying, while all three of our hearts were pierced by her "love gift" for God. Out of her poverty she gave "all the living that she had", equivalent to twenty cents in USA currency. (Lk. 21:4)

The third **faithbuilder** occurred as one of my disciples, a young man who later became a pastor, had gone to visit a small neighborhood and had come back during our lunch hour begging me to immediately come with him. As we approached a nice small house, I heard "thump, thump, thump" as a cataract-eyed man with no legs propelled himself using only his arms to the doorway. He had anxiously awaited my companion's return and held something in his hand as he smiled. He began to tell us of his personal journey with Christ that started with hearing a sermon from a WIVV broadcast on his little transistor radio many years ago. After a lengthy time of great fellowship, he handed me a twenty-dollar bill that had been folded so tightly for so long that when he opened it into my hand it immediately folded back up! This precious half-blind saint lived out the Biblical truths that the righteous are generous in their sacrificial love gifts to God, and that God loves a cheerful giver. (Prov. 21:26; 2 Cor. 9:7) Every man according as he purposeth in his heart, so let him give; not grudgingly, or of necessity; for God loveth a cheerful giver.

Now what enabled these dear saints to live out their joy-filled faith in such a powerful way? Why do so few Christians today have Jesus' joy manifested habitually in their lives as a testimony to God's grace empowering us? If God, as the Husbandman, constantly waters His precious vineyard, His fruit-bearing church, then why does so little fruit of joy, which the Spirit provides, hang on His branches? (Jn. 15:1) The answer lies in the simple fact that few saints daily abide in Christ's love as the inspiring Source of internal and eternal joy as God guards our well-watered souls that receive and believe His truths for fruit bearing. (Isa. 27:2-3; Jn. 1:12; 15:7, 9, ⑪) These things have I spoken unto you, that my joy might remain in you, and that your joy might be full.

As Jesus soon faced the cross, knowing His mission on earth was almost finished, He taught His beloved disciples that they needed utter dependency on God to bear eternal fruits for his glory. (Jn.15:16) Our Lord knew His beloved disciples would struggle as their feelings would seduce their faith in Gethsemane, at the mockery of His trial, at the cross, and after His burial. Their only hope for joy and maximum fruit-bearing resided in God's faithfulness as Husbandman to His Bride, providing all they needed for their struggles in life and godliness. (Jn. 15:5; 2 Pet. 1:1-4) The key enabling factor for their joy depended on their abiding in Jesus' inspiring love, the first fruit of character the Spirit provides daily. (Jn. 15:9; Rom. 5:5; Gal. 5:22) Jesus' calling for their abiding in Him would be empowered by His fervent effectual prayers that they might practically understand that the *exact* same love God has for Him as His beloved Son He also has for them as His dearly beloved sons. (Jn. 17:23, 26)

The challenge will come as His disciples learn to stay yoked to Jesus' love as they work out their own salvation with fear and trembling, remembering He would never leave or forsake them. (Heb. 13:5) Sometimes today's saints need to also remember that as we work out our salvation, God works in us daily to do His will and to do His good pleasure. (Phil. 2:12-13) Our gracious God always grants us the desire and ability to do all He asks of us as His soldiers who strive to fight the good fight of faith. Imagine our confusion if God gave us desire but no ability. We would be so frustrated! Also what if He gave us ability, but granted us no desire. Then we would get nothing done. However, thanks be to God for His unsearchable riches that give us both desire and ability through the fullness of our divine nature empowered by the exact same Spirit that filled Jesus to fulfill His mission! (2 Pet. 1:1-4; Eph. 5:18)

There exist two yokes in Scripture, Jesus' *easy yoke* that makes our burdens light as He carries them and the heavy *iron yoke* of self-destruction as people serve this world. (Deut. 28:48; Jer. 28:14) Jesus loves seeing His servants habitually and prayerfully coming to Him with their burdens so He can give much needed rest and joy for weary souls that listen to Him and humbly learn that His ways are best. (Mt. 11:28-30; Jn. 14:13-14) Solomon learned the hard way that "knowledge is easy to him that understandeth" as full submission to His absolute authority grants us all insight we need to relax in Him. (Prov. 14:6) However, scorners choose to live daily under the iron yoke of a miserable life as they daily ignore God's provisions!

As an application of **submission,** we need to often determine why God uses this specific word to express the key to joy in the Scriptures. The word has two parts, the prefix "sub" and the main word "mission". Now "sub" means under, so saints must place their personal mission or agendas in life **under** God's supreme will and mission for us to please Him joyfully. That's why when Jesus prayed for His disciples to be kept from evil, He prayed in the next verse for them to be mindful that they don't fit into this evil world as pilgrims on a journey to another world, heaven. (Jn. 17:15-16) This blessing would only come as they were sanctified in this truth, which Jesus Himself would guarantee. (17:17) Jesus constantly sanctifies His servants in truths to give us His joy. (Heb. 2:11, 14; 10:10, 14) That's why Jesus previously prayed for us to have His personal joy filling us as we would be sanctified as His ambassadors to a needy world. (Jn. 17:13, 18) Our Lord knew personally the great need for joy for His disciples to endure the coming trials that Satan would bring to paralyze their joy. (Heb. 12:1-2)

God tells us "deep calleth unto deep" and that mature saints know the "deep things of God" as we search the Scriptures, comparing Scripture with Scripture. (Ps. 42:7; I Cor. 2:10, 13) To rightly divide God's Word mandates that saints study their Bibles diligently, lest they be ashamed at what they believe simply because someone lied to them about Jesus' truths, as the Pharisees and Sadducees did constantly. (2 Tim. 2:15) For example, we must understand the "pregnant" meaning, full of life, in the word "understandeth" in Prov.14:6, which reminds us that scorners will never know God's wisdom. This precious word breaks down into three very important parts: under, stand, and –eth. "Understand" reminds us we must "stand" *under* the authority of God's infallible holy Word. The suffix "-eth" tells us that this is a present active participle. Being a college prep English teacher before I entered ministry, I praise God for the training that helps me understand the significance of verbs to interpret the Word correctly. A present active participle is simply a verb where the person must act of his own free will presently (daily) to actively (-eth as a participle) work out salvation in an understanding way by applying diligent disciplines of faith that God rewards. (Acts 17:11; Heb. 11:6)

On top of the good yoke of rest, Jesus also grants the full power of His Spirit to maintain the daily perspective we need motivating us to have joy no man or circumstance can take away as we pray effectually. (Jn. 16:22, 24; Eph. 5:18; Jas. 5:16) God's Spirit sheds abroad into our hearts daily a fresh love for Jesus to anchor our souls to in the normal storms of life. (Rom. 5:5; Heb. 6:19) Remember every Jewish man knew the importance of an anchor, as the Sea of Galilee was filled with a sandy bottom and thus, anchoring to rock was difficult at best while fishing. An anchor is no good in the boat, as our anchors must be outside of ourselves prayerfully trusting Jesus as our "Rock of Ages". Also, the anchor was a symbol written on walls of caves to remind believers of the God of the impossible, as persecuted Jewish Christians often cried out "Increase our faith" in times of potential martyrdom. (Luke 17:5)

God also reminds saints that the same Spirit that constrained

Jesus to go to the cross, in spite of His Gethsemane agonies, constrains us not to serve ourselves but Him, proving we are new creatures in Christ. (2 Cor. 5:14-17) David as the "sweet Psalmist" trusted God's Spirit to create in him a clean and broken heart daily that he might shepherd Israel as God's anointed king. (2 Sam. 23:1; Ps. 51:10, 17) When was the last time you, as a Christian, asked God to give you a broken and contrite heart that you might have His integrity guard your heart as you wait on Him prayerfully? (Ps. 25:12, 21)

The joy that mature saints possess abides in them by faith that the Lord Jesus Christ shepherds their eternal souls daily. (Ps. 23; 91:1) They lack fear of Jesus being their Judge at the Bema Seat because abiding enables us to walk worthy of our calling, trusting Jesus to protect us from sliding. (Ps. 26:1) Do you think that it is a coincidence that the word "backsliding" is nowhere in the New Testament? Backsliding pertains to apostasy, and true saints cannot be apostates since Jesus is their wisdom, righteousness, sanctification, and redemption! (I Cor. 1:30) Jesus paid it all, and all to Him I owe as a debtor. "It is finished", as our salvation decision is settled in heaven forever as our names are written in the Lamb's Book of Life. Nowhere in Scripture does God erase the names of truly born again Christians. Praise God that our Redeemer is also our Judge after the rapture of His Beloved Bride, the church! (Jn. 19:30)

Nor is it a coincidence that the phrases "**eternal life**" and "**the faith**" are nowhere found in the Old Testament. These two unsearchable gifts came only after Jesus crushed Satan at the cross, and through His resurrection as our Lord now holds the keys of hell and death. (Heb. 2:14; Rev. 1:18) Eternal life engrafted into our souls guarantees that Jesus' joy is available to all saints daily through the precious promises that give us a precious faith; God's precious seeds grant infallible truths that are the final authority in all matters of life and death. (Ps. 126:6; 2 Pet. 1:1-4) God's holy seed also never returns void, but always accomplishes what He sends it forth to do for His glorious will to be done on earth as it is in heaven. (Isa. 55:11) The phrase **"the faith"** first occurs in Acts 3:16 when the man lame from birth was healed by faith, and joy filled his praiseful heart. Paul reminds saints in the battle for the Bible in Galatia that we possess **"the faith"** of Jesus Himself, Who loved us and gave Himself for us personally. (Gal. 2:20) In light of this indescribable gift of **"the faith"**, Christians must daily live a crucified selfless life joyfully serving our Savior and King (Gal. 6:14). Paul spoke his last words to the carnally-prone Corinthians warning them to examine themselves to prove **"the faith"** of Jesus ruled their lives unless they be reprobate counterfeits. (2 Cor. 13:5) Paul encouraged the Ephesians to have boldness in accessing God's throne by **"the faith "**of Jesus, their Intercessor who answers prayer exceedingly above and beyond our requests. (Eph. 3:12, 20) Finally, just before Paul died he stated his legacy, "I have fought a good fight, I have finished my course, I have kept **'the faith'**." John's last words stated, "Here is the patience of the saints: here are they that keep the commandments of God and **'the faith'** of Jesus." Praise be to our magnanimous God that all spiritual blessings are ours in Christ through the joyful gift of **"the faith"** of Jesus our Lord whose love will keep us to the very end of time. (Jn. 13:1)

FOOD FOR THOUGHT (Phil. 4:8): "One thing I have desired...to behold the beauty of the Lord" (Ps. 27:4)

1. **How do you seek the Lord with all your heart, strengthened by His joy? (Neh. 8:8, 10)**

So they read in the book in the law of God distinctly, and gave some sense, and caused them to understand the reading.

2. **How do you hide your soul daily in the Rock of God's perfect watch care? (Ps. 27:5; 91:1)**

He that dwelleth in the secret place of the most High shall abide under the shadow of the Almighty.

3. **How are you a teachable, joyful servant of the King of kings? (Ps. 27:11)** Teach me thy way, O Lord, and lead me in a plain path, because of mine enemies.

4. **How do you possess "the faith" of Jesus that gives your soul rest daily? (Ps. 27:13; Gal. 2:20)**

[12] Deliver me not over unto the will of mine enemies: for false witnesses are risen up against me, and such as breath out cruelty. [13] I had fainted, unless I had believed to see the goodness of the LORD in the land of the living.

5. **How do you patiently wait on God prayerfully in key decisions? (Ps. 27:14)** Wait on the LORD: be of good courage, and he shall strengthen thine heart: wait, I say, on the LORD.

6. **Does Jesus' constant love joyfully meet you daily "face to face"? (Gen. 32:20; Heb. 13:8)** And say ye, moreover, Behold, thy servant Jacob is behind us. For he said, I will appease him with the present that goeth before me, and afterward I will see his face; peradventure he will accept of me.

7. Do you enjoy iron sharpening iron fellowship to keep you on God's path? (Prov. 2:20)

That thou mayest walk in the way of good men, and keep the paths of the righteous.

8. How do you pursue God and His wisdom effectually? (Ps. 63:5-8; Prov. 4:5-7, 23) 23: keep thy ♡ with all dilligence; for out of it are the issues of life.

9. Are you a joyful servant who has "lacked nothing" in life? (Neh. 9:21) yea, forty years didst thou sustain them in the wilderness, so that they lacked nothing; their clothes waxed not old, and their feet swelled not.

10. When was the last time God revived your soul to love Him more? (Ps. 119:159)

Consider how I love thy precepts: quicken me, o Lord, according to thy lovingkindness.

11. How does God's gift of eternal peace flow from your heart? (Ps. 37:37; 119:165; Isa. 26:3)

|165| great peace have they which love thy law: and nothing shall offend them.

35-37 I have seen the wicked in great power, and spreading himself like a green bay tree.

36. yet he passed away, and low, he was not: yea, I sought him, but he could not be found.

|37| Mark the perfect man, and behold the upright: for the end of that man is peace.

104

|26:3| Thou wilt keep him in perfect peace, whose mind is stayed on thee: because he trusteth in thee.

[5] my soul shall be satisfied as with marrow and fatness, and my mouth shall ⟨?⟩ thee ⟨?⟩ ⟨?⟩ lips: [6] When I remember thee upon my bed, and meditate on thee in the night watches@Because thou hast been my help, therefore in the shadow of thy wings will I rejoice. [8] My soul followeth hard after thee: thy right hand upholdeth me.

FAITHBUILDERS OF ABIDING LOVE
"Abide in my love"... (Jn. 15:10)
CHAPTER TWELVE

Now we will make a small shift from personal **faithbuilders** to examining some Biblical **faithbuilders** that God reveals in our Scriptures. Jesus, in His last days on earth, gave an intimate invitation to His dearly beloved disciples, "As the Father hath loved me, so have I loved you: continue ye in my love." (Jn. 15:9) Our loving Lord wanted His servant soldiers to understand the durable riches of His unconditional love; He would pray a short time later "I have declared unto them thy Name, and will declare it: (cause and effect noted by the colon) that **the love** wherewith thou hast loved me may be in them, and I in them." (Jn. 17:26) Jesus wanted His disciples to understand the depth, width, breadth, and height of eternal love. This is the character of love that God has for His beloved Son which will be given them by God's Spirit as the first fruit of His unsearchable riches that will shape their character and conduct. (Gal. 5:22; Eph. 3:8; Rom. 11:33)

The disciples, as they grew in grace, needed insight into the **"intimacy factor"** of faithfulness. There are degrees of intimacy in the Christian life. We can be as close to Jesus as we choose to when we exercise the diligent disciplines of seeking Him with all our hearts. (Jer. 29:11-13; Jas. 4:7-8) This is our choice because Jesus is no respecter of persons and loves all men and saints the same. Nearness is likeness as saints grow from faith to faith to be "Jesus with skin on" in this world, as God daily conforms us into His image. (Rom. 8:28-29; I Jn. 4:17) As a word picture, the moon only has one purpose, to reflect the sun, as we have one purpose as saints, to reflect the Son Jesus Christ. (Mt. 5:16; 2 Cor. 3:18)

For example the **"intimacy factor"** illustrated in the Old Testament occurred when God called Moses to the mountain top of Sinai for forty days to see His glory as a consuming fire in the burning bush of revelation. (Ex. 3:2-3) However, at the same time God limited Israel's mixed multitude's approach to Mt. Sinai warning them not to ascend or touch Mt. Sinai as they would die immediately; God knew well their evil hearts prone to build golden calves of vain religion and empty worship. (Ex. 19:11-12)

So Moses ascended with Aaron and some of Israel's leaders and they beheld God and ate and drank in intimate fellowship as a *potential* **faithbuilder** for their future faithfulness in serving God. They experienced a deeper fellowship than ever as they observed God's holy transcendence in the pavement of sapphire, clear as the sky. (Ex. 24:9-11) However, this experience effected *no* permanent life change in most of the leaders as they later worshipped the golden calf; most of them were not ready for the deeper fellowship at the top of the mountain reserved by God for Joshua and Moses as their **faithbuilder**. (I Pet. 2:1-3)

Next, Moses and Joshua went further up to the mountain for their divine appointment to grow in intimacy, as they warned the elders to come no further but to wait. (Ex. 24:13-14) Please note how small this next level of intimacy is, as only two men could ascend, reminding us that narrow is the path of righteousness, and few find it. (Mt. 7:14) We know Moses' specific calling as God's deliverer servant, but what qualified Joshua for such a **faithbuilder**? First, recall that Moses only trained one faithful disciple, Joshua, who habitually loved to serve and worship. (Heb. 12:28-29) In chapter 33, when Moses alone saw God face to face, as God's beloved friend, and returned to camp, Joshua would not depart from the tent where God's glory rested in Moses. Joshua, having tasted of God's glory, would settle for nothing less, as he wanted to be where God dwelled! (Acts 17:28) That's why many truly born again Christians crave the divine faithful fellowship of iron sharpening iron friendships and, consequently, attend church whenever the doors are opened. (Prov. 27:17; Mt. 5:6, 8)

Ultimately, only Moses as a type of Christ tasted the top level of the glory of the Lord as a consuming fire on the top of Mt. Sinai. The mixed multitude only saw the consuming fire from a great distance and *feared* the God they knew about but did not know personally; Moses *worshipped* as he absorbed God's glory, reflecting God's character as he came down the mountain. As all true servants who reflect Jesus to this dark world, Moses didn't realize he had absorbed God's light but simply reflected Him as a result of the intimacy of faithful fellowship because he had listened to God's words. (Ex. 34:29; Luke 8:8; Acts 4:13) To illustrate this absorbing of light, our children owned a white cross that glowed in the dark if they held it to light before the room darkened. Then after a while, the reflective light faded and went out altogether. That's why Paul challenged the Corinthians to behold or absorb God's glory from His enlightening Word daily to be changed from glory to glory into His image, just as Moses did on Mt. Sinai. (2 Cor. 3:13-18)

Part of Moses' **faithbuilder** resulted from His ravenous appetite for intimacy and his consequent boldness to ask God "Let me know thy ways...show me thy glory", as he spoke "mouth to mouth" passionately to God as his friend. (Ex. 33:11,13,18; Num.12:8) However, Moses did not see God's full glory but only the afterglow that his Lord left behind when God hid him in the cleft of the rock as He passed by Moses. (Ex. 33:20-23)

If you and I had been at Mt. Sinai on that day, which experience would we have had, and which level of intimacy would we have tasted? Would we have had to stay at the bottom in fear, as we may know much about God, but do we really know Him intimately and personally? (Phil. 3:10) Are we immature leaders in our church who can only go so far because we have never been discipled and can't take others farther than we have gone with God? (Luke 6:40) Are we a teachable humble Joshua who is being discipled to reproduce reproducers who meditate on God's Word and lead our homes to serve our great God? (Josh. 1:8-9; 24:14-16) Are we key God-fearing leaders, working out our own salvation with fear and trembling, who reflect Jesus consistently as we grow from glory to glory, leaving a legacy for all to see? (Rev. 14:12-13) Intimacy is a choice! What godly choices are you making consistently with God, spouse, family and friends? (Prov. 25:12)

Jesus also had different tiers of intimacy with His beloved disciples. Our Lord started out calling His true disciples "servants ", then "friends", then finally "brethren" as they grew in grace and better understood His unconditional love. (Jn. 13:1; 15:15; 20:17) However, only one disciple, John, knew Jesus so intimately that he was called the one "whom Jesus loved." John's Biblical writings clearly show his heart filled with God's love. (Jn. 13:23, 25; 19:26; 20:2; 21:7, 20)

The next tier of intimacy includes the three constant companions of Jesus: Peter, James, and John, who traveled with Him to ministry settings where great **faithbuilders** occurred that the other disciples did not experience. Jesus grew their precious faith that learned to believe His precious promises starting at Jairus' house when Jesus, as the Gentle Shepherd, raised his daughter from the dead. (Luke 8:51) This miracle foreshadowed our Lord as "the resurrection and the life" as He later raised Lazarus from the dead, which John wrote about. (Jn. 11)

Then our Lord took this inner circle of three to the Mount of Transfiguration with Him as Jesus previewed His eternal glory that would eventually be shown to the whole world at His second coming. (Mt. 17:1; Rev. 19) Peter would later write of this life changing **faithbuilder** as "eyewitnesses of His majesty." (I Pet. 1:16) John also penned "We beheld His glory." (Jn. 1:14)

Note how much God used John and Peter to write inspired Scriptures to share with us what they experienced in their journey of intimacy onto the Mount of Transfiguration.

Finally Jesus took them into Gethsemane with Him that they might pray for Him as he agonized about the cross to come and to learn valuable lessons on spiritual warfare. (Mt. 26:37) Jesus didn't choose these three men to get special privileges, but they chose this level of intimacy by their loving service for Him in spite of their personal weaknesses. Peter denied Christ after being warned! John and James argued over being the greatest! Saints do reap what they sow in love and labor for God. (Gal. 6:7) Christians must remember Jesus' declaration about the intimacy factor when He said, "whosoever does the will of God, he is my brother and sister and mother." (Mk. 3:35) When saints are driven by God's Spirit, they passionately fulfill their mission in life to glorify God by finishing the work he called them to do. (Jn. 17:4; Eph. 5:18) Their hunger for holiness is lived out in their daily practice of godliness, as they possess an insatiable thirst for Jesus' righteousness. (Ps. 63:8; I Cor. 1:30; I Tim. 4:7-9; Heb. 12:14)

Anyone can choose to crawl up into Jesus' lap daily, to lean on His chest in love as John did, if we are willing to count the cost of the durable riches of deep intimacy through obedient love. (Rom. 1:5,17; 5:5; Heb. 4:12) None of us have an excuse for not loving and serving Him as He has loved and served us. (Jn. 15:9; 17:26; 2 Cor. 5:14, 17; Heb. 5:8-9) What a **faithbuilder**! What a faithful Savior who prays for us daily that we might love Him more. (Jn. 13:1; 17; Heb. 7:25)

However, God also warns us that to whom much is given, much is required. (Luke 12:48) That's why Paul warned the church and especially the Israelites, "Behold therefore the goodness and the severity of God" as it's very dangerous to ignore or reject His intimate gift of love. (Rom. 11:22) God's severity fell on Jesus at the cross as sin had to be judged; a price had to be paid for man's violating His holy standards of truth, the ten commandments of law which are a schoolmaster to lead us to our Savior's love. (Gal. 3:24) That gracious gift of God's love is the only source of redemption for our sinful souls. (Jn. 14:6; Rom. 3:23; 6:23; 1 Tim. 2:3-6) Those who reject that love gift choose God's wrath of an eternal hell as a result of refusing the precious blood of the Lamb who takes away the sins of the whole world. (Jn. 1:29; 1 Pet. 1:19) So choose wisely!

FOOD FOR THOUGHT (Phil. 4:8): "Consider how I love thy precepts: quicken me, O LORD, according to thy lovingkindness" (Ps. 119:159)

1. How does your growing love for God produce obedience habitually? (Ps. 119:167)

2. How do you allow God's love to protect you daily from life's offenses? (119:165)

3. How does God's love protect you daily from foolish thoughts? (119:113)

4. How do you allow God's love to guard you from materialistic thinking? (119:127)

5. How do you maintain a God-conscious love for Jesus that fills your heart? (119:97)

6. How does your love enable you to faithfully wait on God? (Isa. 64:4; 1 Cor. 2:9)

7. Do you feast on God's durable riches of love to strengthen your faith? (Prov. 8:18; 15:15)

8. As an act of love, how do you abstain from all appearances of evil? (I Thess. 5:22-23)

9. How does your growing intimacy with God satisfy your soul practically? (Ps. 90:14-16)

A FAITHBUILDER OF FORGIVENESS
"Tender hearted, forgiving one another"... (Eph.4:32)
CHAPTER THIRTEEN

One of the patterns in Scripture that must be understood is how God changes a life and consequently blesses the sinner's soul. This **faithbuilder** always starts with man believing that God loves sinners who sincerely repent and ask forgiveness for their sins. (Jn. 3:16; 2 Cor. 7:10) God then not only forgives those sins, but His Spirit also starts powerfully planting the incorruptible seeds of eternal truth into forgiven hearts. Those supernatural seeds will bear fruits of faith, proving the person is forgiven as a born again Christian. (Gal. 5:22; 2 Cor. 7:11; 1 Pet. 1:23)

This process powerfully works every time by this merciful pattern of divine grace: (Eph. 2:8-9)

1. The sinner humbly receives and believes by faith the truths of God. (Jn. 1:12; Heb. 11:6)
2. The saved sinner then experiences God-engrafting those **beliefs** into their hearts. (Jas. 1:21)
3. The saint then experiences those **beliefs** empowering changed **behavior**. (Jas. 1:22)
4. The saint then grows from faith to faith as God enlarges the heart (Ro. 1:17; Ps. 119:32).
5. The saint then is constrained by God's eternal love to obey Him. (Ro.1:5; 2 Cor. 5:14, 17)

Let's now examine how this **faithbuilder** works in Matthew nine. Jesus enters His own city, where faithful Christian friends bring a bedridden man sick with palsy or paralysis. (v 1-2) Jesus sees their faith by the fruits of their actions, as He had taught earlier in His radical Sermon on the Mount: good trees of faith always bear visible good fruits. (Mt. 7:18-20)

Jesus then declared the paralyzed man forgiven, telling him to be of good cheer. The Lord accomplished two glorious goals here. First He equated divine healing with divine forgiveness, as when a sinner is forgiven by God, Jesus in the flesh, he is healed of sin's dominating power over His life. (Rom. 6:4, 11, 22-23) Second, Jesus was deliberately confronting the Jewish religious leaders who denied His deity and consequent absolute authority over the sin nature.

Then the Satan-inspired counterfeit scribes say "within themselves" that Jesus the Son of God, is a blasphemer of God, as they had been doing throughout Jesus' entire ministry. The irony here is "the pot calling the kettle black", as the true diabolical blasphemers were Jerusalem's religious leaders who were mocking Jesus their Messiah! The Pharisees and Sadducees constantly accused Jesus of committing the sins that they were actually committing.

Next Jesus proves His deity further by revealing their evil thoughts which flowed from evil hearts that were desperately wicked. (v4; Jer. 17:7, 10) Remember in verse three these vile men spoke "within themselves" not aloud, but only within their minds!

Jesus had a similar encounter in Matthew 12:22-30 when the religious liars declared that Jesus' Messianic miracles were empowered by Beelzebub the prince of devils. God left them only two choices after Jesus did so many miracles infallibly proving His deity as the Messiah: Jesus was either Satan's messenger or God's! Such power could only come from God, as He had prophesied seven-hundred years earlier that the Messiah's arrival on earth would be obvious by His doing miracles that had never been done in Israel's history. (Isa. 35:5-8) That's why Jesus finally said that you're either with Me or against Me. You either gather people to Me by your beliefs, or you scatter people from Me by your unbelief. (Mt. 12:30) That truth still applies today to all professing Christians. (Mt. 7:15-23)

Then Jesus challenges their willfully blind hard-heartedness with a rhetorical question. What is easier, to tell you his sins are forgiven, or to prove to you infallibly by telling him to arise and walk, miraculously proving my deity and absolute authority over sin, thus proving I am God in the flesh? (v 5-6)

Jesus consistently for three years proved His undeniable deity as the only begotten Son of God to all who would "come and see" if He was indeed the promised Messiah. (Jn. 1:39) Our Lord's infallible words were always proven true by His infallible works. (Jn. 14:10-11)

One of the Old Testament promises the Israelites, who had the eternal prophecies of God in writing, were accountable to know and believe was that Jesus was eternally God. Therefore, no one could stop Him from fulfilling His mission on earth. (Isa. 43:13; Jn. 1:1; 17:4)

When Jesus used the term "the Son of man" in verse 6, the scribes should have immediately recognized that their most beloved prophet Daniel also used that term to describe their Messiah. (Dan. 7:13) Our Lord often used Old Testament quotes to validate that His absolute visible proofs of deity, as the "Ancient of Days" proved His absolute invisible power to be that of God when He said, "I and my father are One." (Jn. 10:30)

The healed man, to prove Jesus' authority as God in the flesh to forgive sin, arose and departed home with a **faithbuilder** of forgiveness which he would **NEVER** forget! This precious gift was promised as an eternal gift from God, as He not only forgives our sins, but He also casts them into the deepest sea, never to be retrieved; and He casts them into infinity, as far as east is from west. (Mic. 7:19; Ps. 103:12) Note that God doesn't say from North to South, because that is measurable by the North and South Poles. However, East to West has no final stopping point, thus infinite eternal forgiveness is promised as God graciously chooses to remember our sins no more. (Heb. 10:17)

Many years ago I knew a man who had been in absolute bondage as an alcoholic for forty years. His children begged their loving Christian mother to throw him out and divorce him, but she told them that she loved her husband unconditionally just as her Jesus loved her. The godly mother worked diligently to see her needy husband through Jesus' eyes. This lady fulfilled Jude 21-22, "Keep yourselves in the love of God, looking for the mercy of our Lord Jesus Christ unto eternal life. And of some have compassion, making a difference."

God eventually answered her forty years of prayer as she "earnestly contended for **the faith**" of Jesus Christ by trying to win him over without a word of nagging. (Jude 3; 1 Pet. 3:1-2) God broke her husband of the dominion of sin and alcoholism, and he never again took a single drink - proof that when God forgives, He heals us of self-destructive sins. What a **faithbuilder** for a faithful loving prayer warrior who simply trusted God for a miracle of impossibility!

Her saved husband soon began ministering to inner city youth through his athletic wear sales position, reaching out to needy athletes who couldn't afford much. He became "Jesus with skin on" to our community, proving Jesus' words that he who has been forgiven much, loves much. (Luke 7:47)

Years ago, as a relatively new Christian, I wrestled with how often I asked God to forgive the same sins. I began to wonder if God ever got tired of forgiving the exact same sinful confessions or whether there was a limit to His forgiveness. Then I heard a pastor on the radio state that when we begin to think this way, God states, "I do not remember you being here at my throne before regarding this sin confession". Praise God for His forgiveness and love, as He stated to the obstinate sinful Israelites in captivity, that although our sins be as scarlet, He makes them white as snow. (Isa. 1:18)

The truths of Matthew's gospel to God's dearly beloved Jews were closed out by Jesus saying, "All power is given unto me in heaven and in earth. Go ye therefore, and teach all nations...teaching them to observe all things whatsoever I have commanded you: and lo I am with you alway, even unto the end of the world. Amen." (Mt. 28:18-20)

This divine declaration is called the Great Commission as we are all called to reproduce reproducing disciples who bear eternal fruits for God's holy glory. (Jn. 15:15; 2 Tim. 2:2) All God-fearing and Christ-honoring, obedient saints need to be in disciple-making churches in order to fulfill our mission to reproduce after our kind as did the Apostle Paul. (2 Tim. 4:7) Jesus devoted most of His time over His three years of ministry pouring Himself into twelve men, after praying all night which men to choose, as the ultimate Disciple Maker. He did this in order to fulfill His precious promise to give us precious faith that He would build His glorious church and that the gates of hell would not prevail against it. (Mt. 16:18)

As a pastor and counselor of thirty-seven years, I have had many beloved saints struggle severely with an unforgiving spirit of bitterness. Often their hardest offenses to deal with are those inflicted by professing Christians. Some of these struggling believers remind me of a word picture God gave my wife and me on a stormy, windy night when our electricity went partially out, and all our lights dimmed to fifty percent capacity. We called our neighbor, who worked for the electric company, and he quickly came to our house. As soon as he walked in the door he said, "I see you have a brownout".

I told him I had heard of blackouts but had never heard of a brownout. He proceeded to take me outside as the storm had stopped, and he began looking up into our pine trees that the electric lines ran through. After some examination, he spotted the problem as a limb had partially damaged the line. He said, "There's the cause of your brownout. The limb seems to have barely severed your electric power, and that's why you still have partial power". Fortunately for us, he made a call and had service repairmen to our home quickly as they were throughout the neighborhood due to the storm's damage.

I use this "brownout" illustration with godly people struggling with bitterness to teach them they have allowed Satan to partially sever their lifeline of God's love which quenches His Spirit's love within their hearts. (I Thess. 5:19). Forgiveness is a choice of heart, as we allow God's grace to divinely enable us to love others in spite of their sinful offenses. Paul encouraged the mature saints of Ephesus to be kind and tenderhearted in dealing with bitterness and forgiveness just as God had forgiven them in Christ. (Eph. 4:31-32) Only God's unconditional love helps us not grieve His Spirit who has sealed our hearts in His gift of eternal and internal love. (Eph. 3:16-20; 4:30)

Another tool I use in counseling is the "**3 R's**" principle of faith that forgives: **repent**, **release** and **remember**. As we prayerfully tell God we truly want to forgive, our sincere **repentance** radically changes our mind's attitude as the word "repent" actually means a divine change of mind. Then God eradicates bitterness and grants us godly, loving zeal to see others through His forgiving eyes that Jesus used at the cross. (2 Cor. 7:10-11) Our Lord then uses our purified hearts to **release** the offending party "seventy times seven", a Jewish idiom for innumerable, to His perfect vengeance. (Mt. 18:22; Rom. 12:19) God does not need our help in sentencing His justice, as all sin is against God as David learned! (Ps. 51:4) We must **remember** that the enemy is not flesh and blood but merely Satan's pawn in spiritual warfare. God's grace then empowers us to depersonalize the warfare as "Jesus with skin on" to "overcome evil with good" as His beloved children. (Rom. 12:18-21; I Jn. 4:17)

Sometimes I also remind unforgiving people of the damage they are doing to their own peace of mind, as there is "no peace for the wicked." (Isa. 48:18, 22) God hates an unforgiving spirit that allows Satan to disable saints from serving Him effectively. Some saints forget that bitterness is like the offended party taking poison pills and waiting for the offensive party to die! Think about the foolishness of locking yourself in your own prison cell of sorrow because you *won't* trust God. (Isa. 50:10-11) Note that I didn't say, *can't* trust God! Forgiveness is a choice! God tells us to forget the past for He is totally in charge of all events we encounter, and He will do "new things" to "make a way in the wilderness" of our bitter journey in which

<u>we are lost, if we let Him.</u> (Isa. 43:18-19) There are special "treasures of darkness, and hidden riches of secret places" that we might know Him far better as the God who not only forgives us but chooses to forget our sins. (Isa. 45:3; Heb. 10:17)

Whether I like to admit it or not, some saints ignore all Scriptural solutions to their unforgiving attitudes. As a counselor, I never know what God will ultimately use to soften a heart from the hardness of bitterness, but I do know His Word always wins in the end because it is incorruptible seed, which Peter had to learn the hard way! (1 Pet. 1:23) I often use illustrations because some people, like David, need word pictures to "turn on the light" of humility and brokenness. (Ps. 51:10, 17)

For example, I often pose the scenario in my counseling training classes of a bitter person standing by a fresh flowing mountain stream. They have grown thirsty from the long walk up the mountain and see this gift from God that will satisfy their deep need flowing before their eyes. As they look at the stream, however, they also notice a swirling filthy cesspool of brown foam and miscellaneous garbage and sticks floating off their right shoulder. They now have a choice to make as a bitter unforgiving person. Do they use their cup to get fresh living water from the hand of God's mercy, or do they choose to drink from Satan's cesspool of yesterday's bitter exhausting pain?!

The powerful choice of forgiveness always successfully flows from how deeply we truly love Jesus. When we remember He forgave the people who conspired and crucified Him, His Spirit enables us as His "beloved" children to work out our own salvation with fear and trembling that we might shine as bright lights of forgiveness in a dark and bitter world. (Phil. 2:12-15) God reminds us He loves those who love Him, and who seek Him early to start their day. Those hungry saints receive durable riches of God's favor of righteousness, as we find life to be fulfilling in His love alone. (Prov. 8:17-21, 34-35) When we, as His children, have truly feasted at His banqueting table of mercy, He reminds us that nothing can separate from the love of God as we are more than conquerors over life's offenses. (Rom. 8:28-39)

That's why God calls us, as His children, to know well what He requires of us: to do just what Jesus would do, to love mercy, and to walk humbly with our God. (Mic. 6:8) Remember the Old Testament term for "mercy" means unconditional love that flows from the loyalty of a written covenant. Praise God for His forgiving love that flows from the throne of grace and the Word of grace daily!

I remember a story I read years ago about Betsie and Corrie Ten Boom who had spent time during the Nazi Holocaust at Ravensbruck concentration camp. Betsie's unconditional love and forgiveness in the midst of vicious atrocities had pierced her sister Corrie's heart many times before Corrie was released in December of 1944 shortly after Betsie had died. Many years later, Corrie saw a big man who looked familiar in a church service in Germany where she was speaking a message on forgiveness. He approached her to say he had become a Christian as he sought her forgiveness for being a prison guard of great cruelty at Ravensbruck. As he stretched forth his hand he told her he knew God had forgiven him, but that he needed to hear her forgiveness too for all the sins he had committed against her. As Corrie's emotions ran wild in bad memories, she had a hard time raising her hand to meet his in forgiveness. Then she remembered that forgiveness is not an emotion but a choice! So she released him into God's love as she gripped his hand as a dear brother in Christ. Jesus' love poured from her heart through her hand to give her an inspiring **faithbuilder** of "Father forgive them, for they know not what they do." (Luke 23:34)

Ro 5:5 And hope maketh not ashamed; because the love of God is shed abroad in our hearts by the Holy Spirit Ghost which is given unto us.

Jn 15:11 These things have I spoken unto you, that my joy might remain in you, and that your joy might be full.

Gal 5:22 But the fruit of the Spirit is love, joy, peace, longsuffering, gentleness, goodness, faith, (23) meekness, temperance; againts such there is no law.

Phil 4:6- Be careful for nothing: but in everything by prayer and 7 supplication with thanksgiving let your requests be made known unto God (7) and the peace of God, which passeth all understanding, shall keep your hearts and minds through Christ 124 Jesus.

FOOD FOR THOUGHT (Phil.4:8): "For we wrestle not against flesh and blood..." (Eph. 6:12)

1. Has God granted you a faithbuilder of forgiveness, as He ransomed you with songs of everlasting joy and gladness, with sorrow and sighing fleeing away? (Isa. 35:10) *and the ransomed of the LORD shall return, and come to Zion with songs and everlasting joy upon their heads: they shall obtain joy and gladness, and sorrow and sighing shall flee away.*

2. How does God's Spirit, as Comforter, comfort you in the battles of life? (Is. 40:1-2)

3. How does Jesus as your King save you daily from yourself? (Isa. 33:22; Jer. 17:9, 14) *[22] for the Lord is our judge, the Lord is our lawgiver; The Lord is our King; he will save us. [9] The heart is deceitful above all things, and desperately wicked: who can know it? [14] Heal me, o Lord, and I shall be healed; save me, and I shall be saved: for thou art my praise.*

4. As a future inhabitant of heaven, do you trust God daily for forgiveness? (Isa. 33:24) *and the inhabitant shall not say, I am sick: the people that dwell therein shall be forgiven their iniquity.*

5. Because of forgiveness, do you see the fruit of God's Spirit in your life, starting with Jesus' love touching you daily, (Rom. 5:5) then His joy overflowing you (Jn. 15:11) and His peace that passes all understanding enabling you to rest in His grace? (Gal. 5:22; Phil. 4:6-7)

← verses

93:1 The Lord reigneth, he is clothed with majesty: the Lord is clothed with strength, wherewith he hath girded himself: the world also is stablished, that it cannot be moved.

Faithbuilders

6. How does God's sovereign Lordship stabilize your heart in faithfulness? (Ps. 93:1, 5) 93:5 Thy testimonies are very sure: holiness becometh thine house, O Lord, for ever.

7. How do Jesus' stripes heal you daily of self? (Jer. 17:9, 14; Isa. 33:22; 53:5; I Pet. 2:24) Isa 53:5 But he was wounded for our transgressions, he was bruised for our iniquities: the chastisement of our peace was upon him; and with his stripes we are healed.

8. How does Jesus' soul strengthen your soul to forgive others? (Isa. 53:12) Therefore will I divide him a portion with the great, and he shall divide the spoil with the strong; because he hath poured out his soul unto death; and he was numbered with the transgressors; and he bare the sin of many, and made intercession for the transgressors.

9. How has God's forgiveness put wisdom and understanding into your heart? (Job 38:36) Who hath put wisdom in the inward parts? or who hath given understanding to the heart?

10. When's the last time you thanked God for His daily forgiveness for your sins? (Ps. 103:1-5)

1. Bless the Lord, O my soul: and all that is within me, bless his holy name

2. Bless the Lord, O my soul, and forget not all his benefits:

3. Who forgiveth all thine iniquities; who healeth all thy diseases;

4. Who redeemeth thy life from destruction; who crowneth thee with lovingkindness and tender mercies;

5. Who satisfieth thy mouth with good things; so that thy youth is renewed like the 126 eagle's.

FAITHBUILDERS FROM DOUBT STORMS

"O thou of little faith, wherefore didst thou doubt?"...
(Prov.3:5)
CHAPTER FOURTEEN

Doubt storms rumble into our lives as the winds and waves of confusion smash into our rocking boat of life. Peter certainly experienced doubts as Jesus called him onto the water only to quickly find his body sinking in the sea as Satan distracted him from his mission of faith. Although Jesus earlier told him not to be afraid, fear filled his heart as he cried out to Jesus saying, "Lord save me." (Mt.14:30) Immediately Jesus grabbed Peter with His holy hand of deliverance granting a **faithbuilder** as the disciples who chose to stay in the boat soon worshiped Him as the Son of God. We will examine Peter's **faithbuilders** more thoroughly in the next chapter.

Many years ago, I received a call from a missionary friend, Don Luttrell, who served the Lord faithfully in his ministry, WIVV, West Indies Voice of Victory, which broadcast the Word of God into the Virgin Islands of the Caribbean. We had teamed up for six years taking my high school seniors there over spring break to do "cold turkey" door-to-door evangelism with the result of over 10,000 professions of faith. This ministry design created great **faithbuilders** for my seniors, many of whom later became missionaries, pastors, and pastor's wives. Don's call requested that I ask our church to be praying for him to be able to buy a small airplane for these trips because the ticket costs were outrageous for us to be flying the teens to these islands and for his follow-up trips.

A few months later he called to tell me his great doubt storm when the plane he wanted was bought by a company that had out bid him. A few weeks after that he called crying to tell me the same plane exploded in flight killing all passengers on board. His doubt storm became a great **faithbuilder** as he had seen the Lord's divine protection again. This blessing, however, penetrated his heart deeply because he was quite angry with God for not answering his prayer the way he thought that He should have! Praise God, our cloud by day and pillar of fire by night, for how He goes before us and behind us protecting us as He did for the Israelites in the Exodus for forty years. (Exod. 1:30, 33; 8:4; 3:22)

The Bible is filled with Old and New Testament **faithbuilders** in days of *doubt storms* that remind saints that God often has agendas much different than ours. (Isa. 55: 8-11) Even Jesus, after asking God in Gethsemane's garden to spare Him the cup of His wrath on the cross, said "Nevertheless, Thy will be done". Faith frequently paves the path of **faithbuilders** as rewards from God for our diligence in trusting Him in spite of the circumstances that cause doubts. (Heb.11:6)

Sometimes as Christians we ask, "Why me God?" when *doubt storms* bring piercing pain into our souls through life's circumstances. The Shunammite woman, old and childless, experienced God's gracious birth of a son. Her faith drew her prayerfully to "the holy man of God," Elisha the prophet, which led to her **faithbuilder** as an old barren woman. (2 Kg. 4: 9-17; Eph. 3:20)

Then her son died, probably either from sunstroke or an aneurysm, "my head...my head". (v19) <u>God creates a trial here to test and purify His gold as He is always</u> refining our faith so we grow from faith to faith. (I Pet. 1:7) So this faithful woman laid the boy on Elisha's bed as her crisis revealed the depth of her Christian character, just as it does for all saints in trial, such as Job. In faith, the mother made no burial preparations as she marched as a "good soldier" over sixteen weary hot miles of desert with fervent faith stating "It shall be well." (v23)

Elisha sees her from a mountaintop and sends his servant Gehazi running to her to see if all is well. She says, "Yes!" (v26) What an amazing statement of unwavering faith!

Then she humbly bows before him, grabbing him by his feet. Her vexed soul was filled with confusion, as she referred to their previous interaction when she said to Elisha, "Do not deceive me." (v16-17, 28) Elisha stated that God did not reveal this death to him (v27). Sometimes in life we all need to cry out in days of confusion, "Lord I believe; help Thou mine unbelief." (Mark 9:24)

Elisha then sends Gehazi with his staff, representing Elisha's authority, to heal the boy, but the Shunammite refuses to leave Elisha so they travel together to her house. (v29-32) Gehazi arrives and lays the staff on the boy's face but nothing happens. Note Gehazi's lack of prayer. Had he learned nothing from Elisha's effectual fervent prayer life passed down from his mentor Elijah? (Jas. 5:16) Remember that Gehazi's name means "denier", as he was a type of Judas Iscariot, who absolutely failed in his mission to glorify God because he used Jesus for his own agendas. Gehazi would later use God's Name in vain as he lies to Naaman. (2 Kg. 5)

Elisha arrives and "behold, the child was dead," so he shuts the door, as he's not there to put on "a show," and prays effectually, as he lays on top the boy. "The flesh of the child waxed warm", as he then sneezed seven times and opened his eyes. The mother then enters and bows herself to the ground before Elisha, taking up her son and leaving, as her **doubt storm** becomes a God glorifying **faithbuilder**. This precious woman's **faithbuilder** is remembered in Hebrews 11:33 and 35, as her faith obtained precious promises as one of the women who saw her loved ones resurrected. Remember that Naaman in 2 Kings 5 had to dip himself seven times in the Jordan River for the **faithbuilder** of being cleansed from leprosy, as God often uses the number seven to remind us that when He starts something, He always finishes it perfectly. (Num. 23:19)

One of the powerful patterns in Scripture regarding **doubt storms** reminds us that often after great victories there arise great vulnerabilities. For example, after John the Baptist's faithful ministry as the Forerunner of Jesus, he is sitting full of doubt storms in a prison cell awaiting death by beheading for obeying God. Similarly, after the Shunammite's miraculous gift of a son to her barren womb of old age, he dies. She reminds Elisha of their previous discussion when she asked him not to deceive her. She doubts even though she has fervent faith. In Genesis 50, Joseph learned in his trials that what Satan intends for evil, God intends for good. God uses these Biblical *doubt storms* to create **faithbuilders** that deepen the roots of righteousness in saints who remain teachable as soft clay in the Potter's hands. (Prov. 12:12; Isa. 64:8; Jer. 18:6; Lam. 4:2)

I experienced severe *doubt storms* in days of spiritual warfare many years ago as a doctor friend of mine named Rich, who witnessed of Jesus' love consistently, came down with cancer at a young age. He helped many people in his medical practice who couldn't afford health care, and he also offered spiritual guidance to hopeless souls who saw no way out of their trials of life. Rich was truly one of God's gifts to our church and community. When God finally took him home to glory I was somewhat confused as a young pastor because Rich also left behind a loving Christian wife and children. Sometimes we may wonder why God ends some lives yet allows other "less deserving" people to live. However, in the end we must conclude with Job that the all-wise Lord gives, and the Lord takes away. Blessed be His name.

When God finally asked Job sixty questions in two chapters to refocus Biblical perspective in listening to the right voices, He reminded him of the dangers of *doubt storms*. (Job 41-42) God used the leviathan as a word picture of Satan as "a king over all the children of pride" whose "heart is firm as a stone." (41:24, 34) God instructed him "remember the battle, do no more." (41:8) In other words, quit trying to figure out spiritual warfare! Quit asking "why" and learn what God wants you to learn. Quit trying to make sense of the battles between God and Satan! (Job 1-2) Rest in His easy yoke that makes your burdens light; God will grant you **faithbuilders** that will turn your captivity by Satan into the freedoms of faithfulness as you grow from *"faith to faith"* into "the faith" of Jesus who said "Learn of Me." (Job 42:10; Mt. 11:28-30)

FOOD FOR THOUGHT Phil.4:8) - "Ask in faith, nothing wavering"... (Jas. 1:7)

1. How do **doubt storms** deepen your prayer life and Bible reading? (Ps. 42:7; 1 Cor. 2:10)

2. Do you habitually walk by faith and not by sight? (Ps. 31:15; 2 Cor. 5:7)

3. Do you meditate on God's Word daily so you grow from faith to faith? (Josh. 1:8-9; Rom. 1:17)

4. When was the last time you allowed your feelings to seduce your faith? (I Kg. 19:9-18)

5. How do you protect your heart when God seems to offend you? (Ps. 119:165; Luke 7:23)

6. When was the last time God turned a defeat into a victory for you? (Gen. 50:20; Job 33:28-30)

PETER'S FAITHBUILDERS
"Lord save me"… (Mt. 14:30)
CHAPTER FIFTEEN

Peter's **faithbuilders** in the gospels formed a deep faith that prepared him for his trials as God's prime preacher in the Book of Acts. When the terrifying storm raged in Matthew 14 and the fear-filled disciples saw Jesus walking on the water, only Peter left the boat to meet His Lord. When Peter's eyes focused on the devil's unholy distractions of the wind and the waves, Peter began to sink into unbelief, crying out, "Lord, save me".

Immediately, Jesus grabbed his hand, admonishing him, "O thou of little faith". Jesus as the Master Potter continued His specific strategy to build Peter's faith from clay to rock, foreshadowed when Jesus first met him and changed Peter's name to Cephas. The two of them then entered the ship, and I have often wondered if Jesus made Peter walk on the water back to the boat or whether He carried him! *the point is.. Jesus saves us from our troubles, we may have a lesson: Have to walk back throug where we just came*

Later in Luke 22:31-32, Jesus said, "Simon, Simon *Peter*, behold, Satan hath desired to have you that he may sift you as wheat, but I have prayed for thee, that thy faith fail not: and when thou art converted, strengthen thy brethren." Jesus often forewarned his disciples, as God promised His servants in Amos 3:7, about trials forthcoming. Note first that Jesus called him Simon, not Peter. Simon was his fleshly carnal name reminding Peter of his impetuous pride that always led him to defeat in spite of his "god-talk" ("I will never deny you"). When names were used

134

from, so that we can build faith/trust in christ, some Problems Jesus just solves for us and carries us through them

Rory Wineka

twice, like "Martha, Martha," it was Jesus' warning that His admonitions must be heeded, especially by carnal thinkers. (Heb. 2:1) Notice also that Satan definitely targeted Peter alone, somehow knowing his infinite potential as a key disciple. The devil also realized that Peter was definitely "wheat" and not a Judas-like tare! Praise God for Jesus' daily fervent intercession as God's Perfect High Priest who protects saints as we serve Him to bear fruit faithfully. (Heb. 7:25) Peter's faith would be tested severely, but Jesus would ultimately protect Him as the "apple of His eye," and his faith would eventually "fail not". In the end, indeed, in the book of Acts, Peter would often mightily strengthen his brethren. So Jesus answers His own prayers which He prayed in John 17, as Jesus **ALWAYS** wins in the end! (Rev. 19)

To illustrate this, many years ago a group of seminary students played basketball in a local public school gymnasium weekly to burn off the stress of their academic studies. Each night that they played they observed the custodian, who had to lock up when they were done playing, reading his Bible during his supper break. One night a student came over to the custodian, who was reading the book of Revelation at that moment, to thank him for always being so helpful to them each week. Then the student asked, "Are you getting much out of that most difficult book to understand?"

The custodian replied, "I certainly don't understand it all, but I do know one thing for sure. Jesus wins in the end, and that's all I need to know to rest in His love and truth as a Christian who

135

wonders about the evil growing daily in this world!" (I Jn. 5:18-20)

Then, after Peter denies Jesus three times in Matthew 26, just as Jesus predicted, Jesus is crucified and three days later arises from the dead. Later in Mark 16:7, the angel sends the women, who came to the empty tomb after His resurrection, with these instructions, "Tell his disciples *and Peter*" that Jesus would meet them in Galilee. If anyone needed to hear good news it was Peter, whom the angel pinpointed, knowing Satan's mind games after the three denials and diabolical doubts eating at his soul for betraying his beloved Lord.

Peter's feelings and the fatigue of spiritual warfare of Gethsemane's Garden may have seduced his faith for a while as he denied Christ. Surely Satan's fiery darts hit the bullseye of his pride, but Jesus will once again deliver Peter from sin's guilt, giving him the shield of faith to defeat the devil. (Eph. 6:16)

In John 21 the exhausted and perplexed Peter goes back to his trade of fishing and catches nothing, a picture of what happens to saints not doing God's will. But Jesus comes and calls to His disciples, "Children, have ye any meat?" Then Jesus tells them, the "professional fishermen", to cast their net on the right side of the boat, and they caught one-hundred and fifty-three fish. The net was not broken, and God granted His weary disciples, especially Peter, another **faithbuilder**!

Then Jesus questions Peter, calling him by his carnal proud

name "Simon," asking him three times if he really loved Jesus. Peter was grieved the third time his Lord questioned him and said, "Lord thou knowest that I love Thee".

Finally, as Jesus reminded Peter that his mission to feed His sheep (still) needed fulfilled, Peter knew he was not disqualified by his sins of denial. His repentance, demonstrated by his bitter tears of godly sorrow, would bear beautiful fruits in the book of Acts. (Mk. 15:72; 2 Cor. 7:10-11) *Satan wants to keep us deflated so that we are not profitable! We must still continue in His work.*

After God uses Peter to preach a powerful sermon on repentance and salvation in Acts 2, in fulfillment of Jesus' prophecy that He would build His church, (Mt. 16:18) we later find Peter in prison in Acts 12. The chapter opens with, "About that time" Herod persecuted God's church.

A pattern throughout the Bible, and especially in Acts, is that when God goes to work building His kingdom of light and truth, Satan goes to work building his kingdom of darkness and lies, often using his murderous conspirators like Herod. In the gospels, Jesus boldly blamed the religious leaders in Jerusalem for all the confusion about God and His Word, teaching the Pharisees and Sadducees that their father Satan is the father of lies and murder. (Jn. 8:44) Therefore as Satan's sons, they would murder Him as they told conspiratorial lies at His trial. Jesus also taught that a disciple always ends up like his master teacher. (Lk.6:40) Consequently, evil people always choose evil leaders, like the Israelites chose King Saul, rather than God as their king. (I Sam. 8-9)

Therefore, Acts 12 opens with Herod killing James as the church's first martyr and then planning next to kill Peter for political profit. Peter is imprisoned, guarded by sixteen soldiers to guarantee he doesn't escape.

"But prayer was made without ceasing of the church of God for him." (Acts 12:5) Peter slept peacefully, chained between two soldiers, while a keeper guarded the door. The **faithbuilder** for God's beloved servant began! (Jas.5:16)

"Behold, the angel of the Lord came...and a light shined in the prison." (Acts 12:7) The angel awakened the peacefully sleeping Peter, lifted him up as the chains fell off, and told him to get dressed and to follow him.

All this time Peter thought he is dreaming until they passed the second guard station (v10) and came to the gate which opened on its own! And then the angel, no longer needed, departed.

Now Peter had to press on by faith. In **faithbuilders,** God acts to do His part, then we must act by faith to work out our own salvation with fear and trembling, as He always enables His saints to do what He asks them to do. (Phil. 2:12-16)

"Now I know of a surety." (Acts 12:11) Peter fully came to his senses convicting him to head to the safe house of Mary where the warfare intercessors were effectually praying. (I Thess. 5:17) Peter knocked and Rhoda heard his voice and ran in with the glad news, (v14) but she was rebuked by their illusion that an angel was at the door; Jewish superstition believed guardian angels often took the form of God's people. So Peter kept knocking, and they finally opened the door in astonishment.

Then Peter told them all that God had done. He challenged them to share this much needed **faithbuilder** with their brethren who were so discouraged by the martyrdom of their beloved James.

Herod then killed the guards, reminding us that Satan eats his own children, as he has no loyalty at all for those who serve him blindly. This example continues today amongst Muslims, as the Shiites kill the Sunnis, and the Hamas kill the Fatah, and vice versa. As Ecclesiastes states, there's "nothing new under the sun!"

Then Herod entered the political arena proudly coming to a banquet honoring him for his generosity. As he pompously spoke, the people called him a god, adoration which he gladly received. Note that it was a "set day" on God's calendar to make sure Herod would reap what he had sown as Satan's emissary. Now God sent his angel again for a far different mission, as angels are often weapons of God's judgment as in the book of Revelation. This angel smote Herod in a far different way than when Peter was smitten, as parasitic worms filled Herod's body killing him five days later! Imagine his ongoing pain compared to James short-lived pain when he immediately entered the Presence of Jesus upon martyrdom! Jewish and Roman historians record Herod's agonizing death occurring in

44 A.D. Remember that God is the God of all world history, "His Story"!

God historically dealt severely with men and angels who messed with His holy Glory which He refuses to give to another. (Isa. 42:8; Rom. 1:18-23) Nebuchadnezzar stole glory from God and lived like an animal eating grass. Moses struck the rock twice and could not enter the Promised Land. Lucifer, as the "shining one", tried to take over heaven and he and his evil angels will pay a final price in the eternal lake of fire.

In spite of Satan's efforts to damage and destroy God's church, "the Word of God grew and prevailed," providing yet another **faithbuilder** to God's persecuted saints, as it would happen again in Acts 19:20.

As saints we are better off not trying to figure out spiritual warfare, as we by faith trust our loving sovereign God who never makes mistakes. (Rom. 8:28-38) For example, both James and Peter were imprisoned, but God only allowed James to be martyred. Someone could ask, "Who won, James or Peter?"

The answer is, "God!" They both won because God always takes care of His own children. James went immediately to heaven, and Peter served God until he was later martyred.

Twenty years ago I experienced a great loss I couldn't understand. I had gone to Alaska to work with a mission's agency to send our college students for the whole summer to serve Jesus in Indian villages and fishing camps and to do Vacation Bible School. As we were flying from Petersburg to Anchorage we encountered horrible turbulence from the updrafts and downdrafts that make that area one of the most dangerous small plane flight patterns in the world. We all, including our pilot, thought we would probably die. By the grace of God we arrived safely, though very nauseous and exhausted from fervently praying for God's sovereign protection. (Rom. 8:31-39)

Three months later, the same plane on the same flight went down, never to be found. The mission agency lost several key missionaries and key administrators. I personally had a very hard time understanding why he spared me and my pastor whom I was flying with to set up these trips. Yet God chose to take the lives of faithful servants under the same conditions. I simply had to rest by faith in God's Word that tells us that the righteous die to be spared of the further evil of this world, and that every breath is a gift from God. Therefore, when God sovereignly chooses to give us our least breath, we will die. (Isa. 57:1; Dan. 5:23)

Concerning all the books written about "life after death" scenarios, I have a great problem with both the Christian and non-Christian having the exact same experiences. Just because some doctor declares you dead, and then you see light and hear voices that you enjoy, doesn't mean that vision of "experience" was real. Satan is the master counterfeiter, masquerading as an angel of light. (2 Cor. 11:13-14) However, when God declares you dead, only then are you truly dead. Let's trust our God and only measure life's experiences through Scripture alone and not through feelings of what we think happened! Let God be true and every man a liar. (Rom. 3:4)

Recall also that Job asked God "why" over a dozen times regarding trials he faced. Yet, in the end, Job learned that we are not to ask, "Why," but to ask "God, what do you want me to learn from this?" God is not always a God of explanations, but He is always a God of precious promises that grow our precious faith, from faith to faith, if we will believe those promises. God often uses such circumstances to give us stones to stack, as in Joshua's day, as personal **faithbuilders**, as Peter learned quite often in his trial filled life. (Josh. 4:1-7; 1 Pet. 1:1-4)

2:21 For even hereunto were ye called: because Christ also ← suffered for us, leaving us an example, that ye should follow his steps.

3:12 For the eyes of the Lord are over the righteous, and his ears are open unto their prayer: but the face of the Lord is against them that do evil.

3:14 But, and if ye suffer for righteousness sake, happy are ye; be not afraid of their terror, neither be troubled.

5:6 Humble yourselves therefore under the mighty hand of God, that he may exalt you in due time:

5:7 Casting all your care upon him, for he careth for you.

5:8 Be sober, be vigilant; because your adversary the devil, as a roaring lion, walketh about, seeking whom he may devour:

5:9 whom resist steadfast in the faith, knowing that the same afflictions are accomplished in your brethren that are in the world

5:10 But, the God of all grace, who hath called us unto his eternal glory by Christ Jesus, after that ye have suffered a while, make you perfect, stablish, 142 strengthen, settle you.

5:11 To him be glory and dominion for ever and ever. Amen

Rory Wineka

FOOD FOR THOUGHT (Phil.4:8) -"For my thoughts are not your thoughts"... (Isa. 55:8)

1. Why would God allow such a fine servant-disciple as James to be martyred? (Phil. 1:21)

    For to me to live is Christ, and to die is gain.

2. Why does God allow people to be taken at younger ages? (Isa. 57:1-2) The righteous perisheth and no man layeth it to heart: and merciful men are taken away, none considering that the righteous is taken away from the evil to come.

3. What did Peter learn through his trials? (I Pet. 1:7; 2:2, 21; 3:12, 14; 5:6-11; 2 Pet. 1:1-4) 1:7 That the trial of your Faith, being much more precious than of gold that perisheth, though it be tried with fire, might be found unto praise and honor and glory at the appearing of Jesus Christ.

4. Describe a time when God turned evil circumstances into good for you? (Gen. 50:20) But as for you, ye thought evil against me; but God meant it unto good, to bring to pass, as it is this day, to save much people alive.

5. How do you practically number your days to live wisely? (Ps. 90:12)

    So teach us to number our days, that we may apply our hearts to unto wisdom.

6. Do you believe that saints are daily under God's holy protection? (Ps. 91:1) He that dwelleth in the secret place of the most High shall abide under the shadow of the Almighty.

7. How has God used trials in your life to help you understand your calling? (Ps. 90:13-17)

_13_ Return, O Lord, How long? and let it repent thee concerning thy servents. _14_ O satisfy us early with thy mercy; that we may rejoice and be glad all our days.

8. How do you enjoy peace daily as a blameless saint? (Ps. 37:37) Mark the perfect man, and behold the upright: for the end of that man is peace.

9. Do you believe with all your heart that daily God's hand is on you personally? (Ps. 139:5) Thou hast beset me behind and before, and laid thine hand upon me.

10. What drives the greatest fear into your heart consistently? (Ps. 27:1) The LORD is my light and my salvation, whom shall I fear? the LORD is the strength of my ~~salvation~~ life, of whom shall I be afraid.

11. See **Appendix I** on the challenge for finding Peter-like leaders.

_15_ Make us glad according to the days wherein thou hast afflicted us, and the years wherein we have seen evil.

_16_ Let thy work appear unto thy servents, and thy glory unto their children,

_17_ and let the beauty of the Lord our God be upon us: and establish thou the works of our hands upon us; yea, the work of our hands establish thou it.

FAITHBUILDERS THAT SOFTEN THE HEART
"For God maketh my heart soft"... (Job 23:16)
CHAPTER SIXTEEN

Years ago I spent time each December deer hunting in Southern Ohio with a brute of a man we called "Big Jim" who stood six feet six inches tall. He worked in the local steel mill as a supervisor who ran a "tight ship". Every Friday night the local bar filled with steel workers who often argued and fought before the evening ended, but when Jim stood up and said, "That's all boys," the fighting immediately ceased. No one messed with Big Jim.

Jim's God-fearing, loving Christian wife urged him to attend church, and as Jim's little girl got older she likewise begged her daddy to come worship Jesus, but Jim didn't need Jesus, or so he thought. Then one day his precious little girl contracted leukemia and quickly grew weak. Almighty God used her illness to soften Big Jim's hard heart, and before she died he became a God-honoring Christian, granting his daughter a great **faithbuilder** that she would see her Daddy in heaven.

Everyone in town and at work immediately observed the lifechange in Big Jim's softened heart. Everything changed about Big Jim: language, values, morals, drinking, temperament, impatience, and how he spent his free time, especially Sundays. His new lifestyle shouted as a living epistle for Jesus, "I am a new creation in Christ," as God's eternal love had transformed him into Jesus' glorious image. (Mt. 5:16; 2 Cor. 3:18; 5:14, 17)

Job stated, "For God maketh my heart soft, and the Almighty troubleth me." (Job 23:16) God knows well how to wear a proud man down to the point of surrender and submission, shaping a teachable humble heart, as the Potter shapes clay into vessels fit for His use. (Act 9) When God's mercies touched my life through Jesus' love at Rehoboth Beach, my heart's pride melted and truth plowed the fallow ground in my soul, preparing it for the seeds of righteousness that God would sow. (Hosea 10:12-13) As a heathen, I had fought off religion for years, but how do you defend yourself against the penetrating unconditional love of Almighty God!? (Jn.3:16) My God first had to trouble my soul with conviction that I was a wretched sinner who needed a Savior who loved me, which quickly softened my selfish soul to putty in His hands. (Isa. 64:8; Jer. 18:4; Luke 5:8; Ro. 7:24-25)

That's why Paul fully understood God's plan of Christ's cross when he penned, "Behold therefore the goodness and severity of God." (Ro. 11:22) God's holy severity put His dearly beloved only begotten Son on a cruel cross where he was mercilessly mocked and tortured for hours. This severe act of love has saved the souls of millions of sinners over the centuries reminding people that God's love always has consequences for the good of His precious children. (Heb. 12:5-6) Our loving Lord knows how to shape our will to exercise the diligent disciplines that bear fruits for His glory. (Heb. 12:11, 13)

This goodness and severity principle shines forth in the description of Jesus' crucifixion in Luke 23, which David foreshadowed in a Messianic psalm regarding his trials and Jesus' future trials. This prophetic principle is called "telescoping," where two separate events, years apart in fulfillment, are prophesied in one passage. This title correlates to looking at two mountains, one behind the other, but through the telescope you only see one mountain. As time moves you forward in perspective you eventually see the second mountain hidden behind the first mountain; God gives insight into the two different prophecies contained in one passage of prophecy. David described crucifixion hundreds of years before it ever happened historically in any culture on earth, detailing the agony of bones out of joint, the heart melting like wax, and all strength dried up by the "dust of death." (Ps. 22:14-17) Here God telescoped both David's and Jesus' agony hundreds of years apart in one Messianic prophetic Psalm.

The crucifixion showed the severity of hatred God allowed to fall from the hands of the Jews onto Christ, but also His abounding love when Jesus said, "Father forgive them; for they know not what they do." (Luke 23:34) The two malefactors hung on both sides of our Lord. Both thieves initially mocked Jesus, but one of them changed as his God ordained troubles softened him when he rebuked his fellow malefactor about having no fear of God. The repentant thief reminded his fellow malefactor that they were receiving what they deserved in crucifixion, reaping as they had sown in sins of stealing, and that he needed to fear God. Then he declared, "This man (Jesus) hath done nothing amiss." (Luke 23:40-41)

The term "amiss" reminds us that the word for sin in the original language meant "to miss the mark" of God's holy perfect standard of the Ten Commandments. God in His gracious love, which always tells the truth, uses His law as a "schoolmaster" to draw us to Jesus, teaching us to repent so that our souls might be saved by Jesus' sacrifice that covers our sins as our Kinsman Redeemer. (Gal. 3:24) Remember that Boaz acted in love as Ruth's kinsman redeemer and took her into his care to meet all her needs as a stranger. (Ruth 2-4) Jesus, as our Kinsman, fulfilled the cultural mode of forgiveness of debt or crime for a family member in prison. If a man committed crimes they were written on parchment and nailed onto the door of his cell. A family member could come and pay his fines and set him free as they wrote over top the words of his crimes the word, "Fine," meaning "it is finished," paid for in full, just as Jesus cried out on the cross! (Jn. 19:30)

Since Jesus had done nothing amiss in God's eyes, He could declare to the repentant thief in response to his request that Jesus remember him, "Today thou shalt be with Me in Paradise." (Lk.23:43) The saved thief gave living proof that your **concept** of God always manifests itself by your **conduct,** as your life speaks the words engrafted therein. (Mt. 12:34; Jas. 1:21-22) As the repentant thief observed how Jesus handled crucifixion, forgiving those who unjustly mocked Him, God troubled his heart with convictions that saved his soul as he responded to grace. (Luke 23:34; Ps. 51:10, 17)

A short time later the Roman centurion saw what was done, and glorified God, saying, "Certainly this was a righteous man." Remember that culturally Rome's centurions, tough no-nonsense leaders of over one-hundred soldiers in the best trained army in the world, were not men easily persuaded. They oversaw hundreds of crucifixions, and they heartlessly commanded crowd control tactics to preserve the order of Rome's heartless emperors. God, however, had other agendas this day for a **faithbuilder,** as He troubled this centurion's soul to soften Him with enlightened eyes of understanding to see Jesus as the Son of God. I assure you the centurion had never seen a crucifixion where Love hung on a cross and blessed its mockers and co-conspirators. (Jn. 3:16; Eph. 1:17-18) Here rests another case where God's unsearchable riches fell upon Gentiles; the Jews rejected those riches of God's love to repentant sinners who moved from religion's lies into God's loving truths. (Jn. 8:31-32; Eph. 3:8, 16-19)

I had a close church friend who had lost his job and encountered some financial problems, so I had my wife purchase several bags of groceries for his family. We helped him often until he obtained another job as a welder. One day, a year later, someone knocked on our front door. When I opened the door this same man stood there with several bags of groceries in his arms he wanted me to take anonymously to a family out of work. He wept as he thanked God for his troubles that had softened his heart and wanted to "pay it forward" to this needy family. His wanted his **faithbuilder** to bless others as a "love gift" as he believed that "to whom much is given much is required." (Luke 12:48)

In closing, many years ago one evening a pastor visited a good friend of his who had quit coming to church. The man had sinned and repented but withdrew from his church family due to his shame and pride. The pastor reached for the fireplace poker as he sat encouraging his friend regarding the love of Jesus that healed all hurts. He used the poker to pull one of the hot coals away from the fire. Thirty minutes later the red hot coal turned gray in its coldness. As the pastor talked, his friend got the picture! The lonely man stated, "Thanks pastor. I have suffered alone in a "pity party" since I've chosen to withdraw from the sweet fellowship of our church. You will be seeing me Sunday as God taught me a great lesson tonight. Thanks for your love and gentle admonition of forgiveness."

FOOD FOR THOUGHT (Phil. 4:8): "Open thou mine eyes, that I may behold wondrous things" (Ps. 119:18)

1. How do you receive God' Word in meekness through daily devotions that he might engraft divine enablement within your soul to glorify Him in love? (Ps. 40:8; Jer. 15:16; Jas. 1:21-22).

2. How do you choose to feast on God? (Job 22:21-22; 23:10-12; Ps. 119:40; Prov. 15:15)

3. Do you remember well the day God saved you from afflictions of evil and replaced them with days of joy as you feasted on His merciful truths? (Ps. 85:10; Prov. 15:15)

4. How do you cooperate with God's Spirit so he can enlarge your heart? (Ps. 119:32)

5. As you meditate on God's words, how has He given you success spiritually? (Josh. 1:8-9)

6.   How do you run the race well so you can finish well for Jesus' sake? (Heb. 12:1-3)

7.   How does God daily set you free from self to serve Him fruitfully by faith? (Ps. 119:145)

FAITHBUILDERS FOR SERVANTS

"Serve God acceptably with reverence and godly fear"...
(Heb. 12:28)
CHAPTER SEVENTEEN

Jesus' beloved disciple John penned his gospel, three epistles, and Revelation to tell God's **servant** soldiers how the Spirit's constraining love finishes what God starts as our Alpha and Omega, the Author and Finisher of our faith. God only needs a thirsty soul driving a **servant's** heart to drink His ever flowing water of life freely. (Heb. 12:1-2; Rev. 1:8, 11; 21:6; 22:13) John's opening words in Revelation reminded God's faithful **servants** that He wanted them to know the glorious things which would soon come to pass. God promised blessings to His **servants** who would thirst for His truths by reading, hearing and obeying them diligently, living in anticipation that "the time is at hand" for the imminent return of Jesus in glory. (Rev. 1:1-3)

Then John closes Revelation with "His **servants** shall serve Him" as God "sent his angel to shew unto his **servants** the things which must shortly be done." (Rev. 22:3, 6) God's last inspired words of Revelation remind saints that we are *saved to serve*, not just to go to heaven!

Jesus, after he had washed the feet of His disciples as the sacrificial Servant, reminded them, "If ye know these things, happy are ye if ye do them." (Jn. 13:17) The most joyful saints I have ever met all have one thing in common: they love serving Jesus sacrificially. (Luke 14:28)

- out of Discipline
  or
- out of fave
- Have a right ♡
  attitude.

In days of severe persecution, Paul penned Hebrews to remind Christian Jews that only well-grounded faith would grant divine enablement to persevere in the face of possible martyrdom as they served God to the end of life. The entire chapter of Hebrews 11 focused on the fact that it's impossible to please God without faith, which He always richly rewards. (Heb. 11:6) Then Hebrews 12 challenges true faith to use kingdom grace to inspire us to "serve God acceptably with reverence and godly fear." (Heb. 12:28) Godly fear always flows into teachable hearts in order to make God-glorifying wise choices. (Ps. 86:11; 25:12, 14, 21)

To apply this principle in our daily lives, we need to grasp that what we truly worship is what we will serve with all our hearts. What we serve also proves infallibly what we truly worship. What's really important to me gets my time, talent and treasures. (Mt. 6:24, 33)

The Israelites failed miserably as their vain idolatrous worship led them to serve false gods. Their pattern of destruction flowed from Old Testament to New Testament as their poisonous priorities destroyed their families and nation. Psalm 106 graphically details Israel's downfall as they believed God's words and sang his praise only when He blessed them as they wished. Then they soon forgot his miracles and works of providence and refused to listen to God's counsel. (106:12-13) As the nation spiraled lower spiritually, they lusted exceedingly in the wilderness and tested God with their murmurings. (v14, 25) Next their prayers became carnally selfish, but God answered them and sent famine into their souls, as in the days they asked Samuel for King Saul because God as King wasn't meeting their fleshy expectations. (v15) Then, as they grew more apathetic, they forgot God and despised the Promised Land and its holy provisions, desiring to return to Egypt, as they refused to believe His Word. (v21, 24) The Israelites proved that wicked people have short memories no matter how many miracles God performs. (Job 5:7)

Then the Israelites made the worse choice possible by ultimately crawling into bed with Satan, as they then became pregnant with evil and consequently gave birth to disillusionment that you can mock God fearlessly. (Ps. 7:14) David also wrote that people who have no fear of God never change their ways, as the Jews often proved. (Ps. 55:19) Their pattern of willful disobedience worked out this way: socialize, seduce, and then serve. They **socialized** with God's enemy, they were **seduced**, and then they ended up **serving** the enemy's Canaanite evil gods; eventually Jewish parents burned their own children on the demonic altars of idolatry. Remember the Bible teaches that behind every idol is a demonic force. (Ps. 106:34-37; I Cor. 10:19-20; I Jn. 5:21)

Romans 6 simply declares we all serve somebody, either the holy God of heaven or the unholy god of this world. Jesus said, "You're either with me or against me." (Mt. 12:30) There is no neutral purgatorial ground! When God saves a soul, the saint's heart worships righteous things bearing fruits of holiness in their lifestyle, proving their salvation. (Rom. 6:4-23)

That's why Paul spent so much time teaching the carnal Corinthians to separate themselves from the heathen idols of Rome. He warned them not to be unequally yoked with unbelievers with whom they had nothing in common, as light and darkness cannot co-exist. Christ can have no fellowship or harmony with Satan. God's sons and daughters must abstain from all appearance of evil as God always enables us to do as he asks. (2 Cor. 6:14-18; I Thess. 5:22-24)

As a youth pastor training my teenagers to serve, I kept these principles in front of them, especially in choices of dating. The principle is simple; you will never marry Satan's child if you never date unbelievers! To illustrate this incongruity in relationships, I would mix oil and water in a jar and shake it, and then teach the 2 Cor. 6:14-18 passage. As I taught, the oil and water sitting in front of me on the teaching lectern always separated quickly on its own as I taught the lesson on dating wisely. This word picture helped most of my students who often mistook lustful infatuation for love, but not all of them listened. (Heb. 2:1; 5:11)

For example, three very attractive intelligent young ladies I counseled ended up marrying men who said they were Christians, but all their friends knew otherwise because the men's walk certainly didn't match their talk. In a short time after their marriages, two of the young ladies ended up in the emergency room having been beaten badly by their "Christian" husbands, and the third was brutally raped by her husband who never went to church once after their wedding day. All three women ended up divorced because they ignored God's holy protection. (Ps. 90:12; 91:1) Be not deceived; God is not mocked, as we do reap what we sow as we choose whom we will serve. (Gal. 6:7) Hasty people most often make horrible choices of severe consequence as they ignore God's words of loving protection. (Prov. 21:6)

However, in sharp contrast, one of my greatest **faithbuilders** regards the seventy-one weddings I have done over a thirty-seven year period of ministry. To the best of my knowledge sixty-five of those couples are still married today, with most of them glorifying God with homes that radiate for Jesus Christ as they raise their beloved children in the nurture and admonition of the Lord. A big part of my pre-marital counseling focuses on five key principles:

1. What you truly love you will serve, and what you serve you eventually worship. (Mt. 6:21)
2. Growing Christians always have marriages that grow in grace and love. (2 Pet. 3:18)
3. You will only love your spouse to the degree you love your Lord Jesus. (Ro. 5:5; 2 Cor. 5:14)
4. Stay Spirit-filled by memorizing and meditating on Scriptures, and God will seal your heart in a "vehement flame" of His priceless riches of durable love. (Prov. 8:17-18; Song of Sol. 8:6-7)
5. Help each other daily grow from faith to faith, into the faith of Jesus, and He will surely bless you with many

faithbuilders in years of marriage to come. (Jer. 33:3; Eph. 3:20; Ro. 1:17)

Many years after I left youth ministry to become a senior pastor, one of my former students, who participated in all our youth activities and ministries of discipleship and missions, called me for a lunch appointment. He immediately began to share how his life had degenerated into a "train wreck" due to bad choices. After hearing him pour out his broken heart, I asked him a simple question: "When was the happiest span of your life that you vividly recall?"

Immediately he shared "When I was serving God at camp, when I was in a Bible study in my home, when I was being discipled one-on-one, and when I went on mission trips. By far those were the happiest days of my thirty years of life!"

My response was, "Well then, you know the answer to your own question as to why you are so miserable. It's because you no longer possess the joy Jesus promised to His servants, a joy no man can take away." (Jn. 16:24; 17:13) He left the restaurant saying his life would change, but I never saw him again or heard from him, sad to say.

At times I remind my congregation, "Where would our church be if everyone served as you are serving? Are you a servant soldier who could leave a legacy at the end of your life stating as Paul did: that he had fought a good fight, that he had finished his course, and that he had kept the faith of Jesus Christ his Lord; even as he suffered in a prison cell for doing exactly what Jesus had called him to do on that Damascus Road, he still served God as he wrote the Scriptures. (Acts 9:16; 2 Tim. 4:7)

God's small remnant of true servants are called oak trees of righteousness as a word picture of a sturdy faith that survives all trials. (Isa. 6:13; 61:3) Oak trees have deep sturdy roots as a picture of righteousness, a term used fifty times by Isaiah to paint a sharp contrast with most of the nation who were hardhearted apostates. Also oak trees get their leaves last in the spring and keep them the longest after other shallow rooted trees shed their leaves in early fall. White oak trees bear acorns, the food of many forest creatures, especially deer. A good reminder of the powerful persistent oak as a thriving saint sits in our backyard. When we first moved to our house a small stump from a pin oak tree had a tiny branch coming out of its side. A neighbor wanted to dig the stump out, and my wife and I refused even though it had only one branch on it. Today, forty years later, that branch has grown into a seventy foot tall almost three feet wide pin oak tree that houses squirrels and provides shade for half our backyard. What a beautiful **faithbuilder** as a reminder of what a mature Christian should look like as an oak tree planted by God Himself to feed others His riches of righteousness. (Ps. 1:3; Jer. 17:8)

FOOD FOR THOUGHT: "My servant Job... there is none like him that feareth God" (Job 1:8; 2:3)

1. How do you serve God acceptably with reverence and godly fear? (Heb. 12:28-29)

2. How do you maintain a healthy fear of God that satisfies your soul daily? (Prov. 19:23)

3. Do you appreciate God's fire and water of trials and truth that help you abide? (Num. 31:23)

4. Do you fully grasp how God's merciful truths preserve your life? (Ps. 61:7)

5. How do you experience stability in your life through absorbing God's Word? (Jas. 1:6-8)

6. How do you see the conscious holiness of your repentance leading you to unconscious holy patterns of you serving God fruitfully? (2 Cor. 7:10-11; Heb. 12:1-3, 14)

7. What are the visible fruits of you having "a mind to work" for God? (Neh. 4:6; 6:15)

FAITHBUILDERS FOR FIGHTING THE GOOD FIGHT
EPHESIANS 6:10-18
CHAPTER EIGHTEEN

As a pastor, I have watched Satan effectively carry out his specific diabolical strategies to literally destroy churches, pastors, saints and families who got careless in their keeping their hearts with all diligence. (Prov. 4:23) Well-discipled soldiers of Jesus, our Commander-in Chief of God's army, know how to use the indestructible weapons of faith to defend themselves against Satan's deceptive schemes. The key piece of armor is "above all, taking the shield of faith, wherewith ye shall be able to quench *all* the fiery darts of the wicked." (Eph. 6:16)

God lays out in distinctive detail the process of Satan's strategy to keep people from knowing Jesus as Savior in Luke 8. The battle always regards the heart. As God sows His holy seed on earth daily for all to hear, Satan first comes to snatch it from hearts so people cannot be saved from sin and Satan's fatherhood. (v12; cf. Jn. 8:43-47)

Then for those that hear God's Word with joy for awhile, as merely an emotional response to truth, Satan rushes in with temptations of unholy distractions to keep truth from taking root. This prevents the divine fruits that ultimately prove the soul's salvation. (v13; cf. Jn.15)

Then there are people who are pricked daily by the thorns of life, the cares, riches, and carnal pleasures that Satan so fully offers as he did to Jesus in His temptations; here there exists no harvest of fruits for God's glory, as man's selfish agendas feed his egocentric nature. (v14)

Finally, God reminds us that when His holy incorruptible seeds of truth reach good soil, a bountiful harvest always shines as a light for all to see that God has saved a soul and changed a life. Honest good hearts keep the truth patiently as they persevere in growing from faith to faith, living by faith a life that habitually produces obedience out of love. (v15-16; cf. Rom. 1:5, 17; 5:5)

Psalm 1 declares a beautiful word picture that whenever God plants a tree, it always bears fruit because He plants it by living waters of divine nourishment. That's why the Bible teaches that when God, as our Alpha and Omega, the first and last letters of the Greek alphabet, starts salvation, He always finishes it. (Jn. 10:27-30; Phil. 1:6; Heb. 12:1-2) His Name and glory are at stake as His children represent Him as His ambassadors of light to this dark world. (Mt. 5:16)

Satan has assaulted God's people from Genesis to Revelation reminding us of the Biblical principle that saints must train their ears to listen to the right voices. For years, all of us have seen the little cartoons and advertisements of a man trying to make a hard choice while an angel sat by one ear, and a devil sat by the other ear, both beings whispering what he should choose.

In the Garden of Eden, after God had given strict specific

instructions to Adam and Eve about not eating from the tree of the knowledge of good and evil, Satan shows up as a subtle serpent, questioning God's authority, saying, "Yea hath God said?" (Gen.3)

God's absolute final authority as Lord of heaven and earth is always challenged by the devil, knowing our weakness to want to be our own gods, as Satan offered Eve. (3:5) The question was subtle in appealing to the lust of Eve's eyes, (v6) but Satan never stops there. He went on to lie, creating confusion in her mind about not eating of *any* of the trees of the garden. (v1) God is never the author of confusion, so when saints lose their peace, often they are not listening to the right voices. (I Cor. 14:33) When we listen to Satan's wicked lies we become wicked people, as the Israelites did. (Isa. 48:18, 22)

Job is another example of a Satanic assault by the "roaring lion" of evil who stalks God's people, looking for our most vulnerable moments, as Peter learned the hard way. (I Pet. 5:7-8) Satan had been going "to and fro in the earth" and boldly approached God for permission to attack Job, a God-fearing upright saint who hated evil. (1:6-8) Satan eventually took all that was important from Job, but in the end God's tender mercies used what Satan intended for evil for God's glorious good, as God also did for Joseph. (Gen. 50:20; Jas. 5:11) For in all Satan's scheming assaults, Job sinned not. (1:22) Job declared as part of his **faithbuilder**, "Though he slay me, yet will I trust Him." (13:15) God gave Job confidence in the furnace of the battle field as he said, "When he hath tried me, I shall come forth as gold." (23:10) Even if Job died, he would declare, "For I know that my Redeemer liveth." (19:25) Job's shield of faith enabled him to grow from faith to faith as he treasured the Word of God more than his daily needed food! (23:12; cf. Rom. 1:17)

Satan quite often attacks when saints are at their weakest. He assaulted Christ in the temptations of Matthew 4 after Jesus had fasted for forty days and nights. The challenge was logical and appealed to the real need of hunger. "If thou be the Son of God, command that these stones be made bread." (v3) As the three battles ended, each was answered with the same weapon all saints have: the authority of God's written Word (Mt. 4:4, 7, 10)! Please note that assured victory for our **faithbuilders** always comes from knowing and obeying "every word that proceedeth out of the mouth of God." (v4) That's why faithful saints habitually meditate on and memorize God's precious words which build faith, giving us daily all we need for life and godliness. God then graciously makes all our ways prosperous and successful. (Josh. 1:8-9; Ps. 119:11; 2 Pet. 1:1-4)

Jesus forewarned Peter that Satan had asked permission to sift Peter like wheat, but Jesus prayed for him knowing this assault would prepare him for ministry in the book of Acts. This temptation was used by God to fulfill Jesus' promise that He would build His church and the gates of hell would not prevail against it, in spite of Satan's temptations of God's finest soldiers. Count it a privilege beloved saint when Satan assaults you, as that means you're a bright light for the kingdom of God's glory. Satan wants that light destroyed, as he martyred

Stephen in Acts 7, so his kingdom of darkness can ultimately prevail. (2 Cor.3:18)

God allowed a messenger of Satan to afflict the Apostle Paul through a difficult illness, in spite of Paul's three-fold prayers; God wanted Paul to learn that, "My grace is sufficient for thee: for my strength is made perfect in weakness." (2 Cor. 12:9) Satan eventually conspired with his evil political Jewish leaders to have Paul imprisoned in Rome to shut him up once for all, but Almighty God used this to spread God's Word all over the world as Paul penned epistles that we are still reading today. Praise God for fulfilling His promise that he would preserve His holy Word which would preserve His saints for His eternal glory. (Ps. 12:6-7; 25:21, 12; Prov. 30:5-6; Mt. 24:35) May all saints be eternally grateful that when our gracious God speaks, He faithfully always acts for our good and for His glory. (Nu. 23:19)

As Satan's final strategy to stop God's promised plans unfolds in the book of Revelation, we see the Antichrist scheming to finally murder all Jews as the apple of God's eye; Satan has failed historically by using Hitler and many Muslim murderous leaders of countries such as Iran and Iraq or as in the "Six Day War" surprise attack on Israel. Remember that Satan believes Jesus' promise that He will not return to earth to redeem Israel until the repentant Jews cry out, "Blessed is He that comes in the name of the Lord." (Mt. 23:39) Consequently, if Satan kills all Jews, then Jesus has no reason to return because He has no Jewish Kingdom to build!

Recall that the Jews dangerously declared in their pursuit to crucify their Messiah, "His blood be on us and our children." (Mt. 27:25) God answered their request and sent leanness into their souls for their mockery of His Beloved Son. The Jews proved wicked people have short memories which willfully refuse infallible proofs of miracles and messages which astonished the Jewish people for a short time. (Ps. 106:13, 15)

For forty years after the crucifixion, death, burial, and resurrection of Jesus, grace prevailed and God's Word was preached as described in the book of Acts. But then God allowed Titus' Roman army to kill over one million Jews and to destroy their temple as Jesus predicted. Since then and up to today all the Jews have had left is their "wailing wall" as a visible daily reminder of the "goodness and severity of God." (Rom. 11:22) Praise God that Paul writes promises in Romans 9-11 that He still has a redemption plan for the Jewish remnant that is engraved upon the palms of His loving hands. (Isa. 49:16)

Now that we have Biblically examined Satan's scheming strategy to destroy God's eternal plans and people, let's examine the strategy saints today must have to put on their armor daily to fight the good fight of faith. Believing that God has given us all we need for life and godliness, we are responsible to have a personal plan to guard our lives, homes, marriages, children, churches, and ministries, knowing Jesus' command, "Occupy till I come." (Luke 19:13) Paul used many analogies of saints being good soldiers who needed discipled to fight the good fight, to finish their course and calling, and to keep **"the faith"** of Jesus, wanting to hear "well done" at the Bema seat. (2 Tim. 2:2-4, 15; 3:15-17; 4:7)

Many years ago I had the privilege of a special friendship with a sweet godly servant named Marge who did all our food ordering and preparing for thirty people on our six trips into the West Indies. She had always loved discipling teenage girls and held annual Bible studies in her home for neighboring high school young ladies. When I asked her to help us on these short term mission trips, she stepped right in and went far and above the call of duty. Marge set menus for all we needed and fed us well with three meals a day, as well as recruited a retired couple to help serve too. After our sixth trip I learned Marge had stage four cancer that quickly hospitalized her. I went to see and pray with her one day knowing this would be hard for me to have the right words of encouragement. However, when I walked into her room, her smile melted by heart as she radiated peaceful joy no man could take away. (Jn. 16:24; 17:13) Marge immediately shared that her only burden was her son's salvation. She stated that if it took her dying of cancer to reach him, she would gladly pay that price! Her funeral exalted Christ in a praise celebration for her testimony to many people over the years as she fought the good fight of faith to the very end. (Ps. 115:1)

Jesus' last words of "watch and pray" reminded his finest disciples in Gethsemane that the Spirit is willing and ready but the flesh is weak at best. (Mk. 14:38) Paul taught about the war of the flesh against the Spirit for all true saints living in Satan's world. (Rom. 7; Gal. 5) Therefore, we are accountable to have a personal Biblical daily strategy to counter Satan's warfare tactics to destroy us, as God has forewarned us that to whom much is given, much is required. (Luke 12:48) God has given us specific pieces of armor in Ephesians 6, but how do we practically put it on daily to take a stand for Jesus in our God-mocking world run by the spirit of Antichrist today?

Personally, as a Christian and a pastor, I keep a daily praise and prayer journal to help me stay faithfully focused on my calling and mission in life to glorify God. In order for me to protect my family and flock of disciples, I constantly work on memorizing and reviewing over two-hundred verses, many of which are written in my prayer journal and changed as needed for the warfare going on at the time in people's lives. I write out four simple objectives that I must live by daily in order to have the helmet of salvation. I must put His thoughts into my mind to guard my heart with the breastplate of His righteous will, with all diligence for my issues of life that currently confront me. (Prov. 4:23; Eph. 6:14, 16-17) *"Above all"* other armor, I strategize the needed shield of faith to quench all Satan's diabolical darts that try to quench the Spirit's work within me. (v16)

My first strategy: I must grow from **"faith to faith"** to obey God daily... (Ro. 1:5, 17)

1. Giving all diligence to add to my faith, virtue (Luke 6:19; 2 Pet. 1:3,5)

2. Maturing into **"the faith"** of Jesus Himself (2 Co.13:5; Gal. 2:20; Eph. 4:13; Col. 2:6-7)

3. Trusting God to engraft His righteousness within me (Prov. 12:3, 12; Ro. 11:16)

4. Striving to leave a legacy of faith at my death (2 Tim. 4:7; Heb. 11:4; Rev. 14:12-13)

My second strategy: I must **"abstain from all appearance of evil"** ... (I Thess. 5:22-24)

1. Repenting quickly and often to see **fruits** of repentance (Hos. 10:12; 2 Cor. 7:10-11)

2. Pursuing holiness to practice godliness (Ps. 63:1-8; 1Tim. 4:6-9; Heb. 12:1-2, 14)

3. Absorbing Jesus' light, dispelling all darkness (Ps. 119:11; Eph. 1:18; 2 Cor. 3:18)

My third strategy: I must **"work out my own salvation with fear and trembling"** ... (Phil. 2:12-15)

1. Being humble and teachable to grow in faithfulness (Ps. 86:11; 25:12, 14, 21)

2. Receiving truth in meekness and appetite (Mt. 5:6, 8; I Cor. 2:10, 13; Jas. 1:21-22)

3. Allowing God to enlarge my heart (Josh. 1:8-9; Ps. 119:11, 32, 97, 105, 130, 159)

My fourth strategy: I must focus to **fulfill my calling as Jesus' soldier** (Rom. 8:28-29; Jn. 17:4ff.)

1. Knowing my **mission** as Christ's personal ambassador (Jn. 17:18; Acts 1:8; 2 Tim. 2:2)
2. Knowing my **vision**, to see people through His eyes (Pro. 29:18; Jn. 17:21; Eph. 5:15)
3. Knowing my **passion** to reproduce reproducers (Jn. 17:26; 2 Tim. 2:2-7; Titus 2:3-5)

As I strive to live my strategy, Jesus encourages me daily through His enabling Word as I remember He's praying for me to finish my race well as His servant who wants to be more in love with Him daily. (Ro. 5:5; 2 Cor. 5:14-17; Heb. 7:25; 12:1-2)

My nephew, Brian, fought the good fight as Jesus' soldier-servant as he battled cancer the last ten years of his life granting our family a beautiful **faithbuilder**. He went home to be with Jesus November 2, 1994, at the age of twenty-seven. As a teenager he had gone to a doctor regarding a lump in his back but was told that the lump was only a muscle pull. A short time later, he enlisted for the Navy and the doctors told him that the lump needed further testing, as it certainly wasn't a pulled muscle. The testing revealed a very rare form of cancer, usually only found in children, and he was given a year to live at best.

This battle with cancer broke him and led him to a deep personal relationship with Christ that motivated him to work with our children and teens at church. Brian often shared with our young people that God had to break his selfish legs, throw him onto His shoulders, and carry him to green pastures of truth and life change. One evening as he was picking up a child, his arm broke from a tumor within the bone. His surgery was one of many he had over nine years to remove the cancer.

Our best time together, outside of the day I baptized him, occurred as we fulfilled his last wish to go on a fishing trip to Golden Lake in Ontario, Canada. Brian smiled all week long as he caught more bass in seven days than he had his whole life. God's creation reminded Brian that God is always faithful and totally in charge of all He created, and that "from the rising of the sun unto the going down of the same, the LORD's name is to be praised." (Ps. 113:3) Because of fishing so much and being so weak, he depended much on his morphine pump and afternoon naps to cope with the pain and exhaustion. We had also taken a doctor with us as a precautionary measure of watch-care. Nevertheless at the end of the week, Brian said, "It's all been worth it!"

The cancer eventually took his eyesight as he went blind in both eyes, yet he maintained a deep faith as God sustained him miraculously to praise Jesus sacrificially, no matter what he suffered. (Heb. 13:15) Brian truly had peace that passed understanding and Jesus' joy that no man or circumstance could take away. (Jn. 15:7, 11; 16:24; 17:13; Phil. 4:6-7) One afternoon as I climbed the stairs of the hospital to see him after he lost his eyesight and had begun experiencing much internal bleeding, I agonized what I would say to him as his Pastor, uncle, friend and counselor. When I got to his room, he immediately shared his joy for Jesus' companionship and comfort as His all sufficient Great Physician. He proceeded to thank God for putting him in the hospital, even with both nostrils plugged with cotton due to the blood rushing out his nose. Brian then shared his perspective that God was teaching him, that he was far better off than others, as the nurse had just taken a bitter and angry man, also dying of cancer, out of the room as he cursed her. This angry cancer patient's family quit coming because of his vile angry outbursts focused on them. Brian praised Jesus that one day soon he would be walking heaven's golden streets talking with Jesus, with eyesight restored and no more pain and surgeries. Brian's consistent testimony reminded me "that a faith that can't be tested, can't be trusted." (Job 23:10; I Pet. 1:7-9)

At Brian's funeral celebration we simply worshipped Jesus. Afterwards an attorney approached me saying, "I am a Catholic attorney who has been at many funerals of clients. I represent the hospital where Brian worked as a pharmacist's assistant. I have never seen a faith like his or a funeral of joyful peace like this ever. Every Catholic funeral I have ever attended has been depressing because the priest could never tell us if the deceased was in heaven. There was no hope, joy or celebration at all! I don't know what you people have faith wise, but I sure need to find out!" Several hundred fellow hospital employees also came to pay their respects to a vibrant young man who had been "Jesus with skin on" to so many people. (2 Cor. 4:10-11; I Jn. 4:17)

The funeral reminded me of all the **faithbuilders** that God intimately granted Brian in his ten year battle with cancer, surgeries, and pain. I watched him grow from faith to faith, into the "the faith" of Jesus Himself as he fought the good fight to the very end, fulfilling his mission on earth as God's faithful servant. I'm absolutely sure that when Brian saw Jesus he heard "Well done thou good and faithful servant. Enter the joy of your Lord." (Mt. 25:21; Rom. 1:17; Gal. 2:20; 2 Tim. 4:7)

After thirty-seven years of ministering to dying saints, I praise God for His tender mercies to His beloved children, especially in hospice settings where the caregivers always notice the consistency of a testimony of deep faith. Hospice nurses have shared with me how great a difference there is between the bitter, angry lost souls who die miserably, and the peaceful and joyful believers who have great anticipation of seeing their Savior face to face. (I Jn.3:2-3) How we live our lives will certainly be reflected by the way we die and pass on into eternity. (Matt. 5:16; Luke 23:34; Acts 7:59-60)

FOOD FOR THOUGHT: "Precious in the sight of the Lord is the death of His saints" (Ps. 116:15)

1. Why did Jesus weep at Lazarus' grave, knowing he would live soon? (Jn. 11:35-36)

2. What was the key question Jesus asked about His delay in coming ? (Jn. 11:15, 26)

3. What are the "gains" of saints at death? (2 Cor. 5:7-8; Phil. 1:21; Rev. 21:4-6; 22:4-5)

4. Is heaven merely your destination, or your driving motivation as a saint? (Mt. 25:21)

5. Why does God give such great strength to His saints facing death? (Prov. 24:10)

6. As you fight the good fight, who helps you most? (Ps. 46:1, 10)

7. How do you choose to get real close to Jesus daily? (Mt. 11:28-30; Jas. 4:7-8)

8. How does your soul daily follow hard after God Biblically? (Ps. 63:8)

9. In dark days of life, from where do you draw insight? (Dan. 2:22)

10. Does praise flow from your heart to your mouth consistently? (Ps. 145:1-3)

11. What people do you fellowship with who sharpen you to finish your race well so you leave a legacy for your children to follow? How exactly do they sharpen you in diligent disciplines to fight the good fight of faith? (Prov. 27:17; 2 Tim. 4:7; Heb. 11:6)

12. What are the divine battles God has you engaged in today? (I Jn. 4:1-4; Jude 3, 21)

DANIEL'S FAITHBUILDERS
"The root of the righteous yieldeth fruit..." (Prov.12:3)
CHAPTER NINETEEN

After Solomon had failed so many times regarding the temptations of worldliness, God finally taught him many lessons on leadership and holiness that he wrote in Proverbs. Two key lessons all godly servant leaders need to learn pertain to righteousness in **character** that produces the fruits of righteousness in **conduct**. The first promise of character and conduct God gives is that "the root of the righteous shall not be moved" because it is attached firmly by faith in Jesus Christ the Vine. (Prov. 11:28; 12:3; Jn. 15:1-11) The second character/conduct promise flows from the first as "the root of the righteous yieldeth fruit" habitually, as noted by the suffix "-eth," a participle verb ending. *Character → conduct: who you are → determines what you do.*

Paul taught these same principles as he challenged faithful saints to remember that, "if the root be holy, so are the branches". (Rom. 11:16) Paul's Jewish audience fully grasped this growth principle of flourishing fruit bearing because of their agricultural background, especially regarding the value of the root system to healthy vineyards. Biblically healthy roots of faith always produce healthy fruits that remain eternally. (Jn. 15:16)

John declared also that Jesus was the Root of David, as the Lion of the tribe of Judah, the slain Worthy Lamb who would come to open the seven seals of judgment in the end times. (Rev. 5:5)

At the end of the book, John reminded church saints that the Root of David was also the Bright Morning Star who would turn all the darkness of the Great Tribulation period into the Light of His glory, as our Lord would finally be fully revealed as King of kings and Lord of Lords. (Rev. 19:16; 22:16)

With these principles of *character* and *conduct* in mind, let us now examine Daniel's faithfulness as the only Old Testament saint called "greatly beloved" by God. An angel had come from heaven to touch the mourning Daniel with encouragement and a **faithbuilder** regarding prayer and warfare in the second heaven, which we will examine more of later. (Dan. 10:2, 11)

To set the context before we study Daniel 3, Nebuchadnezzar besieged Jerusalem and took Daniel and his three friends as captives and changed their names in an attempt to change their identity as God's children. (1:7) God's people always seriously chose their children's names because your name represented your character. For example, Daniel's name meant "God is my Judge". So this Satanic attempt to eradicate their character and change their conduct had the ultimate goal for them to forget their righteous roots and who they really were as God's ambassadors.

But Daniel knew the wiles of Satan and "purposed in his heart" not to eat the king's food as a word picture that saints don't feast on the devil's dainties. (v8; cf. Prov. 15:15) Beloved once you have feasted at God's banqueting table of grace as a born _never if I choose to stay the course + stay faithful._

again saint, you never will eat again from the garbage cans of this world! (I Pet. 2:2-3)

Then God blesses Daniel's refusal by bringing great favor and "tender love" with the prince that watched over them. (v9) So Daniel and his friends ate differently and God used this **faithbuilder** to make them healthier physically and spiritually as skilled men in all wisdom, understanding, and knowledge, which greatly comes into play later. (v 14-20) This decision of Daniel also reminds saints that people who feast on God have their hearts united to His in a healthy fear that always enables good decision making. (Ps. 86:11; 25:12, 21)

Next, God deepens Daniel's righteous roots of character as He revealed "deep and secret" principles of enlightenment within him for the coming dark challenges of chapter three. (2:22) That's why Paul challenged the carnal Corinthians living in a dark, evil city to learn the deep things of God in order to escape temptations that would defile their souls as newborn babies. (I Cor. 2:10; 3:1)

At the end of chapter two, Daniel reveals Nebuchadnezzar's dream by declaring "the God of heaven" will set up an eternal kingdom never to be destroyed, as an interpretation that was sure to come in God's perfect time. (2:44-46) Then the king fell on his face, worshipping Daniel and declaring that Daniel's God is "God of gods, and a Lord of kings, and a revealer of secrets." (2:46-47) Then the king made Daniel a "great man", ruler over all Babylon as "chief of governors", which angered Satan's jealous Babylonian emissaries who would start a deceitful conspiracy in chapter three.

Nebuchadnezzar next decides to build a self-exalting, ninety feet tall, nine feet wide golden image on the plain of Dura so no buildings would overshadow his egotistical statue. (3:1) This statue commonly fostered self-worship in Egypt when pharoahs wanted to perpetuate their own memories as conquerors, similar to Lucifer's desire in Isaiah 14 and the antichrist in Revelation 15. That's why Solomon wrote in Ecclesiastes that there's nothing new under the sun. History simply repeats itself as vain men learn nothing.

Then the king invites people from all nations to his dedication for his image, demanding they bow in worship or die in a fiery furnace, (v2-7) foreshadowing the Jews' tribulations as Babylon the harlot arises again in. (Rev. 17:1-5) In response to the king's demands, Daniel's dear friends, Shadrach, Meshach, and Abednego refuse to bow as they count the cost of being loyal to God alone, as faith takes risks! So the enraged king ignores his shallow confession of counterfeit worship in chapter two and declares in satanic pride, "Who is that God that shall deliver you out of my hands?" (3:15) Remember Pharoah's similar satanic boast before he died in the Red Sea, as God delivered His people in a **faithbuilder**. (Exod. 5:2)

Then the three fearless saints answered the king that they had no worries in this matter, believing by faith that God is able to save His servants out of his evil hands; but even if God allows them to die, they will not serve or worship the golden image. (v 17-18) God once again reminds saints that we worship what we serve and that we serve what we worship. (Mt. 6:24)

Praise God for all the "persuaded saints" in Scripture who faithfully believed that "God is able" to grant perseverance in days of deep trials. Abraham's faith fully persuaded him that what God promised He was also able to perform regarding the **faithbuilder** of the birth of Isaac. (Rom. 4:21) In a prison cell Paul's faith persuaded him that nothing could separate him from God's love, as he was more than a conqueror over Satan's attempts to discourage his ministry, (Rom. 8:38) and also that God is able to keep His promises, even in dark days of severe suffering. (2 Tim. 1:12) Sometimes martyred saints died faithfully as strangers and pilgrims headed to heaven, as they were persuaded by the precious promises they embraced. (Heb. 11:13) Thank God that Jesus is able to perfectly protect the salvation of His beloved children even as they are martyred. (Heb. 7:25)

Then, the furious king commanded that Satan's harmless furnace be heated seven times hotter so God's **faithbuilder** for these three faithful men would even bring Him more glory, as he uses the wrath of man to praise Him! (v19-27; cf. Ps. 76:10) God, however, uses the raging fire to slay the king's soldiers as Satan, who has no loyalties, often eats his own children, just as he used Titus in 70 A.D. to kill the evil generation of the "Crucify Him crowd". Then the **faithbuilder** gets more miraculous as Jesus, the Son of God, arrives in the furnace to protect His beloved servants. (v25) If God be for us who can be against us? (Rom. 8:31-32) The fire burns off the ropes but not their clothes, and there isn't even the smell of smoke on them! (v27) Almighty God quenched the violence of fire to remind His servants that often we are winning when we think we are losing. (Heb. 11:34) Please note that Shadrach, Meshach, and Abednego made no attempt to escape, reminding us again that a faith that can't be tested, can't be trusted. (I Pet. 1:7)

Nebuchadnezzar then blesses God for delivering His faithful servants who refused to worship his golden image, but chose to worship God instead. (v28) Then his royal decree commands all people to worship Daniel's living God Who had miraculously answered Nebuchadnezzar's previous question, "Who is that God that shall deliver you out of my hands?" (v15) Then the king promoted the three faithful God-honoring survivors of the furnace, as God completed **faithbuilder** number two, with two more to come.

Remember that God holds all nations accountable for how they treat the "apple of His eye", the Jewish nation. (Zech. 2:8; Mt. 25:31-46) Christians should pray daily for Israel's peace in Jerusalem. (Ps.122:6) One day God will end "the times of the Gentiles", as Nebuchadnezzar started this era, in which nations are used of the devil to attempt to destroy Israel. (Luke 21:24)

Daniel's third **faithbuilder** occurs twenty years later in the lion's den of chapter five. Belshazzar, whose name means "Baal protects the king", holds a vile feast to boost morale for his people who have been under siege. No feast has ever been recorded in history like this one which worshipped idols of gold and silver. Belshazzar is the grandson of Nebuchadnezzar who will prove "the apple doesn't fall far from the tree", as we reproduce after our kind. (Luke 6:40; I Cor. 11:1)

This event marks a major turning point in world history when the Medes and Persians encamp outside the walls of Babylon in 539 B.C., as the "head of gold" of Babylon, in the previous dream, becomes "the arms and breasts of silver," the Mede-Persian Empire. Belshazzar felt confident that Babylon's eighty-seven foot thick walls, three-hundred and fifty feet high, would be invincible as he threw a drunken feast for his gods. However, he filled the cup of God's wrath to the brim, as the Lord's holy hammer of judgment would crush Babylon. Paul reminded the Roman Empire, which imploded from self-inflicted sins, that God's wrath is revealed from heaven against people who suppress His truths. (Rom. 1:18)

In the exact same hour the feast began, the king trembled in holy fear as his knees knocked together and he saw God's fingers inscribe on the wall, foreshadowing the judicial judgment of Almighty God to come. (v5-6; cf. Jn. 9:41) The king immediately sought out an interpreter, but none of his wise men could answer the supernatural message. (v7-9; cf. Amos 3:7-8) His queen then recommends a holy messenger be sought "in whom is the spirit of the holy gods", remembering a gifted man named Daniel who had helped Nebuchadnezzar with "hard sentences...dissolving doubts." (v11-12)

The king summons Daniel for his "excellent wisdom" of "light and understanding" and offers him gifts, which Daniel refuses. (14-17) Daniel publicly rebukes the king for his sins against Almighty God, telling him he will be punished for his pride in not thanking God even for the daily gift of the breath in his body. (v21-23)

Daniel gives the interpretation of "ME'NE"; God has spoken and your days are numbered, and you are finished; (v26; cf. Ps. 90:12) then "TE'KEL" is interpreted, you are weighed and found wanting as a sinner; (v27; cf. Ps. 62:9; Rom. 3:23) then the revelation of "PE'RES," thy kingdom will be given to the Medes and Persians, (v28) just as God prophesied earlier for not glorifying Him. (v20)

The king then rewards Daniel, and later that same night, October 16, 539 B.C., Belshazzar is slain as history records. Darius takes charge as God prophesied one-hundred and seventy-five years previously. (Isa. 44:28-45:4) Remember that all history is "His story" as God sovereignly speaks and acts from Genesis to Revelation; He tells us well in advance in great prophetic detail of His plan to develop an eternal kingdom ruled by His Son Jesus. (Num. 23:19) All God's holy words are eternally settled in heaven, and we would do well to study and know those words with all our hearts. (Ps. 119:89; Prov. 4:23)

Historians recorded the fall of Babylon in 539 B.C. in great detail. The Medes drained the Euphrates River that flowed through the city of Babylon, and then their army walked in on the dry river bed. The careless, drunk Babylonian guards left the gates unlocked as when God opens doors that no man can shut as He gives **faithbuilders** to the faithful. As my wife tells our grandchildren, "Grandma always wins". God tells His children "God always wins", and tells his enemies in advance too, as the clock of God's judgment is ticking. (Jer. 51:57-58; I Thess. 5:1-3)

Daniel's fourth **faithbuilder** takes him into the lion's den for obeying God just as John the Baptist sat in a prison cell awaiting beheading for doing God's will in confronting King Herod. Sometimes our greatest tests as saints come as we face trials for loving obedience in doing God's holy will; the Bible calls this suffering for righteousness sake, as Jesus did for us on the cross. (2 Cor. 5:21; I Pet. 2:19)

As Daniel chapter six opens, Daniel, now about ninety years old, has a long track record of holy integrity as he has learned how to wait prayerfully with a holy fear of His God who has granted him divine enablement in all his decisions. (Ps. 25:12, 14, 21) King Darius' heart has been moved by God to exalt Daniel as the first of three presidents over his kingdom. (v1-2; cf. Prov. 21:1) The presidents and princes composed a congress that made laws to protect the king and his kingdom so that once a law was ratified by the king, it could not be changed. This governing format will be critical for Daniel later in the chapter. Of course Daniel's exalted role angers his jealous peers and strikes fear into their hearts knowing he will not tolerate their graft and dishonesty so common among politicians. God's ultimate plan in exalting Daniel will greatly enable the return of the remnant of faithful Jews to Judah to rebuild God's temple in Nehemiah and Ezra's days.

As always, when God goes to work, Satan goes to work through conspiracy and deceit as in Jesus' days on earth. So the devil's politicians seek accusations against Daniel but discover his sinless integrity as a faithful servant of God; therefore they must attack the law of his God, just as the Pharisees and Sadducees did with Christ. (v4-5)

As the conspirators consult as liars and murderers, being Satan's sons, they forbid prayer to God for thirty days, with the penalty being death in a lion's den. (v7) These "vipers" deceitfully persuade king Darius to naively pass a permanent law to entrap the prayer warrior Daniel. Darius was most likely flattered by this temptation as kings of the day loved being prayed to as people treated them as gods like they did Herod in Acts 12. (v8-9; cf. Mt. 12:34)

God, however, grants Daniel a fearless faith that immediately goes to prayer openly, reminding us again that a faith that can't be tested can't be trusted. God's beloved children know that faith takes risks as we count the cost of glorifying God in Satan's world. (v10-11; cf. I Jn. 5:18-19)

Then the king is informed, through a lie, that Daniel did not regard him because of Daniel's prayerfulness, and Darius grieved over his proud foolishness that deceived him. So the king set his heart to work hard to free his friend Daniel from the lion's den, but the law had been written. (v12-15)

So God's blameless and harmless servant Daniel is cast into the lion's den. As Darius seals the den with a stone, he encourages Daniel that God will deliver him for his fervent faithful service to his true King. (v17)

With Daniel in the lion's den, sleepless Darius fasts all night in his palace and then rushes to the den in the early morning. The king cries out with pity, "O Daniel, servant of the living God, is thy God whom thou servest continually, able to deliver thee from the lions?" (v20)

Faithfully, loyal Daniel responds, "O king live forever", as he informs Darius that his personal God sent His angel to shut the lions' mouths due to Daniel's integrity. Praise God for His delivering his servants from all fear, saving them out of all troubles, as faith shuts lions' mouths, granting **faithbuilders** to the faithful, as angels often defend those who truly fear God. (Ps. 34:4, 6-7; Heb. 11:33)

Then the king joyfully commanded that Daniel be removed from the den. All onlookers saw that no hurt had come to him due to his faith in his God, as a Deliverer who redeems His servants just as He had done in the fiery furnace in chapter three. (v23; cf. Ps. 34:22)

So King Darius then commanded that the conspirators, their wives and children all suffer the lion's den, and they are crushed by God's holy wrath before they reach the den's floor (v24). God teaches that the sins of the fathers will fall upon their children; you don't mess with God's anointed servants, as you are tampering with God's glory, which killed King Herod. (I Chr. 16:22; Acts 12)

Then Darius, possibly a God-fearing saved man, wrote a decree that all of his kingdom must tremble in fear before Daniel's living God whose eternal kingdom will never be destroyed. The king also received a great **faithbuilder** from seeing God's signs and wonders in heaven and earth, as he spiritually prospered, just as Daniel did in the end of his fourth **faithbuilder**. (v25-28)

Before we examine Daniel's fifth **faithbuilder**, we need to recognize that the lion's den miracle foreshadows Jesus' tomb of death. Remember our Lord's tomb was also sealed to guarantee He would never be seen again, as a stone also covered the opening. God also delivered His blameless and harmless Servant from death and from the conspiracy of deceitful lies that mocked His person and ministry. Finally, God reminds us that once He frees us from death, by grace through faith, we are free forever from the penalty of breaking the king's law. (Rom. 3:23; 6:14, 23) Thanks be to our great and gracious God for His indescribable gift of eternal life through Jesus Christ our Lord. (I Cor. 15:57-58)

Daniel's fifth **faithbuilder** occurs as he has been praying fervently for Israel's restoration as God's "greatly beloved" intercessor. (9:23) The Israelites have been dispersed sixty-eight years for rejecting God's truth and have two more years to go under God's hand of judgment, which also foreshadowed the modern day dispersion of the Jews in 70 A.D. for killing Jesus.

Discouraged, Daniel is mourning and fasting for three weeks as he is heartbroken so few Jews have returned to Jerusalem to rebuild the walls. Only forty-two thousand three hundred and sixty people out of a population of over two million have followed Ezra's call; a majority of Israelites had grown complacent, liking Babylon's pleasures of a sinful lifestyle of apathy and apostasy. He engages in warfare praying as a faithful intercessor for the sinning Israelites, but he gets no answers. (v1-3)

Then he sees and hears Jesus Christ in his exhausting last vision in the same fashion that John saw his Lord in all of His glory. (v4-6; cf. Rev. 1:15-16) Jesus' pre-incarnate appearances also richly blessed and motivated Abraham, Joshua, and Gideon to grant them **faithbuilders** to fight the good fight of faith. (Gen. 18:1-18; Josh. 5:13-15; 6:2; Judg. 6:11-23)

Then Daniel fainted having no strength left from the spiritual warfare that consumed his agonized soul, just as John fainted in his vision of revelation. Then behold as Gabriel's helping hand delivers him from his deep sleep and strengthens him to arise from the ground. Then Gabriel, who also strengthened Daniel in chapters eight and nine, states "O Daniel, a man greatly beloved, understand the words...fear not" for his prayers had been heard. Gabriel has come because of Daniel's effectual fervent righteous prayer that availed much to move God's hand. (v10-12; 8:15-19; 9:20-23; 10:7-11; cf. Jas. 5:16)

However, as Daniel had been praying without ceasing, the Satanic prince of the kingdom of Persia, modern day Iran which is still the devil's number one enemy of Israel, had been battling Gabriel and Michael, God's guardian angel for Israel; this twenty-one day battle of spiritual warfare takes place in the second heaven. This ongoing warfare is common in the battle of God's kingdom and Satan's kingdom, as the kingdom of light and truth battles the kingdom of darkness and deceit. (v13; Jude 9; Rev. 16:12-14)

Sometimes saints get careless in forgetting that Satan has a specific strategy in fighting to destroy Christians and God's kingdom daily. The devil possesses many wicked spirits and well organized principalities, owning many kingdoms and countries in this world. (Mt. 4:8-9; Eph. 2:2; 6:12; I Jn. 5:19) Because Satan is not omnipresent, as is God, he must constantly empower evil princes in human form, like Nero, Hitler, and today's Islamic Jihadists to do his diabolical work. Remember the day Satan entered Judas to betray Jesus with a kiss. (Luke 22:3)

Gabriel specifically came to help the prophet Daniel understand the latter day prophecies for the Jews, which ironically John also wrote about in Revelation. (v14) There is no coincidence that Daniel and John, the only two men in Scripture called "dearly beloved", and "the one whom Jesus loved", wrote all the major prophecies about the remnant of last day Jews who would repent and love God during the Great Tribulation period. That's the reason Satan targeted these two prophets to kill them, knowing their importance to God's fulfilling all His holy covenant promises made regarding Israel's future hope to Abraham, Isaac, Jacob, and David. (Amos 3:1-3, 7-8)

Consequently, Daniel receives new strength after he humbles himself, face to the ground, exhaustedly to God. (v15-21) This type of blessing also revived Isaiah and Paul as God's humble servants and prophets in days of spiritual warfare. (Isa. 6:6-7; 2 Cor. 12:9-10)

Then Daniel receives the angel's touch again, just as Jesus touched the leper as an act of deep intimacy, to grant divine strength of enablement. Note carefully the phrase "**the scripture of truth**" (v21) as God's will always come through God's Word; God Himself promised to preserve His infallible inerrant Word as the primary source for preserving eternally His beloved servants whose faith takes great risks. (Ps. 12:6-7; 16:1; 25:21; 40:11; Isa. 46:9-13; 2 Tim. 4:18)

In conclusion, God's special angels, Michael and Gabriel, together pave the prophetic path for Babylon's predicted destruction. Consequently, the king of the Medes can send the Jewish remnant back to Jerusalem to rebuild the walls and temple in the glorious days of the ministries of Ezra and Nehemiah, to whom God also grants great **faithbuilders**. May all God's dearly beloved children remember that "nothing is impossible" for our great and gracious God who cannot lie. (Luke 1:37; 18:27; Heb. 6:18)

FOOD FOR THOUGHT (Phil.4:8): Without faith it is impossible to please God! (Heb. 11:6)

1. Do you allow yourself the blessing of trusting God daily by tasting His Word? (Ps. 34:8)

2. How do you strengthen your fear of God by faith to have "no wants" in life? (Ps. 34:9)

3. How has God ever deepened your fear of Him through brokenness? (Ps. 34:11, 18)

4. Do you accept "lion's den" trials as normal in your Christian life? (Ps. 34:19; 2 Tim. 3:12)

5. Do you trust God's healing power enough to allow Him to handle vengeance? (Ps. 34:21)

6. How do you deepen trust in God to redeem you of "self"? (Jer. 17:14; Jas. 1:21; Ps. 34:22)

7. Do you absorb God's Word daily to praise Him in spite of trials? (Ps. 56:10-11; Heb. 13:15)

8. What Scriptures are you memorizing to establish patterns of godly thinking? (Ps. 119:11)

9. What diligent disciplines are growing your deeper roots of faith? (I Cor. 2:10, 13; Col. 2:6-7)

10. How do you cooperate with God in working out your own salvation? (Ps. 74:12; Phil. 2:12ff.)

11. What special verses written by David, the "sweet psalmist," minister to you? (2 Sam. 23:1)

FAITHBUILDERS OF DIVINE DISAPPOINTMENTS
"Be still and know that I am God" (Ps.46:10)
CHAPTER TWENTY

Why do bad things happen to God's people? Why did Joseph suffer so much for obeying his father in checking on his brothers and honoring God in maintaining his integrity in Potiphar's house in Egypt? Why did God-fearing Job have to suffer so much as God allowed Satan to assault him and kill his family, taking all he had? Why did Jesus let his friend Lazarus, whom He loved so much, die, bringing so much grief to Mary and Martha whom he also loved dearly? If the Jews are the "apple of God's eye" (Ps.17:8), why did He allow Hitler's Holocaust?

These questions often arise as Christians express divine disappointment when God doesn't seem to make sense in confusing circumstances He causes or allows. For example, these real life scenarios have occurred to saints I know or know of as "foggy days" of life when spiritual warfare unfolded:

1. A drunk driver runs a red light killing a Christian woman and the baby in her womb, and the drunk walks away from the accident without a scratch on his body
2. Three teenagers committed suicide who were raised in Christian homes
3. A pastor has two sons raised with the same nurturing and love: one son is a pastor, the other one is in prison for murder

4. A plane full of top notch missionaries who love Jesus with all their hearts goes down in Alaska never to be found

5. A Christian mom with two little children and a loving Christian husband jumps off a bridge to her immediate death

6. A woman, blinded by the sunset as she pulled into her driveway, kills the godliest teenager in his youth group in a motorcycle accident

7. A godly doctor dies of cancer at a young age leaving his wife and young family behind

8. A young God-fearing, Bible-preaching pastor dies of an aneurysm while sitting in his car

9. A godly man loses his job for consistently doing God's will and his job faithfully as an employee with integrity and work ethic that all in the workplace see

10. Many Christian children whom God loves die of cancer and leukemia

11. A young Christian woman can't get pregnant when other moms abort their babies for no reason or throw newborns into dumpsters or lakes to die

12. A godly young man sells all he has and commits to being a missionary in Tanzania, and then he is killed in a freak accident just before he leaves the USA for the mission field

Sometimes Christians come to me with the good question, "How can God's finest servants and people in general make such bad decisions?" For example, God's saints ponder:

1. Why did Samson, a powerful man of God, let Delilah seduce him into blindness?

2. Why would Moses, a type of Christ, foolishly strike the rock again and disobey God and consequently be disbarred from entering the Promised Land?

3. Why would Absalom, son of David, a man after God's own heart, rebel in conspiracy to take over the kingdom? And why would David's good friend, Ahithophel, join that evil conspiracy in counseling Absalom when to attack David?

4. Why would Miriam mock her God-fearing brother, Moses, and therefore suffer leprosy?

5. How could John the Baptist doubt Jesus' care after declaring Jesus as God's Messiah and then hearing God speak aloud at Jesus' baptism? (Luke 7:18-22)

6. How could Elijah, after the miraculous victory on Mount Carmel, run and hide from Jezebel's threat to kill him after God had so protected him from enemies? (I Kg. 18-19)

7. How could Peter refuse Jesus' attempt to wash his feet? How could he rebuke Christ about His coming death after calling Him "the Christ"? (Jn. 13:8; Mt. 16:16, 23)

8. How could Thomas doubt Christ's resurrection after He predicted it so often? (Jn. 20:27)

9. How could Demas forsake his good friend and mentor Paul to chase after the worldly treasures of Satan? (2 Tim. 4:10)

10. Why would David foolishly commit adultery with Bathsheba and then have her husband Uriah killed to try to

hide his deceitful sin?

11. After God's major miracles during the Passover process and Exodus, how could most of the Israelites so easily begin mocking and murmuring against God who had saved them from bondage in Egypt? (I Cor. 10:1-12)

12. How could Jesus ask God in Gethsemane to remove the "cup" of the world's sins from Him when He came to redeem all men from their sins? Why would Jesus on the cross ask God why He had forsaken Him, when He knew why?

13. How could ninety-eight percent of the Jews who had God's Word and a Psalm book of history in song ignore Messianic messages and miracles of infallible proof of deity and crucify Him? (Isa. 35: 5-8; 53:1-12)

14. How could Jesus live and preach His love and mercy for three years as God in the flesh walking on planet Earth and only five-hundred people receive and believe Him? (I Cor. 15:6)

Joseph's forty years of suffering and confusion best illustrate "*divine disappointments*" that God uses to create powerful **faithbuilders** that grow His children from *faith to faith*. (Rom. 1:17) Joseph "stacked stones" of many precious memories of God's faithfulness that enabled him to persevere when God "seemed so silently far away." Remember Joseph is a type of Christ who suffered much that many souls that God loved could be saved. (Gen. 50:20) Let's examine how his sufferings parallel Jesus' sufferings.

Some of Joseph's **faithbuilders** of suffering that grew him from *"faith to faith"* are:

1. As his jealous brothers hated him for obeying Jacob and conspired to kill him, God preserved his life often in Egypt. (Gen. 37:7-8, 20, 25)
2. As he was sold for the price of a slave, God protected him. (Gen.37:28)
3. As he was tempted by Potiphar's seductive wife and resisted her sinful advances and was then lied about for his integrity, God blessed him for suffering for righteousness sake. (Gen. 39:7-20; 41:41)
4. Even after the prisoners, whom he helped, forgot him, God didn't as He caused Pharoah to dream a dream that needed divine interpretation. (Gen.41)
5. Joseph saved his family from famine as Jesus saves us from the famine in our land of no preaching of God's Word, the bread of life. (Gen. 43; Amos 8:11-12)
6. At the age of thirty, just as Jesus was, he began getting public recognition that would glorify God, as He moved Pharoah to exalt Joseph. Everything is beautiful in God's time. (41:40, 46; Eccles. 3:11)
7. God granted Joseph a son named Manasseh which means "God made me forget" all my problems, and a son Ephraim meaning "God made me fruitful in my afflictions." (41:51-52)
8. As Jesus did, Joseph wept for his brethren whom he loved and forgave them for sinning against him. (45:1-15; 46:29)

9. Joseph saved God's nation as Jesus will eventually. (45:7; Mt. 1:21; Rom. 9-11)
10. God reversed all Satan's evil lies and attacks to exalt His beloved son Joseph, just as God will in our lives and in the life of Israel, whose names are engraved on His hands. (Gen. 49:22; 50:20, 24; Isa. 49:16; I Cor. 2:7-10)

Joseph had a calling as God's man on a mission to suffer for righteousness sake for God's glory. All true saints have that same calling. Christians who truly pursue God's will often suffer from *divine disappointments* as Satan seems to be winning more than God is "stacking stones" of victory for His soldiers. God has given His servants two weapons of perseverance in battle fatigued days of spiritual warfare:

1. *Listening* to the right voices (Prov. 8:34; Mt. 13:43; Luke 8:8; 9:44; Jn. 14:12)
2. *Learning* to not let our feelings seduce our faith (Prov. 1:5; Luke 7:23)

When Jesus first started to preach, the first word out of His mouth was "repent" which means a change of mind. He offered a kingdom of truth to counteract the kingdom of lies the Jewish hireling leaders had offered to God's beloved Israel who were habitually listening to the wrong voices. (Mt. 4:17; Jn.10:12-13) God's true people had to train their hearts to *listen to the right voices*! Then Jesus preached the Sermon on the Mount to teach His disciples that the Jewish religion had it all wrong! Jesus hates the Talmud's religion and all man-made traditions that nullified His truths. (Mt. 15:6; Jn. 14:6) Jesus wanted a life changing relationship with common people who mourn over sin as they hunger and thirst for a relationship with God through repenting of sin. Jesus offered a pure heart that would actually see God at work in growing His children in the grace and knowledge of Jesus Christ the Lord: (Mt.5:3-8; 2 Pet. 3:18)

1. In *faith* that would save their souls (Heb. 4:2; 11:6; Rom. 10:17; Eph. 2:8-9)
2. In growing from *"faith to faith"* by listening to the right voices (Rom.1:17)
3. In maturing into **"the faith"** of Jesus (Acts 3:16; Gal. 2:20; Eph. 4:13; 2 Cor. 13:5)
4. Into eventually **"the faith of God"** because Jesus is God (Rom.3:3)

That's why as John penned his gospel he kept teaching this protective principle of *"listening to the right voices."* Examine this pattern closely of learning God's truth from John chapters 2 to 12:

1. Mary told the people in Cana to listen to and do what Jesus said. (Jn. 2:5)
2. Jesus told Nicodemus to forget his Jewish religion and to "Be born again". Pay close attention to Jesus' words when often He stressed this principle of *listening to the right voices* when He said, "Verily, verily I say unto thee" because they had been lied to and needed to listen to Him instead! (Jn. 3:3) John used the phrase, "verily, verily"

twenty-five times in his gospel. "Verily" can also be translated "amen" or "truth."

3. Jesus told the woman at the well to forget her religious notion of worshipping in a certain place. Worship is a matter of a heart that seeks the truths only He had to offer as the living water of eternal life. (Jn. 4:14, 21-24; 7:38)

4. Jesus challenged the lying Jews who sought to kill him to hear His words to believe on God for the gift of everlasting life. Jesus also reminded them that they had ignored Moses' truths too as God's messenger. (Jn. 5:18, 24, 47)

5. Jesus taught the murmuring Jews who had believed religious lies that He was the true Bread of eternal life, the Manna from God, as many of His disciples refused to listen and left Him never to return. (Jn.6:43, 51, 63, 66)

6. Jesus warned the crowd to listen to His doctrine to really know God, rather than just know about God as He cautioned them about making judgments based on appearances of their own religious imaginations. (Jn. 7:17, 24)

7. Then the battle for truth got intense as Jesus called the religious leaders Satan's children who couldn't *listen to the right voices*. He reminded His beloved disciples that His truths would make them free indeed from religious deceptions **IF** they continued in His truths as His children. (Jn.8:31-32, 36, 44, 47)

8. Jesus then healed a man born blind to prove He was the Messiah by doing a Messianic miracle never done before

in all Israel's history. (Jn. 9:32-33) The Pharisees still refused this irrefutable evidence as they listened to their own vain imaginations inspired by Satan, sealing their souls in damnation. (v 39-41)

9. Next the battle for the truth intensifies again as Jesus calls the religious leaders hirelings who try to steal God's sheep. Jesus reminds his listeners that He knows His sheep by name as the True Shepherd, and His sheep only *listen* to His voice as they follow His will and His Word into an abundant life of faith. (Jn.10:1-13)

10. Then to summarize our lesson on *listening to the right voices*, Jesus raises Lazarus from the dead as he hears Jesus' voice from a tomb! Our Lord reminds Mary and Martha that He loves us enough to always tell us the truth. However, we must all answer the ultimate question of eternal life, "Believest thou this?" Jesus is the way, the truth, and the life. He is the resurrection and the life. Do you believe that Jesus is the only way to a personal relationship of life change and intimacy with God? (Jn. 3:16; 11:25; 14:6)

11. Finally after Jesus finishes His battle for truth, He condemns the religious community for rejecting His light by refusing to *listen* to Him. (Job 38:15) He then informs them that they have now permanently moved from the "would not believe" stage to the "could not believe" stage of apostasy and permanent judicial judgment. In other words, God is done trying to reach them as Isaiah predicted seven-hundred and fifty years earlier. (Isa. 6:9-10) Israel's

leaders had hardened their hearts and seared their consciences, having chosen darkness over light and lies over truth. They proved that they were Satan's children. (Jn. 8:44; 12:35-40) That's why they finalized their three year conspiracy and chose to kill Jesus because He had exposed them as hirelings who were liars and murderers. That's also why God allowed in 70 A.D. the Roman army under Titus to destroy Jerusalem and the temple. Titus killed over one million Jews, mostly by crucifixion, for rejecting God's dearly beloved Son. The only religious thing God left the Jews was the "wailing wall" where very few Jews gather sorrowfully today as most of Israel is atheistic or agnostic in their apostasy. (Isa. 50:11)

God's beloved children who have trained the ears of their souls to **listen to the right voices** will now be protected from allowing their **feelings to seduce their faith**. I love how God pictures His saints' lives "warts and all" in the Bible. God uses John the Baptist and Elijah as the two prominent prophets who fell as victims to Satan's seduction strategy as they failed to listen to God's voice alone.

Jesus declared John the Baptist as the greatest prophet born of women, as he alone was the prophesied forerunner of the Messiah. (Luke 7:28) When John the Baptist waited for his beheading he sent two of his disciples to ask Jesus if He was really the Messiah. Jesus answered them, "Go your way, and tell John what things ye have seen and heard; how that the blind see, the lame walk, the lepers are cleansed, the deaf hear, the dead are raised, to the poor the gospel is preached." (7:19-22) Notice Jesus did not rebuke John the Baptist's feelings that seduced his faith. Our gracious Lord simply asked John to consider the **FACTS**, Jesus' works and words that validated Him as Messiah. (Jn.14:10) Jesus always allows His beloved child to ask honest questions. However, we are accountable to remember what we have seen and heard as we train our eyes to see and ears to hear biblically! Then Jesus proclaimed, "And blessed is he, whosoever shall not be offended in me." (7:23) Our Savior always blesses those who refuse to let their *feelings seduce their faith* by listening to the still small voice that says "Trust God who promises great and perfect peace!" (Ps.119:165; Isa. 26:3)

Elijah *listened* to God's voice as He called him to confront the apostate king Ahab for worshipping the false god, Baal. Therefore, Elijah called upon the Israelites gathered on Mount Carmel to choose: either follow Baal and his eight-hundred and fifty prophets or follow the LORD God alone; you can't follow both! (I Kg. 18:19-22) However, the silent crowd of people refused to choose as religion loves to ride the fence of indifference which always leads to eventual apostasy.

So Elijah set up a test. He challenged the prophets of Baal to set up an offering and an altar to see whose God or gods would send fire from heaven to consume the offering. All the people thought this idea was a good one! (18:24) So Baal's prophets called on their god for six hours with religious frenzy, but no one answered the call. So Elijah mockingly said, "Cry aloud: for he is a god; either he is talking, or he is pursuing (busy), or he is in a journey, or peradventure he sleepeth, and must be awaked." (18:25-27)

Then the religious crowd cried aloud and cut themselves with knives till their blood gushed, which often characterizes Satan worship! This diabolical ceremony lasted until evening and no god answered their cries! God had previously forbid His "holy people" from cutting themselves as only Satan's children try to defile what's made in God's holy image as an act of their counterfeit "worship". (Deut. 14:1-2)

Then Elijah called all the people to come near as he repaired God's altar they had allowed to disintegrate as a picture of their forgetting their true God. (18:30) He reminded them as he chose twelve stones for the altar that they are God's people, Israel by name. (18:31) So Elijah put the sacrifice upon the altar and saturated it with water three times as faith takes risks. Elijah then called on the LORD God of Abraham, Isaac, and Jacob, as he declared his obedience to God's commands as the owner of Israel. (18:36) Then he called on God to let His people know He is the LORD God who will turn the hearts His people. (18:37) Then the fire of the LORD fell from heaven and consumed the sacrifice, and the wood, and the stones, and the dust, and licked up the extra water in the trench. (18:38) The people who saw this all-consuming fire fell on their faces saying, "The LORD, he is the God; the LORD, he is the God." (18:39; cf. Heb. 12:29)

Then Elijah had Baal's prophets killed as God's hand empowered him. (18:40, 46) The lesson for all people here is the simple difference between religion and Christianity. Religion is man's attempt to *arouse God's favor* by good works and vain prayers. (Ps. 66:18) In sharp contrast, Christianity is *God arousing the heart of man* to repent of good works to call on Him by grace through faith in Christ as Savior. (Jn. 14:6; Eph. 2:8-9)

However, often in Scripture great victories lead to great vulnerabilities as fatigue breeds distortion. Physical and emotional drainage often lead to spiritual exhaustion allowing **feelings to seduce our faith**. The roaring lion that has been stalking Elijah is now ready to pounce on him through the vile Jezebel, Ahab's evil wife. (I Pet. 5:8) Jezebel sends a messenger to Elijah telling him he will die before the day is over for killing all her prophets. So he runs into the wilderness to hide and asks God to let him die. (19:1-4) God instead sends his angel to touch him to awaken him to eat and regain strength and perspective to travel to Mount Horeb. (19:5-8) God meets him there to remind him to **listen to the right voice**, His, as Elijah *feels* all alone. (19:9-10) God's still small voice speaks again. (19:12-13) Elijah proclaims his victory but fears losing his life as the only one left serving the true God of heaven. (19:14) God reminds him, however, that He has preserved a small remnant of seven-thousand, who have not bowed to worship Baal. God later blesses faithful and fatigued Elijah with a chariot ride to heaven as Elisha takes his place as God's holy prophet. (2 Kg. 2)

Even Paul wrestled with choices of spiritual fatigue as he sat in a prison cell writing God's Word for us so that we might be reading it today. He agonized over having a desire to go to heaven to see Jesus or a desire to stay on earth to help Christians grow from faith to faith into "the faith" of Jesus. (Phil.1:21-24; Gal. 2:20; Col. 2:6-7)

To make an application in closing, I often, as a pastor, use the illustrations of John the Baptist and Elijah to help struggling saints who have allowed their *feelings to seduce their faith*. We always focus our faith on *listening to the right voices* to rebuild hope in Christ. (Col. 1:27) Jesus often used word pictures like the vineyard and shepherding to help people remember principles He spoke as He realized people are visually oriented in storing memories. Therefore I use a train illustration to help fatigued saints restore their faith in God:

1. We start our word picture with **FACTS** written on the side of the coal car behind the engine of the train which is going up a hill, as Christianity is an uphill battle (**see Appendix IV**).

    a. The **FACTS** we believe about God must be based on clear Scriptures that we know are true, and hopefully can quote. (Acts 17:11; Ps. 119:11)

    b. The **FACTS** need cross-referenced to support our belief system because God tells us to compare Scripture with Scripture. (I Cor. 2:9-10, 13)

    c. As the **FACTS** stoke the engine of our train (heart), God fuels our faith which is the next car in the train. (Job 29:3; Ps. 18:28; Prov. 20:27)

2. The next two boxcars in the train are labeled **FAITH** and **THE FAITH** as God's Biblical facts always fill our hearts with faith that follows the path of the facts in the engine. (Heb. 11:6)

> a. As we humbly receive God's Word daily, He engrafts His incorruptible character within us to grow from *"faith to faith"*, which develops **THE FAITH** of the third boxcar. (Ro. 1:17; Jas. 1:21-22; I Pet. 1:23)
>
> b. As we grow from *"faith to faith"*, God matures us more into *"THE FAITH"* of Jesus' obedience, as He promised we would do greater works than He did as we deepen our roots of faith. (Jn. 14:12; Rom. 1:5; Col. 2:6-7)
>
> c. Finally we should realize that as we have *"THE FAITH"* of Jesus we also possess *"THE FAITH"* of God, because Jesus is God. (Rom.3:3) This is because God is the One conforming us into Jesus' faith. (Prov. 4:18; Rom. 8:29; 2 Cor. 3:18)
>
> d. When the **FACTS** of the engine are well-fired up and the **FAITH** car is following those facts, then the next boxcar of **THE FAITH** grants us a satisfied soul. (Ps. 63:5)

3. The last boxcar contains the **FEELINGS** of a satisfied soul right with God.

> a. The branch abiding in Jesus the Vine has a healthy fear of God that protects **FEELINGS** from

the fears of life's circumstances. (Prov. 19:23)

b. The satisfied soul sees God working even when our **FEELINGS** try to seduce our emotions as life breeds physical fatigue. (Ps. 17:15)

c. The joy of praise enlarges our hearts with faith-fueled **FEELINGS** as Jesus fills us with His intimacy of eternal love. (Ps. 119:32, 97; Eph. 3:17-19)

    i.   As God strengthens our intimacy of love with Him (Jn. 15:9)

    ii.   As God cleanses us from sins that hinder intimacy (Jn. 15:3)

    iii.   As God brings forth fruits of abounding intimacy (Jn.15:5)

    iv.   As God answers intimate prayers exceedingly (Jn. 15:7)

    v.   As God's love grants our hearts fullness of joy (Jn. 15:11)

    vi.   As God's love reminds us we are His beloved friends (Jn. 15:15)

    vii.   As God assures us of the depth of His love (Jn. 17:26)

FINAL THOUGHTS ON **FAITHBUILDERS** - "Beloved...earnestly contend for the faith..." (Jude 3)

1. What daily diligent disciplines enable you to be sound in "the faith"? (Titus 1:13)

2. What sweet fellowship do you enjoy with saints who love you in "the faith"? (Titus 3:15)

3. As a man leading your home, are you a "watchman" strong in "the faith"? (1Cor. 16:13)

4. How do you evaluate "the faith" when Satan attacks your heart and mind? (2 Cor. 13:5)

5. How does Jesus' internal and eternal love strengthen you in "the faith"? (Gal.2:20; 6:14)

6. How does your patience help you in keeping "the faith" of Jesus? (Rev.13:10; 14:12)

7. How have you tasted of the fullness of Jesus by maturing in "the faith"? (Eph.4:13)

8. How does your worshipful gratitude daily establish you in "the faith"? (Col.2:7)

9. How do you purify your conscience to maintain "the faith" of Jesus? (I Tim. 3:9)

10. How does materialistic thinking cripple "the faith" of God's child? (I Tim. 6:10)

11. How does listening to the right voices foster growth in "the faith"? (2 Tim. 2:18)

12. Will your legacy say with Paul that you have kept "the faith"? (2 Tim.4:7)

13. See **Appendix IV** for the full "train illustration".

MARY AND MARTHA'S FAITHBUILDER
"Jesus wept"... (Jn.11:35)
CHAPTER TWENTY-ONE

Jesus Christ proved His Lordship as Israel's Messiah by doing many miracles to validate His messages of love's salvation just as God prophesied in Isaiah 35. His first miracle in Cana of Galilee "manifested forth his glory, and his disciples believed on him." They viewed infallible proof that Jesus was God's divine Messenger and Son. (Jn. 2:11; Acts 1:3) However, the religious Jewish crowd always demanded more miraculous signs and habitually ignored Jesus' messages. (I Cor. 1:22; Jn.9) That is why Jesus confronted Nicodemus' statement about Him being a Rabbi and teacher from God because of the miracles alone. Jesus told Nicodemus, "ye must be born again." (Jn.3:3-7) Nicodemus needed to hear and understand the message that his religion would not get him to heaven. Only a personal relationship with God as a newborn babe in Christ with "enlightened eyes of understanding" could accomplish that. (Jn. 1:11-12; Eph. 3:8) God designed the miracles only to get the Jews' attention so they would believe Jesus' message about eternal life. The Jewish leaders had so defiled who God really was through their vain religious traditions which undermined God's truths that Jesus, as God in the flesh, had to come to earth to straighten out the mess they made as they led the Jewish people astray. (Mt. 15:6) Let's now see how this problem is further solved in the lives and understanding of Mary and Martha.

As Jesus approaches the cross a week before His death, Mary and Martha inform Him that His beloved friend Lazarus is sick in their hometown of Bethany, which means "house of affliction." Notice that these two sisters did not prescribe what they specifically wanted Jesus to do, but they instead merely told Him their need which somehow they knew He would meet. (Mt. 6:33) Instead of immediately coming, Jesus waits two days as He knows that God has holy agendas in this sickness which will bring Him and Jesus much glory. Mary and Martha will be given a rare **faithbuilder** as Jesus will prove His unconditional love for them as they learn well that everything is beautiful in God's time. (Eccles. 3:11; Jn. 11:1-6) God has many special blessings for His beloved children who learn well how to wait on Him in faithful trust as He answers prayers His way and not ours. (Ps. 27:13-14; Isa. 40:31) Jesus wants Mary and Martha to learn two specific lessons as He delays His response and coming. First that God's people are most often winning when they think they are losing, as in the Exodus and at the crucifixion. Second, that He is far more than a healer and miracle worker; He is the only Hope of eternal life as the great "I AM," the Prophet that Moses predicted would come. (Deut. 18:15; Col. 1:27)

Jesus also has agendas that exceed all the people's expectations as He wants His impatient disciples to also learn contentment in trusting that God's ways often differ from theirs. (Isa. 55:8-11) So Jesus summons His disciples to go with Him into a dangerous setting where His enemies recently tried to stone Him to death. (Jn. 11:7-8) The Lord, however, reminds them that light has no fear of the darkness of men's hateful deeds or life's trials, and that ministering to needy people often demands great faith in God's perfect protection. (11:9-10) Remember that these same disciples rebuked the sleeping Christ who accompanied them in a boat in the midst of a great storm, as they asked Him, "Master, carest thou not that we perish?" Jesus then granted them a gracious **faithbuilder** as He calmed the storm and the winds that He created to test their fearful lack of faith. (Mark 4:38-40)

Then Jesus states that Lazarus is asleep, meaning dead, but His disciples misunderstand as they still do not realize they are talking to the Prince of Life. (Acts 3:15) Then Christ states His gladness over the lesson they will learn as God loves to bless and preserve servants who know how to wait on Him by faith. (Isa. 30:18; Ps. 25:21; Jn. 11:11-15) I personally have many **faithbuilders** of this Biblical principle of death merely being sleep for God's beloved saints as I have spent many days in hospice care with dear Christian friends. The internal and eternal joy and peace that surrounds God's child as they take their last breath gives absolute proof to the precious promise that death has "no sting"! (I Cor. 15:56) Their smiles of God's comforting assurances bless all people in the room as our Lord walks with them through the valley of the shadow of death, with them fearing no evil at all. (Ps. 23:4) Dying saints possess contagious confidence that they will rest eternally in everlasting arms that wipe away all tears knowing that "the faith" of Christ has enabled them to finish their race in a legacy for God's glory. (Rev. 14:12-13)

The significant word "therefore" in verse six also foreshadows a divine purpose that Jesus' delay will give time for more people to show up as eyewitnesses for Lazarus' resurrection. (Jn. 11:19) Martha tells her Lord that if He had shown up earlier that her brother would still be alive, but she still believes somehow that God will answer Jesus' prayers for her dead brother. (11:21-22; 14:13-14) But her "little faith" limits the depth of her peace as her double-mindedness doubts Jesus' promise of Lazarus' soon resurrection. (11:23-24) A short time later in verse 39 Martha reveals her "little faith" as she questions Jesus' command to remove the stone after he's been dead for four days for he surely stinks from the heat of the Middle East decomposing his body.

Then Jesus declares as the Prince of life, "I am the resurrection and the life: (colon meaning cause and effect) he that believeth in me, though he were dead, yet shall he live: and whosoever liveth and believeth in me shall never die. Believest thou this?" (11:25-26) These two verses make up the backbone of our Savior's entire ministry as God in the flesh! First, He reminds her that He is the "I AM" of Moses' day, the eternal all-powerful God who meets all His child's needs in His time and in His ways. (Exod. 3:14) Second, Jesus teaches Martha that His resurrection guarantees life for all saints who die by faith in Him. Third, He declares that people who believe God's holy Word by faith never die, but only go to sleep in death; for saints, absent from the body means to be immediately in the Presence of the Lord Jesus Christ in heaven. (2 Cor. 5:7-8)

Jesus makes these bold assertions based on His knowledge that He will in a few days crush Satan, defeat sin, and take permanent hold of the keys of hell and death by His resurrection that be will be witnessed by over five-hundred saints. (I Cor. 15:6; Heb. 2:14; Rev. 1:18) Our Lord, in His final days, states many precious promises to bolster the immature faith of His followers knowing that their "little faith" prevents them from hearing deeper truths that will build a strong foundation for their future ministry. (Jn.16:12) The Jewish people constantly limited God by their lacking "ears to hear" and slipping backwards into apathy and apostasy. (Ps. 78:41; Luke 8:8; Heb. 2:1; 5:11) For example, Martha previously questioned Jesus' care for her as He ate at her house, and He had to rebuke her lack of faith and her double-mindedness. (Luke 10:39-42) Whereas in sharp contrast, Mary's greatest joy came from choosing to grow in intimacy by sitting humbly with a teachable heart at her Lord's feet. (Jn. 3:29-30)

Next, our Lord proves His love again in tears as He proves Isaiah's promise that God is afflicted in all our afflictions. (Isa. 63:9; Jn. 11:33-36) As Jesus groaned in His spirit and wept, even the Jews noted, "Behold how he loved him!" There are very few exclamation points in our Bibles and we need to note carefully where they exist. Here the Jewish audience, most of them religious spectators who came to give shallow comfort by weeping and wailing at a funeral, proclaimed Jesus' love. You never see in Scripture any Pharisees or Sadducees showing love or weeping in their religious circles. Jesus Christ demonstrates His unsearchable riches of love that not only come at a graveside but will also take Him to Calvary's cross to shed His blood for all mankind. (Jn. 3:19; 2 Pet. 3:9)

Why did Jesus weep though, knowing in a few minutes Lazarus would be alive? What troubled Him? What made Him groan? I believe His holy hatred for sin that causes all men to die grieved His holy soul! (Rom. 3:22-23) That's why he agonized in Gethsemane as for the first time in His holy life He would personally be touched by sin, the sins of the whole world at the cross. That's why He asked God to remove the cup of the cross. That's why the whole world turned dark as God's light could no longer fall on the darkened sin-stained shoulders of His dearly beloved Son. (Mt. 27:46) Imagine God's heartache at this moment! We as Christians will never comprehend the holy agony of Jesus' cry as His sinlessness was initially touched by our personal sins.

Finally Jesus performs the ultimate **faithbuilder** for Martha and Mary as He raises Lazarus from the dead. Praise God for all who saw this resurrection miracle and heard Jesus' prayer as God has a burden for all people "which stand by" observing His gracious acts of love to lost sinners. (11:42; Rom.6:23) This **faithbuilder** became personal as many believed in Jesus that day! (11:45)

Do you remember the exact day Jesus took your sins onto His holy shoulders and in turn gave you the indescribable gift of His righteousness? (2 Cor.5:21) Do you remember the freedom God gave you as His holy truth also set you free from the dominion of sin? (Rom. 6:4, 11) Praise God for such a **faithbuilder** of the unsearchable, durable riches of Jesus' love! (Prov. 8:18; Eph. 3:8)

FOOD FOR THOUGHT (Phil.4:8): And the truth shall set you "Free indeed". (Jn. 8:36)

1. What events surrounded the day you heard God's still voice personally? (I Sam. 3:10)

2. How do you in practical ways wait on God for His fullest blessings? (Isa. 30:18)

3. How do you daily practice God's Presence to be filled with His joy? (Ps. 16:11)

4. How do you gather "true bread" from heaven to richly feed your soul? (Jn. 6:32)

5. How does Jesus as the "True Vine" help you bear fruit as a feeble branch? (Jn. 15:1)

6. How does Jesus as the "True Light" enlighten you in dark days of despair? (Jn. 1:9)

7. From what specific sins has Jesus freed you as Lord of your life? (Jn. 8:31-32)

8. How does God's resurrection power enable you in your ministry? (Phil. 3:10)

9. How do you rise up from your days of "O ye of little faith"? (Luke 12:28)

10. How do your roots of faith bud with abundant fruit for God's glory? (Isa. 27:6)

11. How does the fear of the Lord give you a satisfied soul? (Prov. 19:23)

FAITHBUILDERS FOR TEENAGERS
"And Jesus increased in wisdom and stature" ... (Luke 2:52)
CHAPTER TWENTY-TWO

As a youth pastor, my greatest passion for my young people centered on their personally experiencing the joy of Jesus as they grew in wisdom as their Savior did as a teenager. Most of my mature teenagers, many of whom were their high school valedictorians, were bored with life's personal and educational challenges. Therefore, I prayed that God would give me a practical vision to get them out of their religious comfort zones by designing stretching experiences to help them grow from general saving faith in Jesus to "the faith" of the Son of God. (Gal. 2:20) Many of my youth went to Christian schools from kindergarten to high school. Consequently, they could give you all the right answers to spiritual questions, but they had forgotten the life changing meaning of the questions and the accountability they had to God for having such knowledge. (Luke 12:48)

It is one thing for saints to pray for God to grant us wisdom for ministry tasks, but it's quite another to begin searching the Scriptures to find the answers God gives to effectual righteous prayers. (Jn. 5:39; Jas. 1:5; 5:16) As I began comparing Scriptures with Scriptures God shaped my vision of how to train up teenagers in the way He wanted them to mature. (1 Cor. 2:10, 13)

The Biblical design God led me to develop focused on a ministry approach that combined two major goals, one-on-one discipleship, followed by a three tier short term mission's ministry. The teenagers who finished discipleship became my key leaders in all our three annual mission trips. Our **level one** trip involved going out of state to build our high school sophomores' faith that they were valuable as God's servants by helping rural small churches reach children and teens in their communities through VBS or Vacation Bible School. **Level two** took our juniors onto Indian reservations throughout America and Canada to grow them from faith to faith by doing VBS in cross cultural stretching experiences that exposed them to the effects of alcoholism and child neglect. Our **level three** ministry design took our seniors during their spring break into the West Indies to grow them into "the faith" of Jesus through cross cultural door-to-door evangelism with adults. God's agendas far exceeded mine in this discipleship/missions ministry design as He granted our youth many **faithbuilders** over a six year period that eventually put fifty of them into full-time ministry. (Jer. 33:3; Eph. 3:20)

God powerfully used positive peer pressure to take our teenagers from self-serving youth to selfless youth whose greatest joy in life became serving their Lord. We studied throughout our Sunday discipleship lessons that Jesus came not to be served but to serve lost sinners (Mk.10:45). We examined that He proved His love by serving, especially as He washed Judas' feet, and He told His disciples that their happiness would hinge on them following His example. (Jn. 13:1-17) Finally, we studied the book of Revelation and how it opened in verse one and closed in chapter twenty-two and verse six with special blessings of promise to God's servants. God graciously shaped our teenagers' soft hearts in His holy hands as a revival broke out in our ministry that grew from eighty teens to one-hundred and eighty-five in six years. Most of our growth came from teenagers leading their peers at twenty different high schools to a saving faith in Jesus as their light shined for God's glory. (Mt. 5:16; 2 Cor. 3:18)

One young man named Mike, whom I had discipled for a few months as a sophomore, made a great impact on his peers at his high school. He called me one night to share his burden to see his friends come to know Jesus as he had. God had convicted him to start a Bible study in his home and insisted he needed no help but that which came from Jesus through his Bible. He invited me to meet him at a school for lunch that week and as we sat talking about relationships many teens around us listened attentively. Over the course of the next few months, a dozen teens sat regularly to talk about life. Nine months later, Mike's home study grew from four to forty-eight teens, most of whom were new Christians. God pulled together a great cross section of youth to reach all types of young people: athletes, scholars, musicians, singers, actors in drama, valedictorians, and class officers. Several of the teenagers eventually became pastors and missionaries serving all over the world. All this started from one young man's vision for his lost peers.

Now we will examine many of the **faithbuilders** God gave us as a youth group throughout the six years of our short-term missions' trips. Our first outreach evangelism ministry took us to the island of St. Thomas in the West Indies. Our first **faithbuilder** occurred as our team waited for our vans to pick us up in front of a huge apartment complex at day's end on our first day out. As we waited we noticed a children's playground near the complex and went over to minister for about fifty minutes to a dozen children playing there. Soon another twenty children came pouring out of this complex and our teens began playing our well-known VBS games with them. Not long afterwards, a woman walked up to me and asked, "Who are you people? You're certainly not Jehovah's Witnesses or Mormons!"

I responded that we represented the Christian radio station WIVV, West Indies Voice of Victory, and shared what our ministry entailed that day. I then asked, "How do you know we're not Jehovah's Witnesses or Mormons?"

She replied, "Because they nag us to death with their literature and brainwashing; they totally ignore our children and certainly NEVER play with our children. They obviously have no love for us at all, but you people are totally different and I had to come out to talk with you. I have been watching you all from my second floor window for thirty minutes and am amazed, especially that teenagers could be so good with children who are total strangers!"

I then had the privilege to share Christ's love with her softened heart, and she received our Bible lesson and Gospel of John chapter one through three paperback. We visited her again the next day as we spent two days in each neighborhood to follow-up on all calls made on day one, and I believe she accepted Christ as her personal Savior.

This **faithbuilder** really encouraged our youth as we had a praise and prayer time each evening after dinner sharing the things we all learned to be better ambassadors the next day. (2 Cor. 5:20) The first day challenged our teens as fear gripped their precious hearts in going door-to-door trying to minister to strangers in a different culture. Almost all our first day encounters were good, but this one set the tone for day two as the teenagers went out with far less fear and with more holy anticipation that other nationals would sense our love for them; we trusted God to pave His path of grace, mercy and truth for us as His servant-evangelists. (Ps. 85:10; 139:5-6)

The second **faithbuilder** came a few days later as half of our youth took a boat to a small Island called Virgin Gorda. With very little tourism there, the people were far more open and trusting, and in one day over thirty people accepted the Lord. In the previous five days only thirty people had accepted Christ on St. Thomas with our whole group working all day. This fruitful work of God saving souls so motivated our teens that God could do the impossible that they went out the next day in full faith that "if God be for us, who can be against us". (Ro. 8:31)

Our third and final major **faithbuilder** on St. Thomas came as I paid our final bill at the hotel. The owner, "Big Jim", as we called him, stood six feet six inches and weighed about two-hundred and fifty pounds, all muscle. However, he had polio as a boy and his right leg was spindly thin compared to the rest of his body. He cooked for us each evening so we got to know him quite well as a Christian man with a huge heart for his fellow islanders to come to know Christ. His burden grew as the tourism on the island grew because tourism changed the island dramatically. As the money flowed in, so did crime, drugs, robbery, divorce, and broken homes. Consequently, when he observed for a week our teens' love for his people and Jesus Christ, he totally donated our hotel bill of $10,000.00 to WIVV radio station as a "love gift." I asked Jim what moved his heart most about this gift and he shared with me, "You can't out give God. The Lord has richly blessed me financially in the past and I took it all for granted by wasting foolishly the money He granted me as owner of this hotel. I learned a lesson the hard way on stewardship and accountability. So now I am much more of a giver and far less of a taker!"

This really convicted our youth regarding their materialistic thinking as many of them came from wealthy homes, especially in comparison to the very meager lifestyle of the islanders. Most of our teenagers had radical changes occur in their stewardship of time, talent, and treasures as God powerfully reshaped their value system and decision making that week. God had united their hearts to fear Him in a healthy, submissive, teachable way and He helped them all in refining their choices of life and conduct. (Ps. 86:11; 25:12, 21)

The fruits of this trip multiplied over the years as many of the teens reproduced reproducers as they multiplied disciples in full time ministries: two of the teenagers married four years later and have served God weekly, heading up the foreign students ministry on a major campus in Ohio; four young men became full-time Christian counselors in private practices; two young ladies married pastors and now serve God full-time as helpmates for God's glory; another young man serves Jesus as a full-time doctor exalting Christ through medicine; to God be all the glory. (I Cor. 10:31)

The next year, our second trip to the West Indies took us to a tiny island called Tortola. Immediately our team noticed the openness of all the nationals to the gospel. We discussed with the leadership team from WIVV why this contrasted so sharply to the closed mindedness of the people on St. Thomas. That's when God enlightened us far more to the principle that the love of money is the root of *all* evil. (I Tim. 6:10) This little island didn't even have a police force, as the mayor functioned as the law keeper because no major crime existed. The simple, humble, honest people lived contentedly making seventy-five cents per day working in the sugar cane fields. The soft-hearted people heard us gladly as we shared the love of Jesus with them. (Mk. 12:37)

Our first group-wide **faithbuilder** came as we went out in groups of two, walking down goat paths to tiny ten foot square houses that stood in the middle of nowhere. These modest homes had gaping holes where windows or doors should have been, and often four to seven people lived in that corrugated roof house. As we approached the homes, quite often the whole team in different locations experienced people coming out of their houses proclaiming, "Thank you for visiting us as we have been anticipating your arrival as we heard through our radios that you were coming to our little island. Praise Jesus. We have been praying for you for a month. God is so good to send you to us that we might learn more about Jesus."

Our response would often be, "Thank you. How long have you listened to WIVV? How long have you been a Christian?"

Often they would remark, "I have listened to WIVV broadcasts many years, but I am not a Christian. I'm not real sure how to become one, as no one has ever sat down with me to explain how to know Jesus personally!"

We would then start quoting verses to help them understand Jesus' loving salvation plan, and they often finished quoting many of the verses before we could finish! They knew Jesus in their heads but had never opened their hearts to Him by faith. (Eph. 2:8-9) Their teachable hungry hearts inhaled God's Word and salvation plan, and by the time we left Tortola over a thousand people made professions of faith and started in correspondence Bible courses for follow-up with the WIVV staff. (Jas. 1:21-22)

Our evening praise and prayer sessions went on for hours as our youth shared excitedly their experiences of seeing numerous salvations in one-on-one encounters. Many of our youth experienced for the first time actually leading someone through the Scriptures to know Christ. This motivated them to greater boldness with their peers when we returned home. God had paved a path long before we arrived on Tortola as He went before us and behind us daily preparing hearts of good soil for the incorruptible seed of His Word that saved souls for His glory! (Ps. 139:5; Acts 1:8; 1 Pet.1:23)

Often, after people received Christ, they asked us to return the next day as they invited family members who also then received the Lord. They tearfully thanked us for caring enough to come to Tortola to tell them the truth. What amazed them the most was the fact that our team consisted of all high school seniors, and that gave them hope for their children to grow up into teenagers with a heart for God.

At the end of the week, we attended the little church nearby that was filled with new converts who worshipped God with all their hearts. Their singing contagiously moved our hearts as we saw their joy no man could take away as Jesus' joy inspired their worship to their King. (Jn. 16:22,24; 17:13)

The only downside to the Tortola trip occurred as I awoke at midnight with a delirious one-hundred and three degree fever the last night we were in San Juan getting ready to return to America the next day. My teenage roommate, whom I discipled for two years, heard me groaning and felt my hot forehead before I awoke and thought I was dying! The WIVV staff rushed me to the hospital where they did blood work to discover I had contracted dengue fever, most likely from mosquito bites. I suffered the plane flight home as I ate many packages of saltine crackers and drank many cans of Seven-up, and I often visited the bathroom. My first night at home, my fever finally broke as the bed was saturated in sweat. Thank God I regained my strength in two days and went back to ministering to my precious young people in our youth group, whom I couldn't wait to see. God reinforced a lesson well-learned. When God powerfully works in a miraculous ministry fashion, expect to see Satan enter the picture in some form of major trial to test God's servants. (2 Cor.12:7-10) However, in the end, God always wins! (Rom. 8:28-39; Jas. 5:11)

This missions trip transformed the hearts of so many of our youth that we started a one-hundred voice teen choir singing Gaither music in evangelistic outreaches in many rural churches in Ohio and West Virginia. We ministered in our home church on a Sunday night and two-thousand and five-hundred people came to hear testimonies and songs that exalted our precious Savior. Some of our teenagers, who thought they were Christians, confessed that they really weren't, and God changed their lives radically. For the first time in their lives many teens started witnessing boldly in their secular schools. This helped flame a revival in our youth group that led to the powerful penetration of our city as many teenagers came to know Jesus personally and got involved in our discipling ministry. Over the next three years, we saw over one-hundred teenagers being discipled one-on-one, mainly by our college young people, who ministered to help our youth experience what they had experienced as high school teens in our youth ministry. Praise be to God that when He starts something, He always finishes it in ways that we cannot explain, giving His servants **faithbuilders** which transform lives into the image of Jesus. (Eph. 3:20; Phil. 1:6; Heb. 12:1-2)

Our third missions trip **faithbuilder** took us to St. Croix, a very difficult place to minister as the high level tourism there created a dangerous crime rate, especially of robbery. The first night we were there I was awakened by our little air conditioner which was running much harder than when we went to bed. Out of the corner of my eye I spotted movement on the floor as a Rastafarian robber crawled on his hands and knees. I yelled, "Hey you!"

He jumped up as he grabbed my pants which lay across a chair and ran out of the room. Fortunately, my daughters, ages five and three, heard nothing. My wife awoke and saw the man fleeing out the door. I immediately asked her where my wallet containing five-thousand dollars in traveler's checks was as I thought it had fallen out of my pants when I took them off to go to bed. She had put it on the dresser and later, unknowingly, put all our towels on top of it! The only thing of any value he escaped with was my watch inside my pants pocket.

I immediately ran to the adjoining bungalow to awaken two

missionary men from WIVV. They discovered that the thief also had stolen their cameras, watches and wallets.

Then I returned to my room to discover how they had entered by prying open a sliding glass door which very obviously had been pried open many times before as it was permanently bent at the lock. I admonished the owners who knew the vulnerability of this bungalow and I insisted that they drive long screws into the door and the framework. Then, I had to alert our whole team at two A.M. and move all our females into the main lodge area for secured protection. We had already had a long day of travel, and the robberies only added to our emotional and physical exhaustion. However, the trials were just beginning.

The next day as we went door-to-door, we discovered how powerfully the Rastafarian cult controlled the island of St. Croix. You could feel the dark, satanic, presence of evil everywhere you went. This religious cult, in general, smoked marijuana regularly to get close to their evil god, Haile Selassie I, the Ethiopian Emperor from 1930 to 1974, who they believe is God incarnate and their Messiah. They spit on us and slammed doors in our faces. Our team leaders and youth did not expect this reaction at all after the loving reception we had experienced in previous years on the other islands in the British and U.S. Virgin Islands.

One young Rastafarian man snuck into our compound one night to seek us out as he was interested in the gospel and he watched our unconditional love trying to reach his family and friends in spite of the persecution. He informed us that if he did become a Christian he could tell no one for fear of being killed. Nevertheless, he still surrendered his life to Christ and planned to leave the island soon to stay with friends on a nearby island. His boldness granted our team a much needed **faithbuilder** to persevere in our evangelism outreach the next two days.

A few days later, one of my key female leaders became very sick, and she had to be flown to a Puerto Rican hospital. By the grace of God she soon recovered and joined our group when we all got back to San Juan.

Though we experienced less than two-hundred salvation decisions on St. Croix, our team learned many lessons on "counting the cost" in ministry. The key lesson of perseverance in spite of opposition burned its way into our souls as God's servant-ambassadors. (2 Tim. 3:12)

When we arrived home, the teenagers decided to sponsor a special banquet to share the lessons they had learned about God's protection and their own need for more boldness in witnessing for Jesus. At the close of the banquet, the teen leaders called me forward to give me a very special gift from money they collected from our team. They gave me an engraved watch that stated, "Rory feed my sheep, Puerto Rico 1982". I still wear that watch daily to remind me of the many **faithbuilders** God has given me from over fifty short term missions trips of "stretching experiences" from God that shaped their lives and mine for more fervent ministry.

Our fourth missions' trip took our seniors to the little island of Nevis in the West Indies. God powerfully moved on this outreach like no other I have ever led. **Faithbuilders** abounded to the most mature high school teenagers I have ever discipled. From the first day of door-to-door evangelism to the last, Jesus saved souls that eventually totaled over three-thousand.

One of our main **faithbuilders** came as many families had heard we were coming to their neighborhoods and they had already prepared their hearts to hear about Jesus. Many had also invited their whole families from across the island and as many as twelve people would be crowded into a home to ask us questions about God's gospel of love. In one home all twelve family members became Christians in one day in one-on-one fruitful discussions.

Another **faithbuilder** occurred as I saw a smiling young man named Aubrey carrying a boom 'box on his shoulder as he approached me on the street. I could hear the WIVV broadcast he listened to attentively. As I started sharing Bible verses with him, he finished them all word perfect! I asked him how long he had been a Christian as he looked to be about thirty-years-old. He responded, "Oh I'm not a Christian yet. That's serious business, and I'm not ready to get right with God and live according to the standards in my Bible. But one day, I assure you, I will get right with God when I'm ready to repent sincerely of my sins in order to serve Jesus with my whole heart."

Then he whispered, "Hey there's a young man coming up behind you about one-hundred yards away and he REALLY needs Jesus. He just got out of jail for troubles that arose from running with the wrong crowd, but deep inside he's a good boy! See if he will listen to you."

So Aubrey introduced me to the teenager who attentively listened to the gospel and consequently admitted boldly his need for a Savior. He insisted on praying right there on the side of the road to receive forgiveness through believing in Jesus as the only hope of his salvation. (Col.1:27)

Then as our van pulled up to take us back to our lodging for dinner, I heard a voice shouting out, "Don't leave. Don't leave. I need to get saved!" I turned around to see a young man running as fast as he could towards our team. Two of our teenagers pulled him to the side of the road behind our van for privacy as they also led him to the Lord. I've been on many evangelistic trips and outreaches, but this was the only time someone chased us down the street with a passion to get right with God. That **faithbuilder** stuck in our team's minds for many years to come.

My personal **faithbuilder** came in the most unexpected way. About four days into our outreach, I became very ill through dengue fever, as I had on our first trip to St. Thomas. We had been warned to boil all our water before drinking and cooking because you could hold the spigot water to the light and see the nearly invisible parasites moving around. Therefore, we protected our team accordingly. However, I had personally forgotten about the mosquito issue of dengue fever until I got it again.

The **faithbuilder** miracle came as my high school senior young men, all of whom I had discipled for three years, completely took charge as I lay sick for four days unable to keep even water down. They ran the daily schedules, the sharing times, and the prayer sessions. The WIVV staff proclaimed great praise to God for their leadership and maturity when their leader went down ill, and the whole youth team didn't "miss a beat". The lead missionary eventually flew me back to the hospital in San Juan, Puerto Rico.

The final **faithbuilder** of the Nevis trip came many years later as about half this team ended up in full-time ministry that took them all over the world as pastors, pastor's wives, missionaries and missionaries' wives.

Our fifth and sixth trips occurred on the little island of St. Kitts in the West Indies. The nationals received and believed the truths of Jesus and the gospel of good news just as the people on Nevis did and then some. That's why we had to go back there a second year.

Before our daily door-to-door ministry, I received an invitation to preach at the largest church on the island. After a few of our teens shared their personal testimonies of salvation, I walked to the pulpit that stood five feet off the floor to preach. I immediately noticed a big indentation in the right side of the top of the pulpit. After I finished my message, the six foot six inch tall pastor came to the pulpit and greatly overshadowed his much shorter congregation, especially from such a high platform area. He immediately began to rebuke them for not reaching their neighbors for Jesus. He told them they should be ashamed that a group of American teenagers should have to come to their island to evangelize. Then, the pastor rebuked them for not giving more money to the church. All the time he talked he pounded the right side of the pulpit so hard the whole platform shook. Then I realized how the dent got there!

After the morning worship service a lady approached me and invited our whole team to her home for dinner that evening. When we arrived at her simple home we were amazed at the beautiful spread of food: fresh fish, conk, pineapple, coconuts, and papaya from her trees, vegetables from her garden, and loving hospitality that touched our humbled hearts. After a sweet evening we would never forget, she pulled me aside and said, "I don't mean to say anything negative about our pastor, but he always chides us for not doing the work of the ministry. The real problem lies in the fact he has never trained us how to share our faith with family and friends. It breaks our hearts because we love him and would like to be able to share Jesus as your teens have been trained. Can you help us please?" We will get back to that need later.

As we went throughout the island, men crawled out from under cars they were repairing to hear the gospel. Adults came out of their homes before we even entered their yards because they wanted to meet us. Shop owners stopped business to interact over the Word of God. Our entire team was overwhelmed by their love for us. For several hours each evening, we shared about the approximate six-thousand salvation decisions and many other **faithbuilders** that occurred over two years. Most of those new Christians also began personal Bible lessons via correspondence with the WIVV staff in San Juan.

However, God saved one of the best **faithbuilders** of all for last. Our team received an invitation to visit the Hansen Home, a facility that ministered to former lepers who had been healed by God's grace and cared for by a Christian medical team. At first it was awkward seeing these dearly beloved saints come out of their tiny rooms as their deformities included twisted faces, stumps for legs and feet, and missing hands and fingers, but they had beautiful loving hearts. We all gathered in a little room for praise and sharing as we sang many worship songs to God's glory. Our team, however, broke down weeping soon after we started to sing "Amazing Grace" as the seven lepers' voices out sang us as they wept in gratitude for God's mercy that had touched their lives. All the lepers rejoiced in the fact that one day they would all receive new glorified bodies through which they would serve Jesus eternally. This lesson of praising God, in spite of life's trials, burned into our hearts fresh gratitude like that which Jesus dispensed to His disciples on the Emmaus Road in Luke 24.

Going back to the lady's request to help her learn how to share her faith, a few years later I returned to St. Kitts to help start a disciple-making church that preached God's Word unashamedly. To the best of my knowledge, this church and their pastor still do Jesus' work today. Praise God for His gracious **faithbuilders**. I look forward to getting to heaven and seeing all these precious saints exalting Christ in worship as the Worthy Lamb of God! (Rev. 5:12-14)

In conclusion, as the pastors of churches in America have rejected God's truths and preaching His Word, our darkening society has followed this perverted path. As God states, as goes the leadership so goes the church. As goes the church, so goes the nation. When people forget their God, He forgets their children. (Hos. 6:6, 9) Satan has raised a generation of "horse leaches" that cry, "Give me, give me" as the apathetic apostate entitlement crowd mocks God who predicted in Solomon's writings the horror show we are living in today as America's foundations crumble! (Prov. 30:15) This generation mocks their parents in the filthiness of raunchy rebellion. (Prov. 30:11) Young people's teeth are swords that devour everything in their lustful paths. (Prov. 30:14) However, praise God who has preserved a righteous remnant of teenagers who go against the grain of our perverted world.

I had the privilege this summer of watching our church's teenagers, many as key leaders, serve Jesus passionately in our Vacation Bible School ministry. They lovingly taught nearly two-hundred children about the salvation plan of God to save souls, especially of children who are so dear to Him. (Mt. 18:1-6) Then a few weeks later, I had the joy of praying for our church's people who traveled to the dark society of Ireland, which has the second highest suicide rate in the world, to reach children and teenagers with the love of Jesus in a week long mission trip.

God provided numerous **faithbuilders** to all our youth this summer who asked God to stretch their faith as His servants. (Eph. 3:20) Please be praying for revival in our churches, especially as we disciple our teenagers to "dare to be a Daniel," a teenager who went against "the flow" of Israel's apostasy. (Dan. 1:8) Pray for revival in our adults who say they are Christians that America may once again rejoice in her Savior as God's saints! (Ps. 85:6) May God's gracious hand revive our churches as sinners repent with a broken, contrite and humble heart in a healthy fear of Almighty God who is enthroned in His holiness and eternity. (Isa. 57:15) May God be merciful in compassion to all who humbly seek Him. (Lam. 3:21-25)

FOOD FOR THOUGHT (Phil. 4:8) – "Grow in grace and in the knowledge of our Lord" (2 Pet. 3:18)

1. Do you know any teenagers serving Jesus passionately? (Luke 2:52)

2. What is your vision for missions and spreading the gospel? (Mt. 5:16; Acts 1:8)

3. Is there a disciple-making ministry in your church for teens and adults? (2 Tim. 2:2)

4. How are you training up your children to be godly servants? (Prov. 22:6)

5. Are your teens engaged in friendships that make them wise in Christ? (Prov. 13:20)

6. How are you training your teens to be yoked to Jesus' love? (2Cor. 6:14-7:1)

7. What are the "ancient landmarks" you use to train your teenagers? (Prov. 22:28)

8. How are you consistently training your teen's heart and mind? (Prov. 23:7)

FAITHBUILDERS THAT GROW INTIMACY
"Keep yourselves in the love of God"... Jude 21
CHAPTER TWENTY-THREE

Intimacy with Jesus is a *choice* the saint's heart makes daily. God states, "I love them that love me; and those that seek me early shall find me." (Prov. 8:17) All Christians determine how deeply we abide in Jesus' love by the way we spend the first thirty minutes of our day. (Jn. 15:7-11) God told the Israelites to fill their bodies in the morning with manna, the bread of life, the Word of God. Jesus, many years later, called Himself the Manna, the Bread of life, which most Jews refused (Jn.6:66). Some Israelites gathered more, some gathered less, and the murmuring mixed multitude gathered none as the manna filled with worms and stench by midday. (Exod. 16:12-20) God also stated, "Blessed is the man that heareth me, watching daily at my gates, waiting at the posts of my doors. For whoso findeth me findeth life, and shall obtain favor of the LORD." (Prov. 8:34-35) However, God reminds His dearly beloved children that there are degrees of intimacy when He states that some stand watching at a distance at the gates, but some *choose* to get much closer at His doors in prayerful anticipation and waiting. (Isa. 40:31) God graciously promises to favor and to fill hungry saints who habitually *choose* to seek Him with all their heart. (Jer. 29:11-13; Mt. 5:6)

Another word picture about intimacy that Jesus gave His Jewish brethren called them to come unto Him, to learn of Him for rest and to enter His easy yoke that made burdens light. (Mt. 11:28-

30) Now every Jew understood the value of two oxen in a yoke. Biblically, the oxen, as pictures of saints, walked the same path intimately, shoulder to shoulder, just as the beloved John rested his shoulder on Jesus. This yoking process multiplied their workforce as it did in Acts as the churches and disciples multiplied. (Ps. 144:14; Acts 9:31) That's also why Peter wrote that we as saints are to walk in Jesus' steps as proof of our intimate love for Him as true disciples suffer for righteousness sake. (I Pet. 2:21)

However, in sharp contrast to the oxen is the ass in Scripture. This bull-headed stubborn animal symbolizes the lost soul, often religious in its foolish ways of pride. Remember that religion always appeals to the flesh as it tells us what we must do in "good works" to be right with God. In contrast, Christianity teaches that Jesus "paid it all, and all to Him we owe" as He cried out on the cross, "It is finished." (Jn. 3:16; 14:6; 19:30; Eph. 2:8-9) Judas was the only "ass" amongst the disciples.

Of all the five-hundred disciples Jesus influenced in three years of teaching, three were intimately blessed far more than the others: Peter, James, and John. Their greatest **faithbuilder** occurred just a few days before Jesus was crucified and resurrected from the dead. This event happened on the Mount of Transfiguration where these three special disciples would grow greatly in intimacy with their Savior when they would miraculously see Christ their King in all His glory in Matthew 17.

Jesus had just promised to build His church, and then He started talking about dying and being raised again the third day. (Mt. 16:18-21) His disciples were confused, especially Peter who rebuked his Savior, after which Jesus called him Satan. (Mt. 16:22-23) Then Jesus reminded them that in days of confusion they must *choose* to stay close to Him by denying self to follow Him in love. (Mt. 16:24-26) Then Jesus promised that they would see His glory and be rewarded for their intimate works of faithful obedience in sacrificial service as they took up their cross to crucify their selfish agendas. (Mt. 16:27) Finally, Jesus declared that a special group standing there would not die until they personally saw Him "coming in his kingdom," which happened six days later. (Mt. 16:28)

So six days after Jesus gave His kingdom prophecy, He took Peter, James, and John onto a high mountain, apart from the other disciples, to see Him transfigured in glorious shekinah light. (Heb. 1:3) Then Moses and Elijah show up talking with Jesus, probably about the future history of God's beloved Jewish children as these two prophets will help protect Israel, the apple of God's eye, during the Great Tribulation period. (Mt. 17:1-3; Rev. 11:3-14) God deliberately uses a special word "transfigured" because the Greek word gives us our English word "metamorphosis", meaning to change something simple into something beautiful. For example, a common caterpillar, in God's time, becomes a beautiful butterfly. God also uses this special term to describe how ordinary saints grow into transformed mature servants as they behold His Word and absorb His glorious nature, radiating as bright lights into a dark and desperate world. (2 Cor. 3:17-18) This also happened to Moses as he met God on Mt. Sinai and absorbed His glory unknowingly, but the Israelites sure noticed the change when he came down off the mountain in the book of Exodus. This intimate event with His disciples is also the only time on earth He revealed His eternal glory that all saints will see in eternity. This term "transfigured" is also used to describe the new mind of Christ given to all saints at conversion (Ro. 12:1-2) as God makes us new creatures in Christ, obvious enough so all would see the life change. (2 Cor. 5:17) Remember also that this transfiguration of Jesus' glory foreshadows His glorious return as King of Kings and Lord of Lords to finally crush all God's enemies to rescue the remnant of Israel in Revelation 19 and 20.

The Jewish people were often reminded through their songbook of Psalms to honor God by giving Him the glory due His holy Name as they came humbly into His Presence to worship Him. As saints worship God in the "beauty of holiness", as sinners saved by grace, God engrafts healthy submissive fear into our hearts as He unites our hearts to His in worthy worship and service. (Ps. 96:7-9; 86:11) This daily practice of private worship engrafts within us the divine ability to make godly choices to serve Him more intimately and thus, acceptably. (Ps. 25:12; Heb. 12:28)

This **faithbuilder** radically built the intimate faith of these three disciples who often displayed "little faith" in their Lord. Remember Peter rebuked Jesus the day before, and James and

John had argued over which of the two of them would be greatest, besides trying to call thunder from heaven to judge people they disagreed with! The transformed John and Peter later wrote epistles about Jesus' glory which had so pierced their souls with eternal life change. (Jn. 1:14; 2 Pet. 1:12ff.)

Peter so enjoys this experience he asks to "camp out" by making three tents for Jesus, Elijah, and Moses. But God interrupts Peter in a glorious cloud of revelation saying, "This is my beloved Son, in whom I am well pleased; hear ye him." (17:5) Remember how often Jesus had to teach His talkative disciples to be good listeners with the words, "He that has ears to hear, let him hear". (Luke 8:8) There are many days we as saints need to quiet our hearts to hear God say, "Be still and know that I am God."

This humbling admonition from God drove the three disciples onto their faces to the ground in holy fear, but Jesus touches them intimately telling them, "Be not afraid" because He is with them. (17:6-7) The Scriptures often show Jesus touching needy people when He didn't have to. Remember when the faithful woman with the infirmity touched Jesus and His virtue of character immediately entered her? This word picture teaches saints that when we draw close to Jesus in faith, His virtuous character becomes ours as He transforms us into greater levels of intimacy with Him. That's why Peter would write at the end of his life, "Giving all diligence, add to your faith virtue," as he had learned the hard way that we can limit the effect of God's love upon us, as the Israelites did in the their wilderness wanderings for forty years. (Ps. 78:41; 2 Pet. 1:5)

Jesus then took these beloved three disciples back down into the valley of real life to learn more about battles they would fight in the future as they would prove their love for Him as servant-soldiers. They encounter a "lunatic" boy battling epilepsy, as lunacy was called in that day. Satan seems in control as the "faithless and perverse generation" remains clueless as to the spiritual battle at hand. (17:15-17) However, Jesus rebukes the devil and cures the boy immediately, as John learned here and later wrote, "Greater is He that is in you, than he that is the world". (I Jn. 4:4) That's why Jesus said, "Occupy till I come," as then only will the spiritual war end as He conquers all evil permanently. (Luke 19:13)

Once again God's gracious **faithbuilders** remind us that with God nothing is impossible. On top of that blessing, He also teaches us to *choose* intimacy; diligent disciplines keep our hearts in the love of God through meditating on and memorizing His infallible Word fostering effectually fervent prayer based on His precious promises that build our precious faith. (Jude 20-21; Jas. 5:16)

Many years ago I discipled a single school teacher named Russ whose creativity shaped a puppet ministry that beautifully revealed his love for Jesus. Russ made his own puppets and props and wrote scripts to teach the Word of God to children. After watching him minister so effectively with our children at church, I asked him to help me on a high school missions' trip to do children's Vacation Bible School at a rural church in Virginia. After that trip, he grew so much more in love with Jesus and ministry that he informed his fiancée that God convicted him about going to Japan as a missionary; His mother was Japanese, which gave him a burden to evangelize her home country. His fiancée a short time later broke the engagement as she had no interest in ministry or Japan. Although Russ was heartbroken, he decided to go to Japan the next summer for three months without soliciting any financial support, simply trusting God to provide funds to confirm his decision of faith. God answered His prayers giving him a **faithbuilder** confirming his calling by giving him all needed finances and opening vast doors to minister to Japanese children that summer. As grace abounded, God also healed his broken heart and gave him a greater passion to be a full-time missionary. The following year, God raised all needed support to go to Japan, with the church I pastored supporting him well. I stayed in close contact with him, and after a few months Russ informed me that a secular Japanese TV station approached him to televise his ministry nationally and weekly, offering him a nice salary. The ministry so succeeded that Russ wrote me a letter telling me that he no longer needed our church support as the TV station gave him a big pay increase that funded all needs! I have worked with over fifty missionaries supporting them financially over the years, and Russ is the only one who ever asked to stop support due to God's abounding provisions of a financial **faithbuilder**. And as God frequently does, he added another **faithbuilder** as our Lord later granted him a Japanese Christian wife who greatly enhanced the effectiveness and intimacy of his ministry. Russ' faithfulness to fulfill his vision of ministry came as a direct result of godly choices enabled by an intimate walk with Jesus. He had decided daily to draw close to his Lord for the insight to serve Him in the fullness of love's unsearchable riches of durable grace. (Prov. 8:17-21, 32-35; Eph. 1:18; 3:8)

FOOD FOR THOUGHT (Phil. 4:8) - "Keep yourselves in the love of God" (Jude 21)

1. What diligent disciplines keep you close to God's heart? (2 Cor. 3:18)

2. When was the last time God showed you His glory personally? (Exod. 33:18)

3. Who was the last person you influenced through your shining light? (Mt. 5:16)

4. What stones have you stacked recently as **faithbuilders** from God? (Josh. 4:6-7)

5. Do you keep a daily journal of God's grace building love into your life? (Isa. 12:24)

6. How are you more in love with Jesus than a year ago? A month ago? (Ro. 5:5)

7. When did your faith ever cost you something? (2 Cor. 13:5)

8. How do you daily keep yourself intimately in God's enabling love? (Jude 21)

FAITHBUILDERS FOR PEACEMAKERS
"Blessed are the peacemakers"... (Mt.5:9)
CHAPTER TWENTY-FOUR

In thirty-seven years of ministry counseling, the greatest weakness I've seen that consistently entraps Christians is their lack of conflict resolution skills to solve problems that their carnality causes in relationships, especially in marriages. The best Biblical model for effectual conflict resolution can be found in I Samuel 25 as Abigail, "a woman of good understanding", handles a very difficult situation her evil, surly husband Nabal has caused to infuriate King David. (I Sam. 25:3) Remember, the Biblical word "understanding" means a person who willingly **stands under** the authority of God's Word in matters of decision making that is humble. (Prov. 14:6; Ps. 25:12, 14, 21)

To set the general context, Nabal's men experienced peace and goodness working in the fields as king David protected them daily; so David, as he fled from Saul, thought it would be okay to ask for some food rations from Nabal. (v5-9, 17) Nabal knowingly mocks David his king and didn't seek facts before jumping to conclusions and speaking rashly. (I Sam. 25:10-16) He also tended to solve problems through intimidation tactics and manipulation of people, very common weapons of people poor in conflict resolution.

David courteously asks Nabal to seek reliable information from sources to solve this issue, but Nabal refuses. (v10) So David decides to kill his whole family for returning evil for good. (v13, 21) Abigail becomes aware of the confrontation and acts to prevent the problem from becoming a deadly conflict. This key principle in relationships of stopping problems from becoming conflicts is critical to healthy conflict resolution. Abigail steps in as a mediator, as she recalls God's goodness and models how humility solves most problems proactively for God's glory. (v14-24) She acts as an intercessor reminding David that her husband is an evil man, as his name means son of Baal, an evil god. (v17, 25) Nabal is a foreshadowing of the antichrist as David foreshadows Christ and His battles with Satan. David sees God's hand in her submissive act of mediation and withdraws his threat (v24, 32). This humble act of David's allowed God to deal with Nabal just as Abigail recommended.

Now let's look at the specific steps of conflict resolution the **peacemaker** Abigail used to glorify God in stopping a problem from becoming a conflict of disastrous proportions. First, Abigail listened well to gather all important facts of the problem at hand. (v17; Jas. 1:19) Second, in her God-given wisdom she carefully developed a practical Biblical strategy that focused David on God's ability to defend His king, to take his focus off the problem of Nabal's sarcastic mockery of his king. (v28-29; Ps. 37:1-9) Third, she made haste to initiate the positive action of a "forgiveness gift" to counteract the negative offense of her husband to the king who had blessed Nabal. (v19) Fourth, she humbly acted in the strength of bowing as a servant before the "enemy", David, to defuse his anger and pride. This strength of godly humility allows the other party to lay down their defensive weapons to solve the problem. (I Pet. 5:5-8) Fifth, she took a mediator position, as Jesus did on the cross, to neutralize the problem when she said, "Upon me, my lord, upon me let this iniquity be". (v25) Sixth, Abigail highlighted the solution of non-conflict to avoid David's possible costly anger as she challenged him to trust his God to avenge Nabal's hideous offense; she reminded David of the great asset of a clear conscience before God as he obeyed God's truths of conflict resolution. (v26-31) Here, Abigail becomes a living word picture of Isaiah who said, "The Lord GOD hath given me the tongue of the learned, that I should know how to speak a word in season to him that is weary: he wakeneth morning by morning, he wakeneth mine ear to hear as the learned". (Is. 50:4) Lastly, Abigail succeeds in defusing the "bomb" of David's potential vengeance and turned his murdering intentions into powerful praises to his blessed God. She ultimately refused to be a **victim**, but instead she chose to be the **victor**. (v31-35) Abigail took the "high road" of integrity by choosing paths of God's truth, waiting faithfully for God to solve the problems; God preserved her life through His gift of enlightenment and protection. (Ps. 18:28; 25:21; 119:30) As an old pastor once said, "A bulldog can whip a skunk any day, but some battles just aren't worth it!" Choose your battles wisely.

In the end God took His vengeance graphically. Nabal's "heart died," a phrase meaning he had a stroke, and then God later struck him dead in defending David's honor as His chosen king. David then thanked God for protecting him and took Abigail as his wife. (v36-39)

Now let's look at practical ministry applications regarding how problems and conflicts differ in real life, as we learn to be **peacemakers**:

1. Problem solving is proactively **constructive**, fostering Biblical bonding through the humility of brokenness to build relationships and healthy communication, as Abigail modeled. She proved that it is *more important to be godly than it is to be right*; (Ps. 51:10,17; Prov. 18:15) whereas conflict is **destructive** as personalized carnal reactions throw "gasoline on the sparks" of the problem that needs solved, as Nabal unnecessarily did to enflame David.

2. Problem solving focuses on the issue *for* the couple involved which allows God to grow the people from faith to faith in constraining love that builds the relationship; in other words, the couple is much closer having worked things out in Christ's edifying principles of love; (Rom. 5:5; Eph. 4:29; 2 Cor. 5:14) whereas conflict allows the problem to get *in between* the two parties, separating the "oneness" of two Christians; now Satan has a stronghold often labeled as "irreconcilable differences", a common phrase two professing Christians use today to justify unbiblical divorce. (Eph. 4:26-27, 30-32) Remember there are no irreconcilable differences for true Christians who understand the power of the cross and of the blood of Christ! (Gal. 2:20; 6:14) When two professing Christians allow Satan to establish a stronghold that turns a problem into a conflict, often the following happens:

a. Much energy is wasted with the two parties trying to "win" to egotistically prove their point.

b. Emotional exhaustion leads to spiritual and physical exhaustion as both parties throw up their hands in disgust, and Satan wins.

c. Relationships are badly damaged, sometimes taking months or years to recover.

d. Unity evaporates in the home, as there is no peace for the wicked, the chaos ripple effecting onto the children's hearts. (Isa. 48:18, 22)

e. Prayer lives shrink to nothing as the "victims" usually quit reading their Bibles, too.

f. Creative proactive energies die as people keep fighting losing battles of defensive arguments, trying to prove over and over who was right.

g. Attacks become viciously personal as there are "no winners" in these battles.

h. The home turns into an empty shell of a house as the testimony to neighbors and friends dies, as the roots of love shrivel up. (Mt. 12:33-36; Jn. 13:35; 15:9; Jude 21)

3. Problem solving promotes healthy Biblical reactions of love, mercy and humility, as Joseph saw the needs of his family who had betrayed him as more important than his need for vengeance; (Gen. 50:20; Mic.6:8) whereas conflict prompts hyper-overreactions of indifference, pride, jealousy, and eventually hatred, which always bear bitter fruits of destruction. (Prov. 12:16; 13:3; 14:29)

4. Problem solving focuses on the **problem,** knowing God always gives perfect solutions through His infallible Word; (Prov. 3:5-6) whereas conflict keeps **self** as the focus, which is why Judas hung himself.

5. Problem solving stresses clear **Biblical thinking** through the mind of Christ as living sacrifices of love; (Rom. 12:1-2) whereas conflict feeds on irrational **carnal thinking,** like when David wanted to murder Nabal and his whole family; or when David had Uriah, the husband of Bathsheba, murdered to try to solve his problems caused by lustful pride.

6. Problem solving: study Prov. 10:11; 12:16; 13:3; 15:23; 17:24,27; 18:4; 19:23; 20:5, 22

7. Conflict personality: study Prov. 14:6; 15:18; 16:18; 17:19; 18:2, 13; 26:21; 29:22; Ecc.10:3

FOOD FOR THOUGHT (Phil. 4:8)–"Let no corrupt communication proceed out of your mouth" (Eph. 4:29)

1. What does your tongue usually draw from your heart in tough days? (Mt. 12:34)

2. What do your neighbors see in your life that would draw them to Jesus? (Acts 1:8)

3. What conflict resolution skills are you good at? Bad at...? (Mt. 6:33; Jas. 1:19)

4. How do you stay yoked to Jesus daily to be a victor, not a victim? (Mt. 11:28-30)

5. How do you daily maintain peace within your heart? (Isa. 26:3; 48:18, 22)

6. How do your words minister joy to others as a peacemaker? (Prov. 15:23; Mt. 5:9)

7. How do you daily draw wisdom and understanding from God's Word? (Prov. 17:24)

8. How does your fear of God give you soul satisfaction? (Ps. 25:12; Prov. 19:23)

9. How do you draw deep water from God's well? (Prov. 20:5; I Cor. 2:10, 13)

FAITHBUILDERS FOR PARENTS
"Train up a child in the way he should go" – Prov. 22:6
CHAPTER TWENTY-FIVE

As a relatively new Christian I had the privilege of leading a high school Bible study for two years in the home of a very ornery, high-strung young man named Darrel. He would often leave kitchen cabinet doors and drawers open and his cereal bowl and cup on the counter just to irritate his godly mother who kept an immaculate home. He would take his younger sister's clothing from her closet and throw it on the floor of her room to anger her. He exhausted his Christian father and mother's prayer life as they had worked hard to train Darrel up in the way of Jesus, trusting one day, by the grace of God, he would mature in **choosing** to walk in God's paths of life. The key principle in training children comes down to the **choices** they make to shape their lives over the years.

As I got to know Darrel better, our common love for fishing drew our hearts close together. We would sit and make our own lures and spent considerable time fishing in local rivers and on Lake Erie and Lake Michigan for walleye and salmon. This opened big doors for me to disciple him, as I trusted God to make him a "fisher of men". (Mt. 4:19)

The God ordained turning point came in Darrel's life as he entered our high school youth mission's training ministry to go into rural West Virginia to teach Vacation Bible School to children. When the day of our departure arrived, Darrel didn't show up at the designated departure time. As a rule, I always left on time for all activities with our youth to teach them accountability and integrity, but I decided to give Darrel ten extra minutes because I had seen him grow in the past six months of our discipleship. Just as we started the bus engine to leave church, I heard a car screeching tires as it flew into our church parking lot and came to an abrupt halt! Darrel's dad jumped out of the vehicle and went to the other side of the car and physically pulled his son out of the opened door and escorted him to the bus as he said, "Get on that bus right now. You are going on this trip!"

His dad explained to me that Darrel had gotten into a big argument with his mother and informed her he wasn't going to West Virginia just to break her heart. Darrel walked to the back of the bus and sat by himself, visibly demonstrating he did not want to be there. I just let him sit there until he calmed down an hour later. I approached him to question him about what age group he preferred to work with on our VBS trip because he had missed our planning meeting where we chose age grouping the previous Wednesday. Darrel responded, "I hate children. I don't want to really teach them. Can I please possibly work with teenagers instead?"

I told him we would discuss that over lunch as we were just pulling into an area with several restaurants for our youth to eat at to break the trip up a little bit. Over lunch I informed him that if enough teens came to VBS, he could teach them some of the lessons he and I did during our discipleship times.

When we did our Sunday night presentation at the little church we were working with, several teens came and told us they would be bringing friends if we had a class for them. So Darrel's request was honored and he began preparing that night. All week long Darrel greatly impacted the church's young people and also had a godly influence on our group of teens. When the last day of VBS came, I asked Darrel to head up a softball game for all the teens. As I stood on the ball field, I wondered where Darrel was as he was nowhere to be found. Then I heard children delightfully screaming as they ran around on the hill above us while Darrel led them in a game of "duck-duck goose." I just let him work with the children as I led the softball game. The children followed him around for two hours as he looked like the "pied piper" of children's ministry.

A week afterwards our VBS team had the whole Sunday night worship service as over one-thousand people showed up to be blessed beyond all our imaginations. I had asked four teens to share how God had impacted their lives on our mission's trip. Darrel shared, "When I went on this outreach I had a BAD attitude and God had to slap me in the face to get my stubborn attention. God did a 'slam dunk' right in my face to awaken my soul to how precious children are to Him, and I will never be the same."

Over the course of the next few years, Darrel had a major impact on our teens in the high school youth group and later with our college students too. During his summers of his college years he went to Alaska on a three-month ministry in logging camps and fishing villages that I had designed through one of our missionary couples. He ministered to both children and adults to the glory of God. Most of the loggers stood almost a foot taller than Darrel, but he still impacted them greatly by his love for their children, God, and the great outdoors that they too loved so much.

Darrel finished seminary training after he graduated from college. I had the privilege of assisting him on a small scale as he started a new church just outside Portland, Oregon. Shortly after that he became the children's pastor at a large church in Oregon and started writing children's books.

All this happened by God's grace that consumed a young man who "hated children", or so he thought. God alone put together three things: godly prayerful parents who sowed God's seed into their son's heart, Biblical principles of discipleship engrafted one-on-one into good soil, and ministry opportunities to stretch faith to take a teenager out of his carnal comfort zone. With God nothing is impossible! (Luke 1:37)

When Solomon wrote Proverbs 22:6 on training children, he fully understood that it wasn't a promise from God, but it was a principle that reminds parents that incorruptible seed never returns void. Most of Solomon's life, though he started well, mocked God until he matured much later in life. He learned the hard way as he penned at the end of his life, "Fear God and keep his commandments: for this is the whole duty of man". (Eccles. 12:13)

As parents, we must plant the holy seeds of Scripture into hearts of our beloved children, but only God knows if His seeds of life-changing truth will get ever into good soil. (Ezek. 17:8) The problem of fruit bearing is never in the seed, but fruitfulness always depends on the condition of the soil of the human heart as to its receptivity to God's Word. (Mk. 4:20) When a sinner's heart receives and believes holy seeds of truth, his heart will be divinely rooted and grounded in God's love that always produces fruits of righteousness. (Jn. 1:11-12; Col. 2:6-7) However, all children and adults have a free will, just as Adam and Eve had as fallen sinners with a conscience which tried to hide their sin from God in Eden. (Rom. 2:15) God's love always allows His creation to make **choices** that reveal their hearts as to whether they really love God. Moses told God's people to "choose life"! (Deut. 30:19) Joshua, in his last days, challenged his followers, "Choose you this day whom you will serve". (Josh. 24:15) When Peter preached his penetrating sermon at Pentecost, convicted sinners, "pricked in their heart," asked, "What shall we do?" (Acts 2:37) A **choice** had to be made whether to repent of their sins to get saved by faith or to ignore their convictions that cut them to the depth of their souls. (2 Cor. 7:10; Heb. 4:12)

God gave us a model of His expectations of teenagers in the life of Jesus as a teenager when He stated, "And Jesus increased in wisdom and stature and in favor with God and man". (Luke

2:52) That's exactly what I saw God do in Darrel's life and in the lives of hundreds of teenagers; over forty years of faithful seed sowing into good soil of teachable hearts.

Although Jesus did not cease to be God when he was born, He fully chose to be a child and teenager who maintained diligent disciplines to grow in wisdom. We will be examining those disciplines as we learn how to raise children "in the way" they "should go". (Prov. 22:6)

Jesus first **chose** to submit to His parents' authority as the God-ordained influence in His life. A child will never learn to submit to God if they never learn to submit to parents. (Luke 2:51; Jn. 5:19) A big part of a child's learning teachability depends on parents being godly role models of submission to God's authority in their lives. I teach our young married couples to never expect their children to obey them more than they obey Jesus, as they submit to His Word and will for their lives! Jesus humbled Himself to fulfill God's will as a Suffering Servant, and He learned obedience through His sufferings of the cross, too. (Phil. 2:5-8; Heb. 5:8) Parents must be role models and mentors in this learning process of submission. Role models teach things by example, but mentors disciple their children one-on-one over many years and tears of loving training. (Luke 6:40)

As Jesus modeled, humility breeds selfless servanthood. (Isa. 52:12-13; Gal. 4:4; Col. 1:22) Our Lord chose to lay aside His privileges of deity in order to serve others and to save souls.

Our children must see us **choosing** to serve God sacrificially and consistently. (Mt. 11:28-30; Jn. 13:12-17; Heb. 2:14)

Jesus **chose** to become a baby in a humble stable in Bethlehem as proof of His love for us; He could have chosen to be born in a palace, as all kings deserve. (Mic. 5:2) He **chose** to ride into Jerusalem on an ass and to be buried in a borrowed tomb.

Our Lord **chose** to allow His people to conspire to crucify Him on a cruel cross. This form of punishment, which even the Jews despised, was reserved for the vilest criminals. (Deut. 21:23) Our Lord on the cross **chose** to be separated from His loving Father as He cried out, "My God why have you forsaken me?" (Mt. 27:46)

Jesus modeled how growing in stature from a child to teen years develops personal maturity that always precedes spiritual maturity. Many parents often hinder the growth in stature of their children by overprotecting them from life's normal pains of God-ordained development. God effactually uses pain to foster maturity while children learn to make better choices that enlarge and purify their hearts. (Ps. 119:32)

When I taught hardhearted teens in an inner city school for six years, I emphasized repeatedly that their values determined their choices, and that their choices always determined consequences. The Bible declares this as reaping what we sow. (Gal. 6:7) They saw this in everyday life as many of their parents were either dead or in prison from bad choices! Six of my teenage young men ended up in prison for murder before they turned nineteen, and one ended up in prison for multiple murders later in life.

As we instill Biblical values daily into our children's hearts, they at least have the resource for good decision making. Good **choices** eventually foster a personal maturity of a pure heart that **chooses** God's will. (Mt. 5:6, 8) This maturity process also fosters great bonding in a family like Jesus prayed for in John seventeen. Biblical bonding, however, takes shape proportionate to a child understanding Biblical boundaries. That's why God gave us the Ten Commandments. **Boundaries** shape **bonding!** It's only when someone realizes they are a sinner who violated God's perfect law that they come in repentance to Jesus' loving forgiveness to save them from their sins. (Gal. 3:24-25; 2 Cor. 7:10) Parents must lovingly and constantly teach absolute truths of the behavior they expect from their children, just as God does for us. Then there must be consistent-specific consequences when those standards are clearly broken. (Prov. 22:15; 29:15) As God states, love chastens His children to remind us we are His children indeed. (Heb. 12:5-8) God uses a very strong term here (bastard) to describe the child who is not disciplined appropriately because they really do not belong to God as Father or to His family! (Heb. 12:8)

To illustrate this maturity principle of love and discipline, shortly after I became a youth pastor, two of the young men in my class refused to pay attention to the lessons as they distracted the rest of our youth group each Sunday. Although they were both deacons' sons, I threw them out of class publicly because public sin demands public punishment. They didn't return after six months, so I sent one of my key disciplers after them to get them involved in a home Bible study. A short time later they repented of their sins and sincerely apologized to me. I immediately began discipling them for one year, and they became key leaders in my youth group and on missions' trips. Today, both men are married and serving God in missions ministries, one full-time in London, England reaching Muslims for Jesus, and the other on a local college campus ministering to foreign students. God's love never fails to pierce hearts that **choose** to listen to His loving voice. (Acts 9)

As Jesus grew in stature, He came to the maturity that granted Him "favor with God and man". (Luke 2:52) Even though only five hundred of two and a half million Jews **chose** to respond to Jesus' love, at least they had a *choice*. The common, humble people heard Jesus gladly. (Mk. 12:37) They heard Him love them enough to tell them the truth; they saw His humble love perform miracles to validate His healing touch of infallible authority over illness and demons also. (Mt. 7:29; Jn.3:16; 14:6)

Our children need to also see their parents' maturity as God simply wrote out in Ephesians 3-6. When a person fully grasps the saving and enabling love of God in Ephesians 3, that love draws him to a church where God's pastors disciple Christians to walk worthy of Jesus' love in Ephesians 4. Now that a saint is the **person** God wants him to be in Ephesians three and four, he can now become the **partner** God wants him to be in loving their spouse as Jesus loves them in Ephesians 5. Now as God transforms this saint more into Jesus' image, he now becomes the **parent** God wants him to be in Ephesians 6. That's why chapter six starts with, "Children obey your parents in the Lord: for this is right". Godly partners simply help each other become godly parents.

In summary, God's pattern states this order: **person, partner, parent**; that is, only after you mature into the person He wants you to be, then can you mature into the partner He wants you to become; then you become the parent He wants you to be as a bright light of influence into the darkness of your child's selfish soul. Have you, as a parent, ever been surprised how you didn't have to train your one-year-old to be a sinner!? (Rom. 3:23)

This maturity process then enables parents to put on God's armor daily to fight the battles the rest of Ephesians 6 describes for the servant-soldier ready to fight for their family! Our priorities as parents eventually should become the priorities of our children and teens. Jesus will train them up in this process of maturity if parents follow His instructions, just as He followed His father's instructions that revealed God's will through knowing His Word. (Jn. 7:17) Our children must work out their own salvation with fear and trembling as their parents did. (Phil. 2:12-15) When our children make the right **choices,** God will grant them precious promises that produce precious faith. Then God grants them a divine nature with divine power for all they need for life and godliness. (2 Pet. 1:1-4) These unsearchable riches of durable grace will prepare our children if we will train them up in the way they should go, so that when they are mature, they will not depart from God's ways! (Prov. 22:6)

In closing, one fall afternoon I received a call from the high school guidance counselor requesting me to come see her the next day if I could make time. Seeing fifty of our teens went to that high school, I always made time to see her.

As I sat in her office the next afternoon, she immediately asked me, "How well do you know..." and she named two students who the previous year were often in her office and sometimes expelled from school for their frequent bad behavior.

I told her, "Quite well".

She then asked, "What happened to them? Something radically changed these two, and I think it had something to do with your church and its youth group. What happened here?!"

I responded, "They both came to know Jesus personally in May, then got very involved with our teens in positive peer pressure scenarios and have been discipled all summer."

The counselor then explained to me that she too was a born again Christian, but that she had never seen anything like the transformation these two specific teens had gone through. She talked about her church youth group, a disaster of immorality and drugs. Then she asked me to explain this "discipleship thing" in great detail. We sat there for over an hour interacting on how to change the decision making patterns of teenagers, especially those from broken homes.

I closed our meeting with this statement: "There is no more powerful influence on a teenager's life than Christian positive peer pressure. I told my daughter, as she went off to a Christian college, to run with the thoroughbreds because not all professing Christians are really Christians at all." My daughter soon discovered that the "Christian" students least interested in Bible study and discipleship were the children of pastors and missionaries who had allowed familiarity to breed contempt for Jesus, their "so-called" Savior. (Jn. 4:44) These same professing Christians also engaged in drinking, drugs, and immorality. That's why Jesus warned the Jewish people who thought they knew God and who were good at "God-talk" to examine the fruit of their lives. (Mt. 7:16-23) May we, as Christian parents, lovingly warn our children and teenagers of the same Biblical principles as we train them up in the way they should *choose* to go as they increase in wisdom and stature and in favor with God and man. (Luke 2:52) Then may we, as parents, experience "no greater joy" in our lives than seeing our children walk in God's truths. (3 Jn. 4)

As parents train their children consistently in the way they should go as they mature, certain fruits should verify their Biblical practical faith. For example, our three children were always evangelizing their peers. Our older daughter Rebecca took her Bible onto the school bus as a kindergartener to share pictures in her Bible with a friend who needed Jesus. She couldn't read well yet, but that didn't stop her love for her neighbor friend. We never told her to do that, but God obviously did! She led many teens to Christ in her high school and had great impact on her athletic teams as her friends often asked her how to get to heaven for sure. At the end of her senior year, her peers in a large secular high school voted her "most respected" in her class. (Mt. 5:16) Today she works as a counselor at a school for needy teenagers in Montana.

Our younger daughter, Christine, led a childhood friend to Jesus while they played on the "monkey bars" at recess. Chrissy always witnessed to friends and strangers as she lived and shared her faith boldly in love. She received the "Chrysler Youth Award" in her senior year of high school, an honor bestowed by the school's teaching staff and counselors. Later in life she taught and wrote curriculum at one of the largest Jewish schools in the world in Los Angeles. She often answered questions from her students and Jewish co-teachers because they told her, "You know more about the Old Testament and our history than we do"! Today she is the helpmate of her husband who pastors a church in Montana, as they raise four boys, three of them adopted as brothers.

Our son, Stephen, also witnessed constantly throughout his teen years. He took his Bible to school daily and often had numerous opportunities to share Christ and answer questions as his peers approached him while he ate lunch with an open Bible. He was voted class president in his senior year and had the privilege of sharing the gospel at graduation. Today, he is an intern on our church staff after many years of leading Vacation Bible School, our junior and senior high youth ministries, and numerous mission trips to Ireland. He will soon be ordained as a full-time pastor.

In summary, all the glory goes to God alone for the impact our teenagers had on their high school and our communities over many years. (I Cor. 10:31) Obviously, there are no perfect parents or teenagers. However, when parents disciple their children how to consistently make good Biblical choices, God always "fills in the cracks of our mistakes" with the glue of His grace and mercy. His loving hands never leave the soft clay of the hearts of our children and teenagers who are trained to serve God at a young age. Making sure our teens have godly disciplers and youth leaders in their early teen years is critical as "positive peer pressure" makes all the difference in their world and ours. (Prov. 13:20; 27:17)

FOOD FOR THOUGHT: Practical Biblical Principles of Parenting (Prov.22:6)

1. Fathers set the spiritual tone of parenting in the home. (Eph. 6:4)

2. Christianity is better "caught than taught". (Luke 6:40; I Cor. 11:1)

3. Positive peer pressure protects teenagers from evil. (Prov. 13:20; 17:17; 27:17)

4. Teach your child to be a good listener. (Prov. 8:1, 6; 13:1; 14:6; 15:31; Jas. 1:19)

5. Model to your children how to start a day loving God. (Prov. 8:17, 32-35)

6. Teach your children to fear the Lord. (Prov. 1:7; 3:7; 9:10; Eccle. 12:13; Isa. 33:6)

7. Chasten your children as proof of your love for them. (Heb. 12:5-8)

8. Teach your children how to have eternal perspective. (Isa. 33:16-17)

9. Teach children how to feed themselves Biblically. (Ps. 119:9, 11; I Pet. 2:2)

10. Make your home a haven of Biblical peace and rest .(Isa. 32:17; Mt. 18:28-30)

11. Have zero tolerance for a child's rebellion. (I Sam. 15:23; Isa. 30:1, 9)

12. Teach your child how to patiently wait on God. (Ps. 27:14; 37:34; Isa. 40:31)

13. Train your child how to make wise choices. (Prov. 4:7, 23; 21:11)

14. Teach children humility, as it breeds honor in life. (Prov. 15:33; 18:12; 22:4)

15. Train your child to walk in truth. (Ps. 86:11; 25:12,21; Rom. 6:4; I Jn. 2:6; 4:17)

16. Teach teens how to separate themselves from this world. (2 Cor. 6:14-7:1)

17. Teach children how to serve God at home and in life. (Jn. 13:17; Heb. 12:28)

18. Teach your child integrity of character. (Job 2:3, 9; 27:5; 31:6; Ps. 25:21; 26:1,11)

19. Do a Bible study with your older children on Proverbs. (Josh. 1:8-9)

20. Have sharing times often after dinner as the family sits at the table. (Ps. 107:2)

FAITHBUILDERS AND GOD'S WILL
"Thy kingdom come, Thy will be done…" (Mt.6:10)
CHAPTER TWENTY-SIX

Jesus stated, "Behold the kingdom of God is within you." (Luke 17:21) As our Lord prepared His beloved disciples for the battles of the church age, He wanted them to be sure that they knew that the same Spirit that enabled Him to do God's work on earth would enable them to fulfill their mission as His ambassadors. (John 16) God's kingdom would indwell them because Christianity is the only "religion" in the world where its King moves into the souls He has redeemed! That's why saints are called "the temple of God". (I Cor. 3:16) That's also why **faithbuilders** commonly bless God's saints because **"the faith of God"**, a phrase used only one time in Scripture, works His faithful will into their lives. (Rom.3:3)

Now think "Jewish!" Whenever God showed up inside His temple, His glorious light filled the building. That's why in Jesus' first major message, the Sermon on the Mount, He told His disciples, "Ye are the light of the world. A city that is set on a hill cannot be hidden. Let your light so shine before men that they may see your good works, and glorify your father which is in heaven". (Mt. 5: 14, 16) In other words, Jesus was guaranteeing that God's extraordinary will would be done on earth by these ordinary men, most of whom were common fishermen. (Mt.4:19)

Now with that as our context, I never personally had an interest in finding or knowing God at all! However, His holy, loving will found me and opened my eyes in saving my soul. That's why God moved my friend to invite me on his family vacation to Rehoboth Beach, Delaware in July of 1971. God grabbed my heart through the testimony of loving Christians running a tiny coffee house, and Jesus set me "dead center" in His glorious plan for my life to come.

Also, later in my spiritual journey, I had no desire whatsoever to ever leave teaching in the public school which had become my mission field. However, God slammed the door of that field shut when the rules changed in the public schools refusing that the truths about Jesus could be presented in a classroom setting. Ironically, I had to teach the mythological nonsense of the gods of Rome's kingdom in my English and Latin classes but not the life of Jesus who lived at the exact same time in history!

Next, I never had any interest in entering the ministry. But God used two of my mentor pastors to encourage me to pray about ministry as they trained me in lay ministry tasks. The next thing I knew, I'm sitting in seminary classes with no job and with a wife and two very young children at home. My friends told me I was "nuts" to give up teaching which I loved, "where I only worked one-hundred and eighty days a year", for ministry which I wasn't even sure I would like. Also, I had no guarantee I would even have a job when I finished seminary. How would God's will work out all these things in my life?! (Mt. 6:33)

Then the day came when I had no desire to leave youth work even though my mentor forced me into preaching at the church. I entered the pulpit with fear and trembling and no desire to preach. The next day, a dear friend and mentor named Noel Irwin took me to lunch to tell me I had a calling to preach. I told him I didn't hear it! He assured me it was God's will and one day I would hear His still small voice calling me to "preach the Word." (2 Tim. 4:2)

A few years later our Senior Pastor David Burnham resigned, and I was called upon as one of three pastors to do interim preaching. Again, I had no interest and felt no calling for the ministry of preaching. However, I sought God's face with all my heart and begged Him to show me His holy will. I felt I had no choice in the matter because of my great faith in my mentor, pastor Noel, who had pastored successfully for fifty years as a godly man.

A few months later, I was informed that I would be doing a three-week series of sermons in the spring. I resisted but submitted to the challenge as I left for a missions' trip to St. Kitts in the West Indies. Because I had a great leadership team with me to help run the outreach, I had much time to study and pray to prepare my heart for the sermons. Pastor Noel challenged me to always spend more time preparing my heart for the message than time spent preparing for the message itself, and God would bless richly. So I listened well to my beloved mentor.

When the time came, I preached the three messages asking God for visible fruit to validate His will as to whether I truly had a calling to preach. God abundantly answered that prayer as seventy-two people came forward in three weeks to receive Christ or rededicate their lives to God. God's Spirit stunned my soul with His effectiveness in enabling me to do something I had no desire to do, as he fully revealed God's will for my future ministry! Over the course of the next nine months, twenty-eight churches called me to candidate or interview as a senior pastor, and I hadn't sent out even one resume.

The next week my wife invited pastor Noel to dinner one evening. As I walked to the bathroom to wash my hands, Noel, with a big smile on his seventy-year-old face, told my wife, "My light is going out, and his is just starting to shine". Noel passed away a few years later when he moved out of state to care for his elderly sister. I still get teary-eyed today thinking of his deep love for me that inspired me to faithfully trust God's will in spite of my feelings that I had no calling to preach.

Do you get the picture? God fully desires that His children know His will by knowing His Word. Jesus promised, "If any man will do His will, he shall know of the doctrine, whether it be of God, or whether I speak of myself." (Jn. 7:17) My challenge lay in the fact that I had to know if my mentors were right in all their wisdom, or whether my "unholy hunches" were right. After all, none of us love to leave our "comfort zones" of life, especially through "stretching experiences" that force us to trust God with all our hearts as He reveals and accomplishes His will. (Prov. 3:5-6)

Many years later, after I had been a senior pastor for twenty years, I found myself at a spiritual crossroad as I sought God's will for my life. My greatest love had become discipleship and I felt ready to step "backwards" into an associate pastor role for my last years of ministry. So I called another great mentor, Pastor David Burnham, who had always been there for me in challenging days of seeking and knowing God's will. I informed Dave that after looking online at over five-hundred churches I could find no "good fit" and how hard it was to even find a church that had the word "sin" in their doctrinal statement. He laughed but then told me how challenging an associate pastor role would be after twenty years as a senior pastor. Dave warned me, in love, that it would need to be a "perfect fit" and those were rare relationships of ministry indeed.

As my wife and I fervently prayed for God's will to be done, our son Stephen also sought a good church home. By the grace of God, one night he was standing in the kitchen of a Christian family who lived thirty miles south of us. The family asked him exactly where we lived, and they informed him that their church had started a new satellite church near us a short time ago.

The next Sunday we attended that new work named First Baptist Church of Jackson, and God blessed us beyond measure! I met Pastor Tom Gang and we talked on the phone the next week for an hour. He informed me that he had looked at over one-hundred and fifty associate pastor resumes and could find no "perfect fit" for the needs of their church. I then found out that about half the people in the church had been led to Christ by others in the church. The church had a clear vision for world missions and spreading the gospel and discipleship. Then we began meeting weekly for several months and eighty hours of interaction, and he offered me an associate position which I accepted as I had clearly found God's will. The beauty of this calling of God took me back thirty-five years also when God had laid it upon my heart to one day possibly teach in a Bible college. Then I was greatly blessed to discover that Pastor Tom had just started a four-year Bible Institute in which I have been teaching now for ten years.

Several months after I had started, I called Pastor Burnham to share my joy of a richly fulfilling ministry. I now had the privilege to disciple men and teach the Word of God to ravenously hungry hearts that fully believed God's Word was the final authority in their lives. I told him I felt like Peter on the Mount of Transfiguration, and God had let me "camp out" there! God still blesses me daily at First Baptist Church ministering to men and women who reproduce reproducers who love God and labor to stay anchored in the center of God's will. (2 Tim. 2:2)

Christians often struggle with the issue of, "what is God's will for my life?" Seeing Jesus never uttered opinions, what are the clear expectations of God's absolute standards for all people?

God wrote the Bible as His last will and testament to instruct all mankind that He is the Final Authority for all issues of life and death. Our gracious God wants us to see His power and glory as His love alone satisfies the soul that follows hard after His wisdom and His will. (Ps.63:1-8) Let's break down God's will into eight practical factors of faith that come from His infallible Word:

1. Be saved (Rom. 10:9-10)
2. Be sanctified (Heb. 2:11; 10:10, 14)
3. Be Spirit-filled (Eph. 5:18)
4. Be submissive (Jas. 4:7)
5. Be serving (Jn. 13:17)
6. Be a shining light (Mt. 5:16)
7. Be a soldier (2 Tim. 2:3)
8. Be still, waiting on God (Ps.46:10; 62:1)

God's greatest passion fostered His greatest act of love at Calvary's cross that all men might be **saved** through repentance from confession of sin. (Jn. 3:16; Rom. 3:23; 6:23; 10:9-10, 13; 2 Pet. 3:9) Jesus as our Kinsman Redeemer took on flesh and blood to pay sin's ransom and to free all mankind from Satan's bondage. (1 Tim. 2:6; Heb. 2:14) However, God loves mankind so much that He granted us a free will to choose whether to accept His love gift of eternal life by grace through faith. (Eph. 2:8-9) We choose whether to receive and believe His truths about our sinfulness and the consequent need of the Savior to pay our penalty for sin, as without faith it's impossible to please God. (Jn. 1:11-12; Heb. 11:6) Now that God's will has been accepted in salvation, let's look at the next factor of **sanctification**.

Once God saves our souls, our faith must grow from faith to faith in **sanctification** into "the faith" of obedience. (Rom. 1:5, 17) When God, as the Author and Finisher of salvation, saves souls, He guarantees the finished product of conforming us to the image of Jesus through **sanctification** that purifies hearts. (Rom. 8:28-29) That's why Jesus took on flesh and blood in Bethlehem's stable. He came to crush Satan and remove his grip on the power of sin and death. The **sanctification** process is so guaranteed that God declares as He looks down from heaven that He already sees saints as being sanctified fully in Jesus as His brethren. (Heb. 2:11; 10:10, 14) God's perspective differs from ours because He sees all things of life from an eternal perspective. That's why His gift is called "eternal life", a phrase not found anywhere in the Old Testament because only Jesus could provide it as He defeated sin and resurrected from the dead. Eternal life doesn't begin the day we get to heaven; it began the day God put Jesus' eternal Holy Spirit into your soul to sanctify you forever. (Heb. 9:14) "The faith" factor calls saints to work out their own salvation with fear and trembling because it's God giving you the desire and ability to do His will as blameless disciples. (Phil. 2:12-15; 2 Cor. 13:5) Now that God's will has saved you and sanctified you as His dearly beloved child, you must develop the diligent discipline of being **Spirit-filled**.

God's will commands with an imperative verb "be **filled** with the **Spirit.**" (Eph.5:18) Why do we need this loving admonition? Because we leak! As Satan fires his darts, they often hit his target: our vulnerable minds and hearts. (Eph. 6:16) Therefore, God grants us armor, but "above all" is the shield of faith to quench ALL those diabolical darts of destruction. That's why often vulnerable Solomon wrote, "keep thy heart with all diligence; for out of it are the issues of life". (Prov. 4:23) That's why Paul, often assaulted by Satan's darts, wrote about our need for the **Spirit's filling** that comes through discipleship training in Ephesians 4 that perfects saints for the work of ministry. That's why Peter, who often fell hard under Satan's darts, reminded us to be sober and vigilant as the roaring lion stalks weak prey as our adversary devours careless sheep. (I Pet. 5:8) Knowing Satan's deceitfulness, God's beloved children start abstaining from all appearances of evil to protect their testimony for God. (I Thess. 5:22-23) After we cooperate with God's Spirit to stay in God's will, then we must learn the next factor, **submission** to God's will daily.

Submission reminds us that God's will always gives His servants a specific mission in life to fulfill for His glory. Jesus' submission empowered Him to finish "the work" which God gave Him to do. (Jn. 17:4) Again, discipleship trains saints to submit to "the work" of ministry that we might all do our part to build the body of Christ as His dearly beloved Bride. (Eph. 4:12) God saved us for "the work" as we walk worthy of our calling as Spirit-filled saints driven by a passion to please God. (Col.1:10) However, our **submission** demands that our carnal agendas submit to His holy eternal agendas. (Isa. 55:8-9) God's Spirit reminds us often that one day we will all answer to Jesus at the judgment seat of Christ for how we have used our spiritual gifts in doing "the work" of God. (2 Cor. 5:10) God's Spirit daily empowers "the work" of faith as a labor of love for all God's true servants. (I Thess. 1:3) The greatest labor of love comes through our passion for effectual fervent prayer that submits to His will. (Eph. 3:20) This takes us to the next factor of God's will, **servanthood**.

Jesus Christ, above all else in His life, embodied **servanthood** as the Suffering Servant. (Isa. 53) He learned obedience through His sufferings, and so must we as we faithfully count the cost of true discipleship. (Luke 14:28; Heb. 5:8-9) After all, what has your faith cost you lately? We have been saved to serve, not just to go to heaven! All saints are called "God's workmanship" created in Jesus to do good works as proof of our love for Him to fulfill God's will in our lives. (Eph. 2:10) After Jesus washed His disciples' feet, including Judas', He told His men that their joy in life would hinge on doing the same types of humble service. (Jn. 13:17) As all my roommates saw me as a new Christian humbly serving God at church rather than myself, they knew Jesus had changed my life dramatically. My testimony of **servanthood** shined a glorious light for my Savior that I didn't even see, but all my family and friends saw the transformation from glory to glory. (2 Cor. 3:18) That leads us to the next factor of God's will, being **shining lights** of faithfulness.

Saved, sanctified, Spirit-filled, submissive servants shine a blinding light that can't be hidden on the hills of this dark world.

(Mt. 5:14) When God radically saves the souls of alcoholics, drug users, murderers, thieves, and the rest of us sinners, the world notices, especially seekers after truth.

Many years ago, I visited a man named Bob one evening. His wife Joan had been saved a few years, and he seemed to be softening to his need for Jesus. As she left the room to put the children to bed, I asked Bob what he thought of Joan's life change. He responded that her radical new lifestyle had contagiously affected him and that he found her love for Jesus quite attractive. A few minutes later, Bob gave his life to Jesus as His Savior and began his own miraculous journey of faith.

Solomon's light grew dim for a while, but as he matured in God's will he wrote, "the path of the just is as the shining light, that shineth more and more unto the perfect day" when God conforms us to the image of Jesus. (Prov. 4:18) This **shining light** of righteousness phase leads us to the last factor of God's will, the aspect of being a **good soldier** of Christ's.

As Paul sat in a Roman prison cell in his last days on earth, he wrote a letter of encouragement to his young disciple, Timothy. Timothy had the tough challenge of pastoring a church that had begun to leave its first love, the Word of God. (Rev. 2:4). Paul challenged him to fulfill God's will by fighting the good fight of faith as a **good soldier** of Christ, especially in discipling men as leaders in God's church. (2 Tim. 2:1-4) Paul reminded his beloved friend of fifteen aspects of good soldiering throughout 2 Timothy:

1. To ignore fear, relying on God's power, love, and sound mind (2 Tim. 1:7)

2. To be persuaded that God is able to finish the work He started (1:12)

3. To hold fast the weapon of sound doctrine in loving faith (1:13)

4. To be strong in the enabling grace found in Christ Jesus (2:1)

5. To disciple faithful men who will reproduce reproducers (2:2)

6. To endure hardness in persevering disciplines (2:3)

7. To separate himself from the unholy distractions of the world (2:4)

8. To consider truths that allow Jesus to enlighten the heart (2:7)

9. To rightly divide God's Word in diligent study to avoid shame (2:15)

10. To be wary of head knowledge that hinders heart knowledge (3:7)

11. To live godly even as persecution is guaranteed to come (3:12)

12. To allow God's Word of grace to perfect him in good works (3:14-17)

13. To preach the Word even when people don't listen (4:2-4)

14. To always do the work of evangelism as God loves all lost souls (4:5)

15. To pursue the crown of righteousness, living in light of
Jesus' return (4:8)

As Paul came to the end of his life, he could boldly declare how
he had stayed in God's will to do "the work" which God had
called him to accomplish. Paul stated his **faithbuilder** this way:
"I have fought a good fight, I have finished my course, I have
kept the faith." (2 Tim. 4:7) Timothy's dear friend, mentor, and
discipler had diligently kept "the faith" of Jesus as he had fixed
the eyes of his soul upon the Author and Finisher of his faith,
even as he sat in prison. (Gal. 2:20; Heb. 12:2) Good soldiers
also know how to listen to their Commander-in-Chief, Jesus
Christ, our last factor for being in God's will; **be still and wait
on God** .

One of the songs the Israelites sang in their annual pilgrimages
to Jerusalem for feast days focused them to "Be still and know
that I am God". (Ps. 46:10) God's people often forgot that He
was their refuge and strength, a very present help in time of
trouble. (Ps.46:1) Prayerfully *waiting* on God in silence
enlightens eyes of understanding to know His perfect will, and
this factor is the most important of all to safeguard godly
decision making. (Eph.1:18) I have often said in difficult days of
choosing to know God's perfect will that I would rather be ten
steps behind God than one step ahead of Him. When I have
diligently followed this discipline of *waiting*, God has never
failed to show me His path of light and truth. (Ps.16:11) I don't

want to make good choices in serving God. I want to make the best choices possible. One of the hardest discernment factors in decision making is whether my choices are good, better, or best in pleasing my gracious God. Solomon, after making many hasty choices, learned the hard way that time and judgment go hand in hand. (Eccles. 8:5-6) Truth and time go hand in hand in Scripture as the more time that passes prayerfully, the more truth we have to make the best choices as we *wait* to hear from God. (Ps. 25:12) As David, "the sweet psalmist", wrote, "Truly my soul waiteth upon God: from him cometh my salvation." (Ps.62:1)

Job and Isaiah understood this principle of *waiting* on God, because God used them to write Scriptures in days of severe suffering, whether personal or due to the bad choices of the nation of Israel. Job penned the following principles for wisdom to *wait* on God to know His will:

1. "All the days of my appointed time will I wait, till my change come." (14:14) Job knew that God makes His divine changes in our circumstances if we *wait* prayerfully instead of trying to manipulate our issues of life through carnal solutions.
2. Job knew that some of the people we seek counsel from are "physicians of no value" because they have no wisdom that compares to Jesus' wisdom as the Great Physician and Lover of our souls. (13:4)
3. Job consequently "esteemed the words" of God's holy truths more than his necessary food as he *waited* on God.

293

(23:12)

4. Job understood not to jump to conclusions in evaluating circumstances of trials as he *waited* on "the hand of the Lord" to reveal discernment for decision making. (12:9)

5. Job knew that God keeps Satan under His control as "the deceived and the deceiver are his". (12:16) God's "strength and wisdom" in trials remind us in suffering that He has perfect power to carry out His perfect will, even as God lets Satan test us. (Job 1:10-12) Throughout Scripture Satan is God's pawn on a "short leash" to accomplish God's will in the end.

6. Job also understood that God "discovereth deep things out of darkness, and bringeth out to light the shadow of death". (12:22) Job learned many deep things about God as He transformed Job's dark trials into blessings of enlightenment. Even as saints walk through the valley of "the shadow of death", God's hand keeps us in the grip of His tender mercies as we wait to see His face. (Ps. 23:4)

7. At the end of Job's trials, he prayed for his so-called friends, who had wrongfully accused him, as his *waiting* on God came to an end. God "turned the captivity of Job" into unsearchable riches granting Job twice as much as he had before. (42:7, 10)

Isaiah also wrote many principles of faith for saints who *wait* on God prayerfully knowing nothing escapes God's eye when it comes to His child's needs. (Isa. 26:3; Mt. 6:26-34; Heb. 4:13)

1.　　Isaiah had learned well to **wait** on God due to the stubborn refusal of the Israelites in their captivity to listen to their Lord through the mouth of His prophet. This exhausting process moved God to inspire Isaiah to pen, "they that wait upon the LORD shall renew their strength; they shall mount up with wings of eagles; they shall run, and not be weary; and they shall walk and not faint". (40:31) The eagle represents God's finest saints who soar majestically above life's problems by sticking out their wings of powerful faith, flying heavenward into the Presence of God's love. All born again Christians possess eagles' wings! As we learn to **wait** on God in the yoke of faith, He strengthens us through **faithbuilders** as we kneel at His throne. (Ps. 46:1, 10)

2.　　Isaiah discerned that **waiting** on God didn't mean sitting around doing nothing as professing Christians and expect God to bless when they are living in sin as the house of Jacob did. So he wrote, "I will wait upon the Lord, that hideth his face from the house of Jacob, and I will look for him". (8:17) Saints must seek God's face with all their heart in searching His Word as they **wait** in prayerful anticipation for answers. (Jer. 29:13)

3.　　Saints can expect blessings to abound as they **wait** prayerfully on God. Isaiah wrote, "blessed are all they that wait for Him". (30:18) The context of this powerful passage is that God is also **waiting** on us to humbly seek His face in repentance that He may be merciful to us!

4.　　God's people will never be ashamed as they *wait* on God to reveal His will through His Word. That's why Isaiah wrote, "thou shalt know that I am the LORD: for they shall not be ashamed that wait for me". (49:23) We will never know God better than we know His Word because Scripture is God's holy character in holy print!

In closing, remember Jesus Christ *waited* thirty years as God prepared Him to start His ministry that would accomplish God's perfect will. May we prayerfully pursue God knowing "The LORD is good unto them that wait for him, to the soul that seeketh him". (Lam. 3:25) That's why we keep on searching as "deep calleth unto deep" as we learn "the deep things of God." (Ps. 42:7; 1 Cor. 2:10) Praise God for His indescribable gift of **faithbuilders** to those saints seeking the center of His will as they *wait* on Him on their knees with an open Bible. (Ps.46:1, 10; Mt. 6:33)

FOOD FOR THOUGHT (Phil. 4:8) - "I will wait upon the Lord..." (Isa.8:17)

1.   How are you more patient than a year ago as you wait on God to prayerfully discern His holy will? (Isa.40:31)

2.   See **Appendix III** and **IV** for the keys to listening to the right voices to discern God's will

3.   See **Appendix VII** on a deeper lesson on God's will and Word

FAITHBUILDERS FOR REPRODUCERS
"Go ye therefore and teach all nations... " (Mt. 28:19)
CHAPTER TWENTY-SEVEN

Imagine Jesus in heaven after His resurrection and ascension, and greatly confused angels gather around him to question Him. They asked, "What are you doing up here already after only three years of ministering on earth? We thought you promised to build your church and kingdom, and we certainly don't see either! How are you going to accomplish your promise from up here to build a church that the gates of hell cannot stop? (Mt. 16:18) For years we have tried to understand and examine the things of salvation and your church which we see nowhere in the Old Testament plans of God. We are perplexed at best. Please help us here to understand your holy plans so we can help carry them out like we did in the days of your dearly beloved Daniel!" (I Pet. 1:12)

Jesus replied, "You see those eleven disciples I left behind gazing up into heaven after my ascension that the two angels are talking with about my second coming? (Acts 1:10-11) They are my plan! They and their future disciples will finish what I started as they live faithfully and die faithfully for me; I will empower them prayerfully with my Holy Spirit to witness for me and to teach others all that I have taught them." (Acts 1:8; Mt. 28:18-20)

The angels replied, "You have got to be joking! These guys who all ran from the cross, even after you told them they would?

The men who argued over who would be the greatest among them, who fell asleep in Gethsemane after you asked them to just watch with you one hour? (Mt. 26:40) The men who wouldn't believe the women's report after you had resurrected and even doubted after seeing you in your resurrection body? (Mt. 28:17) Peter denied you three times after you warned him Satan would be sifting him through the temptation of denial! (Luke 22:31) Thomas had to see the holes in your body because he refused to believe by faith that you rose from the dead! These men of 'little faith', as you so often labeled them, these are the men who are the source of power for your plan to build your church? You must have another plan!" (Mt. 6:30)

To which questions Jesus replied, "I have no other plan! I will love them unto the end of the world and will be with them as they fulfill my Great Commission to reproduce reproducers, faithful disciples, who will fight the good fight, finishing their race for God's glory". (Mt. 28:20; 2 Tim. 2:2-3; 4:7).

Jesus' plans are always perfect because His authority perfects His precious promises with perfect power to carry out God's plans on earth. God granted Jesus "all power" in heaven and earth because he crushed Satan, sin, and death at the cross when He cried out victoriously, "It is finished". (Mt. 28:18; I Cor. 15:57-58) Our Lord's work to finish building His church, as He had promised, flows from heaven as our Intercessor's effectual prayers are answered by God. (Heb. 7:25; Jas. 5:16)

Let us now examine Jesus' perfect plan of discipleship that had four distinct phases to it:

1. Phase one: "Come and see"… (Jn. 1:38-39, 46) approximately five months of *listening*
2. Phase two: "Follow Me…I will make you fishers of men" … (Mt. 4:19) eleven months of *learning*
3. Phase three: "Ordained twelve that should be with Him"… (Mk. 3:14) twenty months of *laboring*
4. Phase four: "Go ye therefore"… (Mt. 28:19) lifetime of disciple making and *loving souls…*

Phase one began when two of John the Baptist's disciples came to Jesus asking if He was truly the prophesied Messiah that John had called "the Lamb of God" who takes away the sins of the world. (Jn. 1:29-39) Jesus replied, "Come and see". All evangelism starts with a person's hungry heart as a *listener* who has "ears to hear" as a seeker after truth who will "*come and see*". (Jn. 4:24) Jesus tests them as to whether they have an appetite for His truth or whether they are just curiosity seekers playing games with Him, as many religious people do in the gospels. (Jer. 15:16; I Pet. 2:2-3) Religion has a long history of seeking "head-to-head" information only, that merely "tickles the ears," not seeking life change coming through a commitment to God through Jesus alone. (Jn. 14:6; 2 Tim. 4:3-4) That's why Jesus called religion a wide path to destruction that most people will follow. (Mt. 7:13) Paul described the religious counterfeit crowd as people ever "learning" but never coming to really know the Truth, Jesus Christ. They have a form of godliness but deny the power of Christ's gospel. (2 Tim. 3:5, 7)

In sharp contrast, Christianity has a long history of humble, hungry people seeking a personal relationship of "heart-to-heart" intimacy with Jesus that changes the life. (2 Cor. 5:17; Jas. 1:21-22) Jesus taught that very few people find this path in life just as only one good soil received the seeds of truth that bore the eternal fruit of salvation in the parable of the soils. (Mt. 7:14-20; Mark 4:7-18) The boy, Samuel, pictures beautifully the humble teachable heart in a day when there was no vision in the land of Israel. (I Sam. 3) His attitude cried, "Speak Lord, thy servant is listening," with attentive ears to hear. (Luke 8:8) Samuel ended up being a powerful prayer warrior who listened to His God! (Jer. 15:1)

Once Jesus' salvation creates a true disciple who is a *listener* at heart, God's Spirit works passion into their soul to tell others what they have found in Jesus. (Ps. 18:28; Acts 1:8) Andrew immediately calls Peter to **"come and see"** Jesus. Our Lord immediately calls Peter "Cephas" as God knows the potential of His disciples in spite of obvious weaknesses they may have as new babes in Christ. (Jn. 1:42). Then Philip calls Nathaniel, telling him **"come and see"**. (Jn. 1:46)

Jesus chooses ordinary men through whom He will do extraordinary acts of service and ministry, so He gets all the glory. (2 Cor. 4:7, 11) Our Lord trains His disciples in the basics of the faith that they may grow from faith to faith, knowing He will often have to rebuke them later with the admonition of "O ye of little faith". (Matt. 6:30; Rom. 1:17)

As we disciple new Christians we must anchor them in *four* diligent disciplines that God will always reward richly as He trains them to use their senses to discern good and evil in daily battles of life. (Heb. 5:13-14; 11:6) The *first* training tool of **phase one** teaches "babes" how to feed themselves by comparing Scripture with Scripture to rightly divide the truth, especially to withstand the temptations of this world. (Mt. 4:4; I Cor.2:10, 13; 2 Tim. 2:15; 3:16) That's exactly why Jesus asked Peter if he loved Him and then challenged him to prove his love by feeding His sheep. (Jn. 21:16)

The *second* training tool of **phase one** of discipleship equips new Christians in the basics of effectual fervent prayer which will always flow out of personal Bible study and daily devotions. Can you imagine what the disciples learned just from hearing Jesus pray? That's why one day his disciples asked Him, "Lord, teach us to pray". (Luke 11:1) Note they didn't ask Him to teach them to do miracles or to preach, or to heal! They realized they had to learn to talk to God as Jesus did, being the first person to ever use the term "Abba" or Daddy to address God in prayer. (Mk. 14:36) Somehow these new disciples understood there's only two ways to build intimacy with God, by being a *listener* and a communicator who discusses what they learned from listening attentively. God makes it so simple; listen to Me and talk to Me, reminding His beloved children so their minds would never be corrupted from the simplicity of the truths that are found in seeking Christ prayerfully. (Jn. 1:11-12; 3:16; 14:6; 2 Cor. 11:4)

The *third* training tool equips new Christians in the vital importance of iron sharpening iron fellowship with other saints. (Prov. 27:17) We need each other and must never forsake the assembling of ourselves together so we can contagiously spur each other on to new levels of intimate love and good deeds; we must remind one another that Jesus is coming soon to rapture His dearly beloved Bride, the church. (Heb. 10:24-25) Faithful fellowship reminds us that God is not interested in programs that merely keep people busy, but He is keenly interested in ministries that change lives. (2 Cor. 5:17) Always choose people over programs as Jesus did! Remember how the crowd marveled at the life change in the "unlearned and ignorant" Peter and John, recognizing that the power of their boldness came from being with Jesus. (Acts 4:13)

The *fourth* training tool of **phase one** equips new Christians how to share their faith effectively and confidently. I remember well, as a new believer, being challenged to partake in evangelism training that had classes and then immediate application by going with a seasoned Christian man to visit new people who had visited our church. This ministry design gave me the tools and the vision to share my faith with others, just as someone had loved me enough to tell me the truth about Jesus. (Acts 1:8) This last tool reminds new believers that the "bottom line" of all Biblical discipleship is evangelism, and that all Biblical evangelism must have a discipleship ministry to train new "babes" to find out if their professions of faith were sincere. Over many years, I have seen people who thought they were Christian realize their professions of faith, especially as a child, were merely mental assent and not decisions of the heart flowing out of repentance. (2 Cor. 7:10-11) Jesus' first word of His first sermon was, "Repent". (Mt. 4:17) I am amazed at the lack of preaching repentance today in this lukewarm era of "ear tickling" entertainment, when Jesus commanded repentance be preached boldly to all nations and people. (Luke 24:47)

Jesus' **phase one** ministry training took His disciples to normal social events such as the wedding in Cana where He used a miraculous **faithbuilder** to help them grow from faith to faith, knowing that one day this growth process would produce habitual obedience. (Ro. 1:5) Our Lord simply wanted them to see His works and hear His words: the two key tools of His ministry. (Jn. 14) Often I will take my new disciples on hospital calls, visitation or on long ministry-related trips to have quality conversation that fosters growth in our friendship and fellowship. Jesus always taught that Biblical beliefs foster Biblical behavior, so this principle constantly shapes our evaluation process of the discipleship journey of growing in grace. (Luke 5:4-11; 2 Pet. 3:18)

In conclusion, in the **"come and see"** phase of evangelism, allow potential converts time to make Biblical decisions, always being ready to humbly answer every person who asks you of the hope you possess. (I Pet. 3:15) Allow God's Spirit to lovingly draw people to Jesus in His time, remembering God is never in a hurry and never forces Himself on people. (Eccles. 3:11) Be "Jesus with skin on" to hurting people as you pray for them to understand only Jesus can meet their needs and save their souls. (I Jn. 4:17) For example, a few years ago I visited a cancer patient many times for eighteen months as he was often hospitalized. This man thanked God for his Christian daughter, son-in-law and grandchildren who all came to our church, but he wanted nothing to do with their Jesus, although he listened to his daughter as she shared her faith. Then one day, I awoke thinking about him and went to visit him once again in the hospital. For the first time ever, as I entered the room, he declared, "I'm glad you came today as I was hoping to see you. I'm ready to accept Jesus as my Savior!" He humbly confessed his need of Jesus to save him from his sins. A few months later he went home to be with his Lord Jesus, simply because he was willing to "come and see" that Jesus was his only hope of glory. (Col. 1:27)

Phase two of discipleship training turned *listeners* into *learners*, as Jesus focused now on deepening their roots of righteousness as "fishers of men". (Prov. 12:12; Mt. 4:19; Phil. 4:9) Their Savior had prayerfully chosen many men who were fishermen, knowing their diligent disciplines to make a living in a tough occupation that often had them on the dangerous Sea of Galilee. Now Jesus would teach them the difference between making a living to survive and making a life to serve and glorify God in their daily choices. (Deut. 30:19)

When Jesus first saw his disciples, James and John, these fishermen were mending nets so no fish fell through the holes. (Mt. 4:21; Mk. 1:16-20) Their Savior would disciple these *learners* in making spiritual nets that would catch men, allowing no repentant honest souls to fall through the cracks of indifference or religion. Interestingly, the Greek meaning of the word "mend" is to restore, as all lost sinners need restoration with their gracious God. (2 Cor. 5:20-6:2)

Jewish fishermen also were skilled in working as teams in weaving nets, as Jesus prayed His disciples would be one in spirit reaching the world with His love to catch many "fish" as fishers of men. (Isa. 19:9; Jn. 17:18, 21) Paul spent much time discipling teams of men to work together as leaders in all his new church plants too. (2 Tim. 2:2-3)

Fishermen labored hard, often all night long without catching any fish, yet never quit because their obedience in labor kept their families fed. (Luke 5:5) Peter obeyed Jesus' call to "launch out into the deep" one frustrating night as God broke his heart as a sinner who doubted his Lord. Sometimes, we as saints, must dig deeper into prayer and the Word to understand God's commands as Peter did that day. (I Cor. 2:10) Jesus also taught His disciples a parable that the kingdom of heaven was like a net cast into the sea to catch every kind of fish. That's why He sent them all over the world in His love to reach and save all mankind. (I Tim. 2:6)

Also when a fisherman's day ended, he busied himself washing his nets. (Luke 5:2) This discipline prevented the stink that kept fish away from the nets and also prevented nets from rotting. Dirty nets also made fishing harder as they stuck together, and fish are smart enough to stay away from dirty nets that are easily spotted. That's why God's greatest leaders and *learners* in Scripture fervently prayed for God to give them a pure heart to enhance ministry and for God to search the heart and thoughts for weaknesses of faithlessness. (Ps. 51:10; 139:23-24) Praise God for how the Trinity uses three major tools for our cleansing and witnessing: the spirit, the water, and the blood. (I Jn. 5:7-8)

As a fisherman of fifty years, I was well trained in fishing techniques by two of the greatest fishermen I have ever known, one of them was a great Christian friend who owned a charter business in Alaska and Florida. I have gone on dozens of trips with these two men and have always caught bigger and more fish than any other boats in camp or charter boats on the lake. Skilled fishermen have insights into weather, tides, moon phases, barometric pressure, nautical maps, and what baits to use when and where. Jesus, after praying all night, knew exactly which disciples to choose as fishers of men. (Mt. 4:19)

Phase two defined Jesus' calling that would develop over the next three years in a pattern we'll call **M.V.P.** , as God would clearly define the disciples' *mission, vision* and *passion* as His ambassadors. We've already examined the *mission* to reach souls as fishers of men. Jesus prayed for them to fulfill their mission in His high priestly prayer, "As thou hast sent me into the world, even so have I also sent them into the word". (Jn. 17:18) The beauty of our mission as Christians comes in the next verse of His prayer to remind us that He guarantees our purity that will be divinely enabled by God's engrafted truths. (Jn. 17:19; Jas. 1:21)

One of the most precious promises that God gives to His children teaches us that when God saved our souls He placed us into Christ who is our wisdom, righteousness, sanctification, and redemption! (I Cor. 1:30) That's why Paul says that we are "complete in Him". (Col. 2:10) True born again saints can never lose their salvation purchased fully by the precious blood of the Lamb of God. (Rom. 8:28-32; I Pet. 1:19, 22-25)

Romans 6 lays out the picture of this blessing, as Jesus, our wisdom, has engrafted divine enablement within us to walk in righteousness and newness of life. (v4) The ability to habitually serve God obediently, by grace through faith, proves we are His sanctified servants of righteousness. (v6-18) Then as we appropriate His power of being made free from sin's dominion, our servanthood proves fruitfully that we are His holy fishers of men with His eternal life consuming us through God's eternal Spirit. (v22) Praise God for His gift of this **faithbuilder** that grows from glory to glory in a radiant, changed life. (Ro. 6:22-23; 2 Cor. 3:18; 5:17)

Jesus also clarifies the *vision* for His fishers of men, knowing that without vision people perish. (Prov. 29:18) The religious

Rory Wineka

community of Jerusalem had their vision blurred and blinded by the false doctrines of the Pharisees and Sadducees who promoted legalism and liberalism, respectively. The Pharisees added to God's Word, and the Sadducees took from it, dangerously bringing God's judgment of "woes" of damnation upon themselves. (Mt. 23:13-29) That's why Jesus prayed for their unity of *vision* to see the world through God's eyes which would enhance their ministry to an unbelieving world blinded by religion's false doctrines. (Jn. 17:21)

Consequently, Jesus spent much time teaching misguided sheep "You have heard, but I tell you" statements of truth to counter the religious liars who mocked Jesus as they replaced His truths with their religious traditions. (Mt. 15:6) Paul addressed the same issues in Ephesus when he taught that God gives eyes of enlightenment to His children that they might understand a Biblical vision of their eternal hope and riches of inheritance. (Eph. 1:18) That's also why Jesus kept in front of his disciples that the harvest fields were white if they would prayerfully learn to be *laborers* as He prepared them for the next level of His training. (Mt. 9:38)

Then Jesus intensified His discipling to create the *passion* needed to fulfill their *mission* with *vision*. Jesus powerfully closed His high priestly prayer knowing only God can engraft constraining love into hearts to understand the depth of His eternal love. Jesus, at the end of His life, wanted to insure His struggling disciples that the same love God had for Jesus He had for them. (Jn.17:26) Our Lord knew the *passion* needed to enable Him to withstand His temptations in the wilderness, Gethsemane, and the cross, and that only God could place that kind of fire into His servant's soul to dispel the darkness of doubts. (Job 29:3; Ps. 18:28; Prov. 20:27) God even sent angels to minister to Jesus to strengthen His passion to finish His race faithfully as the Author and Finisher of our *mission* on earth. (Mt. 4:11; Luke 22:43)

Phase three enables *listeners*, trained to be *learners*, to now become mature *laborers* in God's white harvest fields to build Jesus' church though the Biblical principle of multiplying disciples and churches. (Acts 6:1, 7; 9:31; 12:24) Jesus' strategy in maturing His disciples to **reproduce reproducers** would take deep root in Acts, as God multiplied disciples through the preaching of His Word by well-seasoned soldiers Jesus trained for three years to build His church. (Mt. 16:18) This twenty month phase finalizes Jesus' training of growing His disciples into *laborers*. Jesus knew the fire-filled furnace of trials that would build their weak faith through "great grace" and many **faithbuilders** to deepen their roots of righteousness. (Prov. 12:12; Acts 4:33; Rom. 11:16)

As *laborers*, Jesus' enlightened disciples will now learn the diligent disciplines through the "strong meat" that will grant them "senses exercised to discern good and evil". (Heb. 5:13) God has used a deliberate training pattern to prepare these men to become "doers" of His Word. He has engrafted convictions into their souls to shape the character and conduct needed for the battles facing them in Acts as Satan will launch an all-out attack from both within the church and from without. (Acts 5)

As Jesus shapes their vision for their **mission** of "love with shoes on", He will send them out into His harvest fields for on the job training that He will supervise. (Mt. 9:37-38; Mk. 3:14) As God shapes practical ministry skills, He will mold the crude clay pot of Peter's pride through numerous stages of humility training and brokenness. (Luke 22:31) James and John will learn to love rather than call down fire from heaven. (Luke 9:54) Philip will become an effective evangelist, but James will be martyred by Herod. (Acts 8; 12) Jesus will clearly confirm to these very ordinary men how proper Biblical discipleship produces **reproducers** of extraordinary divine ability as compassionate **laborers** serving Him sacrificially to glorify God. (I Cor.10:31; Jude 22)

Jesus is done trying to reach the religious community as a whole because they rejected Him as being empowered by Beelzebub, the prince of devils, and not God. So He now devotes all His time to equipping further His soldiers for the battles ahead by teaching them parables only His beloved servants would understand. (Mt. 12:24; 13:3-35)

Phase four would conclude Jesus' training as He challenged His disciples with the Great Commission, assuring them of His Presence that would enable and protect them as "**lovers of souls**" and leaders who would build His church in Acts. (Mt. 16:18; 28:18-20)

This final phase started when Jesus washed the disciples' feet to teach them that servanthood marked the character and conduct of true disciples. (Jn. 13) Our Lord proved His love as the Suffering Servant and so must we. (Isa. 53; Jn. 13:1; 14:21, 23) Jesus fully understood His **mission,** and the disciples needed to fully understand their Great Commission. (Jn. 13:3; 17:4ff.) Note carefully where Jesus' focus is one day before His crucifixion: on His beloved disciples into whom He has poured His soul for three years. His last words are critical just as yours would be to your children the day before you die. If you want to do a life-changing Bible study, examine the last chapter of every book in your Bible to see the last words of God's finest servants to their beloved children!

Peter's pride protests Jesus' loving gesture to wash their feet, but Jesus' rebuke humbles him, a **faithbuilder** he never forgot. (Jn. 13:8-13; I Pet. 5:5-8) The humility of teachability fosters great passion into the heart of true disciples. (Ps. 16:11; 18:29; Jn. 8:31-32) Remember Jesus washed Judas' feet too as a picture that anyone can be forgiven by God's love if they will repent or change their mind about needing a Savior, Jesus Christ the Lord. (2 Cor. 7:10-11; 2 Pet. 3:9)

The last key to this final training phase for **loving souls** involved understanding the roots of Jesus' unconditional gift of eternal and internal love for all sinners. (Jn. 13:34-35) Our Lord taught this being fully aware of Judas' coming betrayal. (Ps. 41:9; Jn. 13:18-21) Judas was such a master counterfeiter that no disciple knew he was the betrayer, just as Satan has planted his tares in disguise in today's churches, especially behind counterfeit pulpits! (2 Cor. 11:13-15)

In conclusion, many years ago a friend of mine went on Christmas break on a mission trip to a children's orphanage in Haiti. To show their love for the children, the team took a Christmas gift for each child so they could later use the gift as a word picture of God's love gift of Christmas, Jesus Christ. When the children received the gifts they just sat their staring at the boxes as they thought the pretty box was the gift! To their delight, they discovered a better gift inside the box. Many religious people today only see Jesus as "a box" offering very little true hope because no one has fully explained to them that there is a "better gift" that saves souls with "better hope". (Heb. 1:4; 6:9; 7:19, 22)

FOOD FOR THOUGHT (Phil. 4:8): Where are you in the four phases of Jesus' discipleship plan? (Luke 6:40)

1.   Are you a **listener** who has clearly seen Jesus working in your life? (Jn. 1:38-39, 46)

2.   Are you a **learner** who is following Jesus with all your heart? (Mt. 4:19; Jn. 10:27; 12:26)

3.   Are you a **laborer** who serves Jesus sacrificially with joy? (Mt. 9:37-38; Mk. 3:14; I Cor. 3:9)

4.   Are you a **lover of souls** who has a vision for the lost? (Prov. 29:18; Mt. 28:19; Acts 1:8)

5.   See **Appendix II** for personal questions of self-examination as a reproducer for God's glory.

6.   See **Appendix V** for Satan's schemes to keep us from reproducing fruit for God's glory.

7. See **Appendix VI** for more information on how Jesus equips saints to reproduce reproducers as servants who demonstrate "love with shoes on" as they "adorn the doctrine of God" in all things. (Titus 2:10)

APPENDIX I
"IT'S ALL IN THE RESUMES"

TO: Jesus, Son of Joseph
    The Woodcrafter's Carpenter Shop
    Nazareth 25922
FROM: Jordan Management Consultants
    Jerusalem 26544
RE: Personnel Evaluations

Thank you for submitting the resumes of the twelve men you have picked for managerial positions in your new organization. All of them have now taken our battery of tests, and we have not only run the results through our computers but also arranged personal interviews for each of them with our psychologist and vocational aptitude consultant. It is the opinion of the staff that most of your nominees are lacking in background, education, and vocational aptitude for the type of enterprise you are undertaking. They do not have the team concept. We would recommend that you continue your search for persons of experience in managerial ability and proven capacity. We have summarized the findings of our study.

Simon Peter is emotional, unstable and given to fits of temper. Andrew has absolutely no quality of leadership. The two brothers James and John, the sons of Zebedee, place personal interests above company loyalty. Thomas demonstrates a questioning attitude that would tend to undermine morale. We believe it is our duty to tell you that Matthew has been blacklisted by the Greater Jerusalem Better Business Bureau. James, the son of Alphaeus, and Thaddeus definitely have radical leanings. Additionally, they both register high scores on the manic depressive scale.

However, one of the candidates shows great potential. He's a man of ability and resourcefulness; he is a great networker; he has a keen business mind and has strong contacts in influential circles. He's highly motivated, very ambitious and adept with financial matters. We recommend Judas Iscariot as your Controller and Chief Operating Officer.

All the other profiles are self-explanatory. We wish you the utmost success in your new venture.

What if Jesus had chosen the twelve based on the modern methods of leadership selection? Most of them would have never had a chance to participate. Jesus chooses people not for who they are, but for what they can become in Him. Aren't you glad that when Jesus looked at you He didn't take you for what you were (a sinner), but He took you for what you could be? Jesus sees the potential in us all and has called us to be disciples. Jesus is still saying "Follow Me!"

Author Unknown

APPENDIX II
QUESTIONS REPRODUCERS ASK THEMSELVES

"Examine yourselves, whether ye be in the faith"...
(2 Corinthians 13:5)

1. What is my first love? (Rev. 2:4)

2. How does God's constraining love affect me daily? (Rom. 5:5; 2 Cor. 5:14)

3. How fervent and effectual in righteousness is my prayer life? (Jas. 5:16)

4. How healthy is my reverential fear of God? (Ps. 86:11; Prov. 9:10)

5. How acceptable is my service to God? (Heb. 12:28-29)

6. Am I so feared by Satan that my name is on his lips? (Luke 22:31; Acts 19:15)

7. How often does sacrificial praise flow from my heart? (Mt. 12:34; Heb. 13:5)

8. What has my faith cost me lately? (2 Sam. 24:24; Heb. 11:6, 33-37)

9. Where are my fruit-bearing disciples? (Luke 6:40; 2 Tim. 2:2; Titus 2:3-5)

10. What level is my fruit bearing in God's eyes...thirty, sixty, one-hundred fold? (Luke 8:8; Jn. 15:16)

11. Where are my **faithbuilders** only God can get glory for? (Jer. 33:3; Eph. 3:20)

12. How hot is the divine flame in my soul? (Ps. 18:28)

13. How effectively do I practice God's presence in fullness of joy? (Ps. 16:11)

14. Is my prayer life fruitful in repentance that's done quickly and often? (2 Cor. 7:10-11)

15. How faithful am I in evangelism as God's ambassador? (Acts 1:8)

16. Do I know God far better in intimacy than I did a month ago? (Phil. 3:10)

17. Do I seek God early daily that I may grow in intimacy with Jesus? (Prov. 8:17)

18. What are the durable divine riches God has granted me recently? (Prov. 8:18-21)

19. When is the last time I found favor with God as His beloved child? (Prov. 8:32-35)

20. What will be the final verdict on my life when I meet Jesus in heaven? (Mt. 5:21)

APPENDIX III
DISCERNMENT FOR LISTENING TO THE RIGHT VOICES

THE VOICE OF THE HOLY SPIRIT – PSALM 103

1. Clarity (Ps.119:9, 18, 30, 32, 105, 130)
2. Intimacy (Prov. 8:17-21; Mt. 11:28-30)
3. Facts (Heb. 11:6; Rom. 10:17; 1:17; 8:1)
4. Growing faith (Col. 2:6-7; 2 Pet. 3:18)
5. Obedience (Rom. 1:5; 6:16; 16:19, 26)
6. Biblical strategy (Prov. 16:3; Eph. 6:10-18)
7. Humility (Prov. 15:33; 22:4; 1 Pet. 5:5-8)
8. Blessing (Gen. 50:20; Mt. 5:3- 16; 2 Pet. 1:1-4)

THE VOICE OF SATAN – PSALM 106

1. Confusion (Gen. 3:1, 4-5; I Cor. 14:33)
2. Destruction (Luke 22:3; Acts 5:3-9)
3. Feelings (Luke 22:31-32; Jn. 18:25, 27)
4. Seduced faith (Jonah 1:3; Luke 17:32)
5. Disobedience (Eph. 2:2; 5:6; Col. 3:6)
6. Carnal strategy (Prov. 28:26; 29:1, 18)
7. Humiliation (Prov. 16:18; Rom. 1:21-26)
8. Judgment (1 Pet. 4:17; 2 Pet. 2:9, 20-22)

APPLICATION: One of the greatest challenges facing Christians who really love Jesus is the daily choices we make that reflect how well we train our hearts to listen to the right voices. When we listen attentively to God's Spirit, He always helps us to apply "above all the shield of faith" that quenches all Satan's fire-filled darts that encourage us to exalt our ways over God's ways. God calls us to self-denial, whereas Satan calls us to self-exaltation! God just wants us to draw close to the cross for the double crucifixion power of Galatians 6:14 so Jesus' love constrains us to obey Him. (Gal. 2:20) Satan wants us to run from the cross as we fear counting the cost of tough choices.

This ongoing battle reminds me of the cartoon-like advertisements when a man is trying to make a choice and an angel sits on one shoulder whispering into his right ear, and a tiny devil sits on the other shoulder whispering into his left ear. It may seem funny in the ad, but it certainly can be fatal in real life choices. Therefore, we Christians must have a well-defined Biblical strategy to discern whose voice is trying to sway us. Maybe this chart will help, as Jesus promised He would guide us in difficult days when Satan "muddies" the waters of life. (Jer. 2:13; Jn. 7:17, 24, 37-38) For your own further study, examine Paul's struggles and how God helped him in Romans 7 and Galatians 5. Compare Paul's struggles with Jeremiah's in Jeremiah 17:9-14. May God help you as His dearly beloved child to choose wisely God's gift of eternal victory as Joseph did, over Satan's goal to defeat us as he did Judas Iscariot in our daily journey of life. (Ps. 25:12, 21) Choose wisely!

THE BATTLE OF FAITH VERSUS FEELINGS
APPENDIX IV
TRAIN ILLUSTRATION EXPANDED

Paul wrote serious admonitions about the daily battle all saints face as our flesh wars against our spirit in an effort to detour us off the narrow path of righteous living for Jesus' sake. To win this battle, Christians must listen to the right voices as we live in Satan's world that shouts all the time that we can't trust God and a Bible written over four-thousand years ago. Jesus always reminded His true disciples to have "ears to hear" as they focused diligently on Biblical **facts** that grew a **faith** that pleased God daily. (Heb. 11:6) Our Lord also promised His disciples that if they held onto those **facts** as the *final authority* in their lives that He would personally set them free from Satan's grip of diabolical belief. (Jn. 8:31-44)

As we examine the train illustration on page 326 we will note that the train is going uphill as Christianity is a daily uphill battle as we go against the grain of this evil world. (Rom. 12:1-2; 2 Cor. 6:14-7:1) Notice the first car behind the engine is a coal car of **facts** which represents that the train's engine must be filled with Biblical facts and fuel to produce Biblical faith and fire which feeds on those divine facts. (Ps. 18:28; Rom. 10:17)

The general **faith boxcar** is then supernaturally followed by **"the faith" boxcar** that moves us down the tracks as we grow from faith to faith into **the faith** of Jesus Himself, as we saw in earlier chapters. (Rom. 1:17; Gal. 2:20)

Then as we allow God to drive the engine of our soul He uses this pattern of growth: (Col. 2:6-7)

1. Biblical **facts** produce Biblical **faith**. (Rom.10:17)
2. Biblical **faith** then grows into **the faith** of Jesus' Biblical obedience. (Rom. 1:5, 17)
3. **The faith** of Jesus eventually grows us into **the faith of God** (Rom.3:3) as He conforms us into the fullness of His holy love that deeply touches our hearts daily. (Rom. 5:5; Eph. 4:19)
4. Then the caboose stays where it belongs. As we live by **the faith** of Jesus, feelings must come last in the "train of life" so our feelings are never allowed to seduce our faith. Remember well how Elijah and John the Baptist allowed feelings to seduce them. The only time Satan can seduce our faith with unbiblical feelings is when we quit fueling our souls with the Word of God. Consequently, Satan's voice overrides God's voice as now the train starts going backwards down the hill to potential destruction of joy and peace as feelings rule the heart.
5. However, we must feed our souls by going to the word of grace. God then He leads us prayerfully to His throne of grace. (Heb. 4:12, 16) Then we will find His grace sufficient to meet our needs in Christ as He enables us to habitually listen to the right voices so His will is done daily in our lives. (Jn. 8: 31-32; 2 Cor. 12:9-10)

SATAN'S SUBTLE SCHEMES
APPENDIX V

Christians must understand Satan's pattern of subtle schemes that defile our character and conduct as Jesus' potential disciples. The serpent is always working to corrupt our minds from the simplicity that is in Jesus' calling to serve Him wisely as "watchmen" on the church's walls of faithfulness. (2 Cor. 11:3-4, 13-15) Satan offers, through vain religion, a counterfeit Jesus, spirit, and gospel to get professing saints off the narrow path of Jesus' righteousness. Paul laid out, in great detail, in the book of Hebrews exactly how Satan works out his subtle plan of deception to get believers focused on selfish agendas. The persecuted church fell victim to this diabolical plan as professing Christians debated going back to the religion of Judaism to avoid possible martyrdom as believers in Christ. I call this pattern "**deviant drift**" and here are the stages:

1. *Drifting* from God one degree at a time as we carelessly listen to Him (Heb. 2:1)
2. *Dullness* of hearing then develops as ears are trained not to hear (Luke 8:8; Heb. 5:11)
3. *Defying* God then hardens hearts in willful disobedience in lifestyle (Heb. 10:29-30)
4. *Denying* a relationship with God as you finally no longer fear Him (Heb. 10:26, 31)

To amplify the understanding of this process, *drifting* is a well-known process fully understood by avid fishermen. When I fish

Lake Erie in Ohio I often travel five to twenty-five miles out to areas where there are no landmarks to measure the accuracy of the location where I want to fish. So using a compass in the old days ensured my accuracy, but if I am one degree off leaving port, I will be many miles off target when I travel far distances. Thus **"deviant drift,"** one degree at a time, creates great danger of not reaching my goal. Unfortunately, many professing Christians sit in churches weekly under heretical "Bible teaching" assuring they will never reach God's ultimate goal of eternal and abundant life as a true disciple of Jesus Christ. (2 Cor. 13:5; I Jn. 4:6)

Satan's simple strategy starts the *drifting* process with his fostering indifference and laziness in people's souls who fail to heed Jesus' habitual call to listen carefully to His voice alone. (Luke 8:8) "Ears to hear" are critical as Eve learned the hard way that Satan's subtleties cost her dearly as she fell to the evil scheme to ignore God's specific commands. (Gen. 3)

The devil knows that the indifference factor in the *drifting* process is one diabolical degree from apathy which unchecked always fosters apostasy. Then apostasy unchecked always drifts into anarchy where men do what's right "in their own eyes" as you study the evil downfall pattern of Israel in the book of Judges and in Solomon's life. (Prov. 30:12)

In order for Satan to deceive professing saints, he must get us to adhere to his devilish carnal wisdom as we consequently *drift* from God's holy and protective wisdom. That's why James warned the persecuted church in his day to ignore the earthly and sensual wisdom that caused envying, strife, and confusion in their lives as Satan led them down a path of eternal destruction. (Jas. 3:15-16) God is never the author of confusion. He leads us with His pure and perfect wisdom that fosters His peace in our souls through His mercy that always bears good fruits of His righteousness in our lives. (Jas. 3:17-18)

The *dullness* stage that follows the *drifting* stage can be compared to a carpenter who works with his hands so much that thick callous develops. After a while, that man can no longer feel pain because his nerve endings are hard as the hard-hearted soil in Jesus' parables. (Mark 4) Eventually dullness creates an attitude that defies God's truths even though you were trained in them. This happened in the infallible Messianic miracle when Jesus healed the man born blind which the Pharisees absolutely refused to believe in spite of irrefutable evidence. In sharp contrast, the common people believed when they heard Jesus gladly and consequently received great **faithbuilders**. (Jn. 9) Humble people are always blessed by God because they do have "ears to hear" the Spirit's clear voice which always drowns out Satan's confusing voice. (Jn. 8:31-32)

One of God's eternal promises about giving humble hearts eternal hope through His eternal Word, lies in the phrase *"covenant of salt"* used in the Old Testament. (Num. 18:19; Levit. 2:13) That's why Jesus told His true disciples that they were indeed the "salt of the earth" in the Sermon on the Mount. (Mt. 5:13) Remember that Matthew is a Jewish book and therefore saints must "think Jewish" when they read it! The disciples Jewish minds should have immediately remembered the Old Testament promises in Jeremiah about the permanent life-change the New Covenant would bring as a *covenant of salt*. Every Jew understood the value of salt in the Middle East where no refrigeration existed. Salt possesses three powerful qualities: it penetrates what it touches; it purifies what it penetrates; it preserves the pure character quality God intends. Therefore saints should have a lifestyle that penetrates society with God's loving truths as true Christianity should purify culture through its character and conduct that enlightens the world for God's will to be done. (Mt.5:16; Acts 1:8)

So consequently when the proud Pharisees' willfully ignored Jesus' "salty" words, their rotten, hard hearts boldly engaged in **defying** God in the flesh, Jesus Christ the Lord. Consequently they willingly entered the **denial** stage that permanently prevented any future truths from piercing their dull, hardened hearts that had drifted from God's holy truths which they had in writing. That's why Jesus as Judge said, "If ye were blind, ye should have no sin: but now ye say, We see; therefore your sin remaineth". (Jn. 9:41) They wanted Jesus to turn off His light of conviction and truth, so He did as He held them accountable to "reap what they had sown" in choosing the Satanic lies and schemes of darkness and delusion. (Gal. 6:7) Whenever people refuse light they choose darkness. (Mt. 12:30)

Praise God, however, that His light always eventually dispels Satan's darkness for those who receive and believe truth and repent of their drifting into denial. That's why it is so important to study Peter's writings about remembering these truths about God's precious promises that grant precious faith to defeat Satan's schemes. (1 Pet. 5:5-8; 2 Pet. 1:1-10) Peter simply repented after his three denials at Jesus' trial and was consequently powerfully used by God in the book of Acts.

However, men like Judas failed to repent of their drifting into the dullness of defiance and denial. Judas chose to commit suicide rather than repent as he continued to the end of his life to listen to Satan's deceptive and destructive voice as the "king over all the children of pride". (Job 41:34)

I trust that someone in your life has loved you enough to tell you the truth that you're a sinner who needs a loving Savior to set you free from Satan's schemes to destroy you eternally. (Jn. 3:16; Rom. 3:23; 6:23; 10:9-10, 13) Please remember that truth is the foundation for all relationships that last because it is eternal in character and quality. May God help you to abstain from ALL appearances of evil that you may be a victor rather than a victim of Satan's schemes as you use "above all" the shield of faith to conquer the devil's fire-filled darts. (Eph. 6:16; I Thess. 5:22) As you daily choose to listen to the right voices, God will grant you **faithbuilders** as your heart seeks His will and wisdom. (Eph. 3:20)

LOVE WITH SHOES ON
APPENDIX VI

"Love with shoes on" dominated Jesus' teaching in level four of His discipleship training. Jesus wanted His disciples to understand that they had to love people just as much as He did. John, "whom Jesus loved", penned chapters 13 to 21 of his gospel to burn this principle of divine love into the souls of His beloved disciples. (Jn. 13:1, 23, 34-35) The disciples needed to also believe with all their hearts that Jesus' love would provide a kingdom after He returned to rapture His Bride, and that He was the only "Way" into that eternal kingdom of hope. (Jn. 3:16; 14:1-6) God's love had sent Jesus to all the earth as His "love gift" to be received and believed as John wrote about Jesus throughout His gospel:

1. As the Bread of life foreshadowed by the manna from heaven (Jn. 6:35)

    a.   As He feeds us with His eternal and internal love (Rom. 5:5)

    b.   As He engrafts His character of love within us (Jas. 1:21-22)

2. As the Eternal One who existed before Abraham was born (Jn. 8:58)

    a.   As He grants us eternal perspective of His eternal love (Gal. 5:22)

    b.   As His eternal character shapes our hearts (2 Cor. 5:14-17)

3. As the Light of the whole world to be seen by all (Jn. 8:12; 12:36)

    a. As He enlightens our eyes with His love for all people (Eph. 1:18)

    b. As His love gives us His vision for souls (Prov. 29:18)

4. As the only Door to eternal abundant life (Jn. 10:7-10)

    a. As His abundant loves meets our daily needs (Phil. 4:19)

    b. As we become His "door" as His ambassadors of truth (Jn. 14:6)

5. As the Good Shepherd who cares lovingly for His sheep (Jn. 10:11)

    a. As we become "Jesus with skin on" as disciplers (I Jn. 4:17)

    b. As He conforms us to His loving image daily (Rom. 8:28-29)

6. As the Resurrection and the Life of eternal hope (Jn. 11:25)

    a. As He daily grants us resurrection power to love others (Phil. 3:10)

    b. As His eternal love covenant enables us to serve Him (2 Pet. 1:1-4)

7. As the True Vine who guarantees His children's fruitfulness (Jn. 15:1-16)

    a. As we bear fruit thirty, sixty and one-hundred fold for His glory (Luke 8:8)

b. As we reproduce reproducers who reach the world (Mt. 28:18-20)

Jesus also instructed them about His Holy Spirit who would empower His love within their minds, emotions, and wills, implanting eventually **"the faith"** of Jesus Himself, the Truth of God in the flesh. (Jn. 14:6; 16; Acts 3;16; Gal. 2:20; 5:22) The first character trait of Jesus' Spirit would be His love that would empower His disciples as *"love with shoes on"* to do everything He asked them to do. Jesus' gift of the Spirit of truth would engraft:

1. Truth that comforts by eliminating sorrow through His love (Jn. 16:6-7)
2. Truth that convicts of sin and righteousness (Jn. 16: 8-11)
3. Truth that comes as we need it, in God's perfect timing (Jn. 16:12; Eccles.3:11)
4. Truth that prepares Jesus' disciples for what's coming (Jn. 16:13)
5. Truth that guards hearts to glorify God alone (Jn. 16:14)
6. Truth that deepens our daily walk fruitfully on righteous paths (Jn. 16:15; Col. 1:10)

GOD'S WILL AND GOD'S WORD
MATTHEW 6:10
APPENDIX VII

Saints who hunger and thirst for righteousness are always filled with God's wisdom that flows from His Word to know His will for daily living. Their pure hearts see God working miraculously as God provides **faithbuilders** in answering prayers exceedingly well above and beyond their requests. (Mt. 5:6, 8; Eph. 3:20) The following Bible study will encourage you to seek God with all your heart knowing His righteousness will meet your daily needs in Christ as you pray effectually and submissively for His will to be done. (Mt. 6:33; Phil. 4:19; Jas. 5:16)

I.   INTRODUCTION: GOD'S WILL AND BIBLICAL PRAYING...(Acts 6:4)

    A.   Job prayed for his "friends" and God restored his blessings two-fold (Job 42:10-15)

    B.   Jacob prayed in brokenness and contriteness...Esau's twenty years of anger died (Hosea 10:12)

    C.   David prayed...his conspiratorial enemy Ahithophel hung himself (2 Sam. 17)

    D.   Moses prayed...God gave a cure for venomous snake bites (serpent/pole) (Num. 21:7)

    E.   Elisha prayed ...and the Shunammite's son was raised from the dead (2 Kg. 4)

F.   Elijah prayed on Mt. Carmel...eight-hundred and fifty of Baal's prophets died and Israelites worshipped (I Kg. 18)

G.   Esther prayed and Haman hung on the gallows he had built for Mordecai (chap. 7)

H.   Nehemiah prayed...a king's heart was moved to do God's will in protecting the Jews (Neh. 1)

I.   Daniel prayed...lions' were afflicted with "lock jaw" by God's protective hand (Dan. 6)

J.   Hezekiah prayed when ill, about to die...God gave him fifteen more years (2 Kg. 20:6)

K.   Jesus prayed and the disciples were equipped for ministry in the book of Acts (John 17)

L.   Epaphras prayed effectually and fervently and saints completed the will of God (Col. 4:12)

M.   Persecuted saints prayed...Peter was delivered from prison (Acts 12); James had been martyred!

    1.   Think...why did God spare Peter and yet allow James to be killed?

    2.   Think about God's will: when does God change His mind in answering our prayers?

II.   INSTRUCTION: THE HOLY HEART BEHIND
EFFECTUAL SUBMISSIVE PRAYER... "Thy will be done"...

A.   We cannot pray "our Father", if we live
selfishly, ignoring His holy Word and
will...(Judas)

B.   We cannot pray "Who art in heaven", if
we have no eternal perspective...(Mt. 6:20)

C.   We cannot pray "hallowed be Thy
Name", if we are not practicing godliness (He.
12:14)

D.   We cannot pray "Thy kingdom come", if
our service does not reflect God's kingdom
(2Cor.3:18)

E.   We cannot pray "Thy will be done", if we
habitually live in willful disobedience (Jn. 14:15)

F.   We cannot pray "in earth as it is in
heaven", if we are not His ambassadors on earth
(2 Cor. 5:20)

G.   We cannot pray "give us this day our
daily bread", if we do not daily feed ourselves
(Job 23:12)

H.   We cannot pray "forgive us our debts", if
we are unforgiving of our debtors (Eph. 4:32)

I.   We cannot pray "lead us not into
temptation", if we place ourselves in Satan's
paths (Ps. 51)

J.   We cannot pray "deliver us from evil", if we don't flee from all appearance of evil (I Thess. 5:22)

K.   We cannot pray "Thine is the kingdom", if we fail to do the King's will (Luke 6:46)

      1.   God's love demands obedience to His will, proving our salvation (Mk. 3:35)

      2.   God wants His will to be well known and done immediately (Jn.7:17)

      3.   God's Spirit intercedes for our obedience to God's will (Rom.8:27)

      4.   God's will fosters joyful fellowship with beloved saints (Rom. 15:32)

      5.   God's will is that we know our calling (I Cor. 1:1; 2 Cor. 1:1; Eph. 1:1; Col. 1:1)

      6.   God's will always shapes a heart of sacrificial giving (2 Cor. 8:5)

      7.   God's will daily delivers us from this evil world's power (Gal. 1:4)

      8.   God's will inspires sacrificial servanthood from the heart (Eph. 6:6)

      9.   God's will flows into our lives from effectual fervent praying (Col. 4:12)

      10.   God's will demands and enables holiness (I Thess. 4:3; 5:22-23)

11. God's will fosters grateful worship at all times (I Thess. 5:17-18)

12. God's will enables patient waiting for His promises to be done (Heb. 10:36)

13. God's will is for our good works to silence foolish ignorance of men (1 Pet.2:15)

14. God's will eventually involves suffering for His Name (I Pet. 3:17)

15. God's will and Word crush the carnal nature of lust (I Pet. 4:2)

16. God's will enables faith to persevere in difficult days of suffering (I Pet. 4:19)

17. God's will and Word inspire daily obedience and assurance of salvation (I Jn. 2:17)

18. God's will and Word received enable all people to be saved (2 Pet. 3:9)

III.   INSIGHT: LAST WILL AND TESTAMENT...THE BIBLE IS GOD'S LAST WORDS OF HIS FINAL AUTHORITY

A.   Christ's last Words (Mt. 28:18-20; Acts 1:8; Jn. 21:16-17; Rev. 22:20)

B.   Joshua's (24:14)

C.   Joseph's (Gen. 50:20)

D.   Job's (42:6)

E.   Solomon's (Eccles. 12:13)

F.   Peter's (2 Pet. 3:18)

G.   Paul's (2 Tim. 4:2)

H.   Luke's (24:47)

I.   John's (Rev. 22:18-19)...the last prayer in the Bible (Rev. 22:20)..."Come Lord Jesus"

FOOD FOR THOUGHT...Is the Bible your final authority for all your decisions in life as you strive to please God?

APPLICATION: If you want a special blessing read the last chapter of every book of the Bible to understand what was most important on God's heart as He closed His message through inspired men who wrote His Scriptures. Their last words were our great God's last words to His dearly beloved children! Compare this with what words you would give to your children to guide them regarding living for Jesus as you lay on your deathbed someday. May our gracious, merciful God inspire you in this endeavor to know and do His will in your daily life as you seek His face through His Holy Scriptures and effectual prayers. (Ps. 90:12)

CPSIA information can be obtained
at www.ICGtesting.com
Printed in the USA
FFOW04n1146230215
11229FF